The Analysis of Mind

BY BERTRAND RUSSELL

1903 *The Principles of Mathematics*
1910 *Philosophical Essays*
1914 *Our Knowledge of the External World*
1916 *Principles of Social Reconstruction*
1917 *Political Ideals*
1918 *Roads to Freedom*
1918 *Mysticism and Logic*
1919 *Introduction to Mathematical Philosophy*
1920 *The Practice and Theory of Bolshevism*
1921 *The Analysis of Mind*
1923 *The Prospects of Industrial Civilization* (with Dora Russell)
1925 *The ABC of Relativity*
1925 *On Education*
1927 *Outline of Philosophy*
1928 *Sceptical Essays*
1929 *Marriage and Morals*
1930 *The Conquest of Happiness*
1932 *Education and Social Order*
1934 *Freedom and Organization: 1814–1914*
1935 *In Praise of Idleness*
1938 *Power*
1940 *An Inquiry into Meaning and Truth*
1945 *History of Western Philosophy*
1948 *Human Knowledge*
1949 *Authority and the Individual*
1950 *Unpopular Essays*
1952 *The Impact of Science on Society*
1954 *Human Society in Ethics and Politics*
1956 *Portraits from Memory*
1957 *Why I Am Not a Christian* (ed by Paul Edwards)
1958 *Bertrand Russell's Best* (ed by Robert Egner)
1959 *My Philosophical Development*
1961 *Fact and Fiction*
1967 *The Autobiography of Bertrand Russell Vol. 1*
1968 *The Autobiography of Bertrand Russell Vol. 2*
1969 *The Autobiography of Bertrand Russell Vol. 3*
1972 *The Collected Stories*
1975 *Mortals and Others* (ed by Henry Ruja)
1983 *The Collected Papers of Bertrand Russell Vol. 1*
1984 *The Collected Papers of Bertrand Russell Vol. 7*
1985 *The Collected Papers of Bertrand Russell Vol. 12*
1986 *The Collected Papers of Bertrand Russell Vol. 8*
1987 *The Collected Papers of Bertrand Russell Vol. 9*

The Analysis of Mind

Bertrand Russell

with an introduction by
Thomas Baldwin

London

First published in Great Britain by George Allen & Unwin
in 1921 as part of the Muirhead Library of Philosophy,
edited by H. D. Lewis
First published in paperback by Unwin® Paperbacks,
an imprint of Unwin Hyman Limited, 1989

Reprinted 1992, 1995 by
Routledge
11 New Fetter Lane, London EC4P 4EE

Introduction © 1995 Thomas Baldwin

Printed in Great Britain by T. J. Press (Padstow) Ltd, Padstow,
Cornwall

A CIP catalogue record for this book is available from the British
Library.

ISBN 0-415-09097-0

CONTENTS

v

INTRODUCTION

RUSSELL wrote *The Analysis of Mind* during one of the most turbulent periods of his life. He began its composition in 1918 while he was in prison for his opposition to the First World War, and completed it in Peking in 1921, where he had been giving some lectures at the National University (it was during this visit that Russell was so seriously ill that his death was announced in the British press, thereby enabling him to read his own obituary notices). In between he had visited Wittgenstein at The Hague, visited Bolshevik Russia with a Labour Party delegation, and begun his relationship with Dora Black, who accompanied him to China and whom he married on their return. Along with all these activities and emotional involvements, Russell continued to write at an extraordinary rate: while in prison his main achievement was the composition of his *Introduction to Mathematical Philosophy* (published in 1919). Once back from Russia he wrote *Practice and Theory of Bolshevism* (published in 1921) – a work of extraordinary prescience and quite unlike the uncritical enthusiasm with which most intellectuals of the time greeted the establishment of the Bolshevik state. And all the time that he was in China he was gathering material for his book *The Problem of China* (published in 1922).

Like most of Russell's philosophical books from 1914 onwards, *The Analysis of Mind* is based on a series of lectures. Although in 1919 Trinity College Cambridge offered to reinstate him to the lectureship from which he had been dismissed in 1916 (because of his anti-war activities), Russell was by then happy to leave Cambridge and he accepted instead a short-term lectureship in London which gave him the opportunity to articulate the reflections on the philosophy of mind which he had begun while in prison. As he says in the preface, he then took these lectures with him to Peking, and completed the book after delivering them there (one rather wonders what his Chinese audience made of them). The initial intellectual stimulus for the book had been provided by Russell's reading of William James' posthumous collection *Essays on Radical Empiricism* (1912), especially the first two essays, 'Does Consciousness Exist?' and 'A World of Pure Experience', both of which were first published in 1904. James here argues that the traditional view that there is a fundamental distinction between 'mind' and 'matter' is a mistake; instead, James suggests, the concepts of mind and matter should be regarded as different, but not incompatible, conceptualizations of aspects of something that is, in itself, neutral as between them – hence the name for this position: 'neutral monism'. James called this neutral substance 'experience'; although Russell remarks that this is not the best word for a supposedly neutral substance because of its idealist connections, he himself regards the neutral substance as 'sensations', and maintains that 'the physical world itself, as known, is infected through and through with subjectivity' (p. 230). So although 'neutral monism' was supposed to be neutral as between idealism and materialism, for Russell, as for James, it is in fact a quasi-idealist doctrine. As such it is in conflict with another prominent aspect of *The Analysis of Mind*, Russell's favourable reception of the behaviourist position advanced by the American psychologist John Watson in his book *Behavior: an Introduction to Comparative Psychology* (1914). For, as Russell was well aware, Watson's behaviourist programme was part of a broadly materialist doctrine according to which all reference to mental states is to be understood in terms of observable patterns of behaviour. Hence Russell devotes a good deal of space in *The Analysis of*

Mind to the attempt to extract what he regards as the genuine insights of behaviourism from their materialist presuppositions.

Although, as I have indicated, *The Analysis of Mind* is Russell's attempt to come to terms with, and reconcile, James' neutral monism and Watson's behaviourism, there is a further question as to why Russell should have felt at just this time that these were important questions that he needed to tackle. I think that the answer to this question lies in his sense that Wittgenstein has shown that his previous philosophy was deeply flawed. That previous philosophy had included the presumption of the correctness of Brentano's thesis that mental phenomena have essential reference to objects (in the light of recent interest in Brentano it is interesting to see how familiar Russell was with his work, even with his talk of 'intentionality' – see pp. 14–15). Under the influence of Moore, Russell had initially conceived of this 'reference to objects' as *consciousness* of objects, and typically as consciousness of those complex objects which he and Moore called 'propositions'. Once Russell came to reject the existence of false propositions he switched to his 'multiple-relation' theory of mind, according to which mental states like belief involve a complex 'multiple' relation, which he still conceived as a form of consciousness, to the objects which he would previously have regarded as constituents of the proposition believed. The details of this position (which can be found in 'On the Nature of Truth and Falsehood' in *Philosophical Essays*) do not matter here; but what is important is that it was this position, as further developed in the 1913 *Theory of Knowledge* manuscript, which Wittgenstein criticized so severely that Russell threw aside that work and 'became filled with utter despair' because he was persuaded by Wittgenstein 'that what wanted doing in logic was too difficult for me' (letter to Ottoline Morrell, 1916 – *Autobiography 1914–44*, Vol. II, p. 57).

My suggestion is, then, that *The Analysis of Mind*, which is Russell's first attempt at original work after receiving Wittgenstein's traumatic criticisms, represents Russell's attempt to establish a new conception of the mind, which would be altogether free from the doctrines that Wittgenstein had criticized so severely and which would enable him to reconstruct his philosophy from an altogether different starting-point – that provided by his eclectic fusion of James' neutral monism, Watson's behaviourism, and his own new causal theory of meaning (which I discuss below). And it is, I think, certainly true that all of Russell's subsequent works bear witness to this attempt to rethink his previous doctrines in the light of the positions he first set out in *The Analysis of Mind*; so that the book provides the foundation for the distinctive character of much of his later philosophical writing.

To say this is not, of course, to imply that all here is new. On the contrary, Russell relies on his previous method of 'logical construction', as worked out in *Our Knowledge of the External World* (1914) to explain the relationship between 'sensations' – the ultimate and supposedly neutral particulars – and material objects, which are conceived of as limiting cases of certain special series of such sensations, namely those whose relations of intrinsic similarity constitutes them as 'perspectives' (see esp. pp. 102–7). There is much here that remains obscure and unpersuasive, e.g. concerning the implied conception of physical space (for an excellent critical discussion, cf. M. Sainsbury, *Russell*, Routledge, London: 1979, pp. 241–61). But what is of more interest is the way in which Russell seeks to combine his *ontological* monism with a *nomological* dualism: he maintains that although material objects are just constructions from suitable series of sensations, the laws of physics are irreducible to the laws of psychology. For the laws of physics deal with causal relationships between these series, whereas the laws of psychology require us to break into these series and consider the causal relationships between particular sensations (see pp. 300–2). Although Russell's way of formulating this position is idiosyncratic, it is one of a type which has subsequently become increasingly influential, most commonly as the position known as 'non-reductive physicalism' according to which psychological laws are not reducible to the laws of physics, although psychological states are invariably constituted by physical ones (for an influential exposition of this position, see J. Fodor, *Psychosemantics*, MIT, Cambridge, Mass.: 1987). Admittedly this modern variant of Russell's position has a physicalist bias which contrasts with Russell's own predilection for sensations as ultimate particulars; but what matters here is Russell's insight that ontological monism, whatever the ultimate particulars may be, does not require a reductive monism that holds that all truths, including in particular natural laws, are of just one type.

Russell begins *The Analysis of Mind* by identifying beliefs and desires as typical mental states, and the conception of psychology that guides his discussion is broadly that of our common sense 'belief-desire' psychology. In particular this psychology provides the context for his discussion of behaviourism: Russell is sympathetic to behaviourist accounts of desire, but he holds that such accounts do not do justice to the structure of beliefs, which depends on words and imagery in a way which behaviourism cannot accommodate. In the case of desires Russell argues (in lecture III) that the basic phenomenon is the occurrence of dispositions to engage in courses of action that bring about a result of a type whose occurrence suffices to switch off the disposition; where there is such a disposition Russell holds that the type of result in question specifies what it is that is desired. Russell acknowledges that this schema will appear too crude to account for sophisticated human desires, and he allows that, because among humans desires are commonly accompanied by beliefs about them, such desires are regarded as 'conscious' and may be such that these beliefs give rise to further desires concerning themselves – as is characteristic of vanity.

It is, in fact, not difficult to see that Russell's account of the primitive phenomenon of desire is too crude: as Wittgenstein observed, one can switch off someone's apparent desire for food by giving them a kick in the stomach, but that does imply that what they really wanted was a kick in the stomach. Most contemporary philosophers would, I think, hold that an account of the kind Russell wants needs to include the concept of a *function*: if we can render legitimate the thesis that desires are states whose proper function is to cause an organism to bring about a result of a certain type, then we can sidestep objections such as Wittgenstein's. Just how the concept of a function is to be understood, however, remains disputed (for a recent discussion of this issue, cf. D. Papineau, *Reality and Representation*, Blackwell, Oxford: 1987). Furthermore, contemporary philosophers would hold that although Russell presents his account of desire as basically behaviourist, it really implies that desires are states which cause 'behaviour-cycles', and is therefore committed to the reality of such states over and beyond behaviour itself. Thus the position is not so much behaviourist as 'functionalist', in that it acknowledges the reality of 'inner' mental states and identifies them by their characteristic causes and effects (for recent discussions of functionalism, cf. W. Lycan, *Mind and Cognition*, Blackwell, Oxford: 1990).

It would have been neat if one could portray Russell's account of belief, which he describes as 'the central problem in the analysis of mind' (p. 231) as similarly functionalist, at least in outline. But in fact in this case his treatment is altogether more complicated. He does briefly discuss the 'behaviourist' (functionalist) view that beliefs can be defined by their causal efficacy in the course of voluntary action, though without spelling out the position in any detail (pp. 244–6);

but he proceeds to reject this view for the reason that many of our beliefs do not in fact enter into the causation of our actions, and even when he has acknowledged that beliefs need be no more than dispositions to act, he holds that this objection is decisive – a claim which functionalists will of course dispute. I think that on this issue Russell's real objection emerges from the alternative theory which he commends, namely that beliefs are basically the combination of a distinctive sensation of assent together with a complex structure of images that constitute the 'content' of what is believed. For this Humean theory shows that on this issue Russell had not altogether freed himself from the seductive illusions of introspective psychology.

Russell of course recognizes that this account of belief is not compatible with the behaviourism to which he is generally sympathetic. He does not seem to regard the reference to sensations (such as 'assent') as especially problematic on this count; for, according to his neutral monism, sensations are the ultimate particulars, and behaviourism has therefore to accommodate itself to them anyway. But he does see that his reference to imagery conflicts with behaviourism, and on this issue he argues that the behaviourist position 'seems to me flatly to contradict experience'. We may well agree with Russell on this point, but still dissent from his Humean thesis that images are basically just 'copies' of sensations. This thesis, however, turns out not to be as central to Russell's position as it was to Hume's; for whereas, according to Hume, what makes an image an image of, say, a dog is defined in terms of the kind of sense-impression it is a copy of, for Russell the issue of the 'meaning' of an image is basically to be handled by means of a causal theory: what makes an image an image of a dog is that it has effects similar to those of dogs. It is not easy to make good sense of Russell's discussion of this issue, for it is not clear how there is a distinctive type of 'effect' that is reliably produced by objects and less reliably by mental imagery. But what is nonetheless striking is that, once the meaning of images is defined in this way, their central role in beliefs implies that the content of beliefs is in the end also defined through a causal theory. So in this roundabout way Russell ends up with a causal theory of the content of beliefs, even if not with a causal theory of belief itself (since that remains defined in terms of the distinctive sensation of assent).

Russell's causal theory of the meaning of images connects directly with his account of the meaning of words, since he holds that in thought the words of 'inner speech' replace or recall images, and that this shows us the 'most essential function of words', namely that through their connection with images, they bring us into touch with what is remote in space and time' (p. 203). It is, therefore, no surprise that he adopts a causal theory of meaning, according to which the meaning of a word is specifiable in terms both of the thing in relation to which the use of the word was first learnt and of the production of effects similar to those produced by that thing. Again the position is only roughly sketched, but it is recognizable as an ancestor of the causal theories of reference which are prominent in contemporary discussions (see, for example, G. Evans, 'The Causal Theory of Names' in his *Collected Papers*, Clarendon, Oxford: 1985). Russell then goes on, as one would expect, to use his causal theory of meaning to provide the basis for a correspondence theory of truth, according to which a word- or image-proposition is true just where the things meant by its constituent words or images constitute a fact. As Russell recognizes, this position is not so very different from that to which his earlier multiple-relation theory of mind had led him; but he does also advert to one of Wittgenstein's criticisms of that position (p. 272) and tries to show how, in the context of his new theory of meaning, he can accommodate that criticism.

Russell connects his discussion of truth with his treatment

of knowledge; and his sympathy for behaviourism, and indeed his incipient functionalism, is again clearly manifest in his 'externalist' approach to knowledge, according to which the possession of knowledge is basically a matter of having, not just true beliefs, but *reliably* true beliefs (pp. 183, 253ff.), where this reliability need not have been achieved through a process of evidential reasoning. Russell develops this position by comparing the situation of one who possesses knowledge with that of an accurate thermometer; the idea is that in both cases changes – in belief in one case, in the level of mercury in the other – are reliably linked to changes in the environment. Russell argues that possessing knowledge is not just a matter of being a reliable instrument (a thermometer does not 'know' the temperature of its environment): the subject of knowledge must also have purposes in relation to which its beliefs are appropriate as well as reliably true. But since he has argued for a behaviourist account of purpose, linked to his account of desire, there is no need on that account to have recourse to any 'internalist' features of the subject's state of mind, although, as we have seen, Russell's account of belief does depend on the alleged sensation of assent – a feature which is especially anomalous in this context.

The fact that Russell's account of knowledge is, in this way, broadly externalist is confirmed by his criticisms of the foundationalist position, that all knowledge requires 'self-evident' foundations, and, equally, of the coherentist position, that knowledge is just a matter of the possession of coherent beliefs. Russell argues that we are not infallible with respect to even the most obvious perceptual truths, and that coherence cannot by itself suffice for knowledge; so against these positions he urges that 'it is better to take a more external and causal view' of verification (p. 270). Equally, however, Russell shows that he does not think that the adoption of an externalist position suffices to provide a complete refutation of philosophical scepticism, which remains 'logically unassailable'. Indeed it is in *The Analysis of Mind* (p. 159) that Russell first introduces the sceptical hypothesis that the world sprang into being five minutes ago in order to fill out his discussion of memory with an account of scepticism about the past, which he holds to be 'logically tenable, but uninteresting' (p. 160).

Current work in epistemology is dominated by sophisticated externalist theories of the kind Russell sketches (sometimes introduced by Russell's own 'thermometer analogy' – cf. D. Armstrong, *Belief, Truth & Knowledge*, Cambridge University Press, Cambridge: 1973, pp. 166ff.). But, curiously, Russell's pioneering work in developing this position passes unrecognized; instead the credit is usually given to Ramsey, on the basis of his essay 'Truth and Probability' (in his *Foundations of Mathematics*, Routledge, London: 1931). Although, to the best of my knowledge, Ramsey does not acknowledge Russell's *The Analysis of Mind*, it seems to me quite likely that in this respect, as in his broad sympathy for a functionalist philosophy of mind, Ramsey was drawing on Russell's earlier work. And in a way I think this situation is all too characteristic of contemporary attitudes to *The Analysis of Mind*. We like to think of Russell as the philosopher whose great works are those which fall within the period from the commencement of his writing of *The Principles of Mathematics* (1900) to the final completion of *Principia Mathematica* (1913). Hence we are prone to regard his later works with suspicion, as evidence of Russell's 'falling off' after he had abandoned his career as a professional teacher of philosophy. But in fact, for all its idiosyncrasies, *The Analysis of Mind* shows Russell to be still capable of deep and enduring originality. Within the analytic tradition of philosophy it was only in the 1970s that the dominance of a philosophy of language that owed much to Russell's early work was successfully challenged by those who held that the study of language was inseparable from an understanding of the mind – a challenge

which has led to the proliferation of sophisticated functionalist theories of mind and externalist theories of knowledge. It
is therefore doubly ironic that fifty years earlier Russell
himself had seen that his philosophy of language needed to be
complemented by a proper philosophy of mind, and that in
doing so he had sketched out a range of positions which are
broadly comparable to those which are most influential today.
Russell's *The Analysis of Mind* is a book which deserves to be
rescued from the unjust oblivion into which it has fallen.

Thomas Baldwin
November 1994

PREFACE

THIS book has grown out of an attempt to harmonize two different tendencies, one in psychology, the other in physics, with both of which I find myself in sympathy, although at first sight they might seem inconsistent. On the one hand, many psychologists, especially those of the behaviourist school, tend to adopt what is essentially a materialistic position, as a matter of method if not of metaphysics. They make psychology increasingly dependent on physiology and external observation, and tend to think of matter as something much more solid and indubitable than mind. Meanwhile the physicists, especially Einstein and other exponents of the theory of relativity, have been making "matter" less and less material. Their world consists of "events," from which "matter" is derived by a logical construction. Whoever reads, for example, Professor Eddington's *Space, Time and Gravitation* (Cambridge University Press, 1920), will see that an old-fashioned materialism can receive no support from modern physics. I think that what has permanent value in the outlook of the behaviourists is the feeling that physics is the most fundamental science at present in existence. But this position cannot be called materialistic, if, as seems to be the case, physics does not assume the existence of matter.

The view that seems to me to reconcile the materialistic tendency of psychology with the anti-materialistic tendency of physics is the view of William James and the American new realists, according to which the "stuff" of the world is neither mental nor material, but a "neutral stuff," out of which both are constructed. I have endeavoured in this work to develop this view in some detail as regards the phenomena with which psychology is concerned.

My thanks are due to Professor John B. Watson and to Dr. T. P. Nunn for reading my MSS. at an early stage and helping me with many valuable suggestions; also to Mr. A. Wohlgemuth for much very useful information as regards important literature. I have also to acknowledge the help of the editor of this Library of Philosophy, Professor Muirhead, for several suggestions by which I have profited.

The work has been given in the form of lectures both in London and Peking, and one lecture, that on Desire, has been published in the *Athenæum*.

There are a few allusions to China in this book, all of which were written before I had been in China, and are not intended to be taken by the reader as geographically accurate. I have used "China" merely as a synonym for "a distant country," when I wanted illustrations of unfamiliar things.

PEKING,
      January 1921.

THE ANALYSIS OF MIND

LECTURE I

RECENT CRITICISMS OF " CONSCIOUSNESS "

THERE are certain occurrences which we are in the habit of calling " mental." Among these we may take as typical *believing* and *desiring*. The exact definition of the word " mental " will, I hope, emerge as the lectures proceed ; for the present, I shall mean by it whatever occurrences would commonly be called mental.

I wish in these lectures to analyse as fully as I can what it is that really takes place when we, e.g. believe or desire. In this first lecture I shall be concerned to refute a theory which is widely held, and which I formerly held myself : the theory that the essence of everything mental is a certain quite peculiar something called " consciousness," conceived either as a relation to objects, or as a pervading quality of psychical phenomena.

The reasons which I shall give against this theory will be mainly derived from previous authors. There are two sorts of reasons, which will divide my lecture into two parts :

   (1) Direct reasons, derived from analysis and its difficulties ;

(2) Indirect reasons, derived from observation of animals (comparative psychology) and of the insane and hysterical (psycho-analysis).

Few things are more firmly established in popular philosophy than the distinction between mind and matter. Those who are not professional metaphysicians are willing to confess that they do not know what mind actually is, or how matter is constituted ; but they remain convinced that there is an impassable gulf between the two, and that both belong to what actually exists in the world. Philosophers, on the other hand, have maintained often that matter is a mere fiction imagined by mind, and sometimes that mind is a mere property of a certain kind of matter. Those who maintain that mind is the reality and matter an evil dream are called " idealists " —a word which has a different meaning in philosophy from that which it bears in ordinary life. Those who argue that matter is the reality and mind a mere property of protoplasm are called " materialists." They have been rare among philosophers, but common, at certain periods, among men of science. Idealists, materialists, and ordinary mortals have been in agreement on one point : that they knew sufficiently what they meant by the words " mind " and " matter " to be able to conduct their debate intelligently. Yet it was just in this point, as to which they were at one, that they seem to me to have been all alike in error.

The stuff of which the world of our experience is composed is, in my belief, neither mind nor matter, but something more primitive than either. Both mind and matter seem to be composite, and the stuff of which they are compounded lies in a sense between the two, in a sense above them both, like a common ancestor. As regards matter, I have set forth my reasons for this view on former occasions,[1] and I shall not now repeat them. But the question of mind is more difficult, and it is this question that I propose to discuss in these lectures. A great deal of what I shall have to say is not original ; indeed, much recent work, in various fields, has tended to show the necessity of such theories as those which I shall be advocating. Accordingly in this first lecture I shall try to give a brief description of the systems of ideas within which our investigation is to be carried on.

If there is one thing that may be said, in the popular estimation, to characterize mind, that one thing is " consciousness." We say that we are " conscious " of what we see and hear, of what we remember, and of our own thoughts and feelings. Most of us believe that tables and chairs are not " conscious." We think that when we sit in a chair, we are aware of sitting in it, but it is not aware of being sat in. It cannot for a moment be doubted that we are right in believing that there is *some* difference between us and the chair in this respect : so much may be taken as fact, and as a datum for our inquiry. But as soon as we try to say what exactly the difference is, we become involved in perplexities. Is " consciousness " ultimate and simple, something to be merely accepted and contemplated ? Or is it something complex, perhaps consisting in our way of behaving in the presence of objects, or, alternatively, in the existence in us of things called " ideas," having a certain relation to objects, though different from them, and only symbolically representative of them ? Such questions are not easy to

[1] *Our Knowledge of the External World* (Allen & Unwin), Chapters III and IV. Also *Mysticism and Logic*, Essays VII and VIII.

answer ; but until they are answered we cannot profess to know what we mean by saying that we are possessed of " consciousness."

Before considering modern theories, let us look first at consciousness from the standpoint of conventional psychology, since this embodies views which naturally occur when we begin to reflect upon the subject. For this purpose, let us as a preliminary consider different ways of being conscious.

First, there is the way of *perception*. We " perceive " tables and chairs, horses and dogs, our friends, traffic passing in the street—in short, anything which we recognize through the senses. I leave on one side for the present the question whether pure sensation is to be regarded as a form of consciousness : what I am speaking of now is perception, where, according to conventional psychology, we go beyond the sensation to the " thing " which it represents. When you hear a donkey bray, you not only hear a noise, but realize that it comes from a donkey. When you see a table, you not only see a coloured surface, but realize that it is hard. The addition of these elements that go beyond crude sensation is said to constitute perception. We shall have more to say about this at a later stage. For the moment, I am merely concerned to note that perception of objects is one of the most obvious examples of what is called " consciousness." We are " conscious " of anything that we perceive.

We may take next the way of *memory*. If I set to work to recall what I did this morning, that is a form of consciousness different from perception, since it is concerned with the past. There are various problems as to how we can be conscious now of what no longer exists. These will be dealt with incidentally when we come to the analysis of memory.

From memory it is an easy step to what are called " ideas "—not in the Platonic sense, but in that of Locke, Berkeley and Hume, in which they are opposed to " impressions." You may be conscious of a friend either by seeing him or by " thinking " of him ; and by " thought " you can be conscious of objects which cannot be seen, such as the human race, or physiology. " Thought " in the narrower sense is that form of consciousness which consists in " ideas " as opposed to impressions or mere memories.

We may end our preliminary catalogue with *belief*, by which I mean that way of being conscious which may be either true or false. We say that a man is " conscious of looking a fool," by which we mean that he believes he looks a fool, and is not mistaken in this belief. This is a different form of consciousness from any of the earlier ones. It is the form which gives " knowledge " in the strict sense, and also error. It is, at least apparently, more complex than our previous forms of consciousness ; though we shall find that they are not so separable from it as they might appear to be.

Besides ways of being conscious there are other things that would ordinarily be called " mental," such as desire and pleasure and pain. These raise problems of their own, which we shall reach in Lecture III. But the hardest problems are those that arise concerning ways of being " conscious." These ways, taken together, are called the " cognitive " elements in mind, and it is these that will occupy us most during the following lectures.

There is one element which *seems* obviously in common among the different ways of being conscious, and that is,

that they are all directed to *objects*. We are conscious
" of " something. The consciousness, it seems, is one
thing, and that of which we are conscious is another thing.
Unless we are to acquiesce in the view that we can never
be conscious of anything outside our own minds, we
must say that the object of consciousness need not be
mental, though the consciousness must be. (I am speaking within the circle of conventional doctrines, not
expressing my own beliefs.) This direction towards
an object is commonly regarded as typical of every form
of cognition, and sometimes of mental life altogether.
We may distinguish two different tendencies in traditional
psychology. There are those who take mental phenomena
naïvely, just as they would physical phenomena. This
school of psychologists tends not to emphasize the object.
On the other hand, there are those whose primary interest
is in the apparent fact that we have *knowledge*, that there
is a world surrounding us of which we are aware. These
men are interested in the mind because of its relation to
the world, because knowledge, if it is a fact, is a very
mysterious one. Their interest in psychology is naturally
centred in the relation of consciousness to its object, a
problem which, properly, belongs rather to theory of
knowledge. We may take as one of the best and most
typical representatives of this school the Austrian psychologist Brentano, whose *Psychology from the Empirical
Standpoint*,[1] though published in 1874, is still influential,
and was the starting-point of a great deal of interesting
work. He says (p. 115) :

" Every psychical phenomenon is characterized by
what the scholastics of the Middle Ages called the inten-

[1] *Psychologie vom empirischen Standpunkte*, vol. i, 1874. (The
second volume was never published.)

tional (also the mental) inexistence of an object, and what we, although with not quite unambiguous expressions, would call relation to a content, direction towards an object (which is not here to be understood as a reality), or immanent objectivity. Each contains something in itself as an object, though not each in the same way. In presentation something is presented, in judgment something is acknowledged or rejected, in love something is loved, in hatred hated, in desire desired, and so on.

" This intentional inexistence is exclusively peculiar to psychical phenomena. No physical phenomenon shows anything similar. And so we can define psychical phenomena by saying that they are phenomena which intentionally contain an object in themselves."

The view here expressed, that relation to an object is an ultimate irreducible characteristic of mental phenomena, is one which I shall be concerned to combat. Like Brentano, I am interested in psychology, not so much for its own sake, as for the light that it may throw on the problem of knowledge. Until very lately I believed, as he did, that mental phenomena have essential reference to objects, except possibly in the case of pleasure and pain. Now I no longer believe this, even in the case of knowledge. I shall try to make my reasons for this rejection clear as we proceed. It must be evident at first glance that the analysis of knowledge is rendered more difficult by the rejection ; but the apparent simplicity of Brentano's view of knowledge will be found, if I am not mistaken, incapable of maintaining itself either against an analytic scrutiny or against a host of facts in psycho-analysis and animal psychology. I do not wish to minimize the problems. I will merely observe, in mitigation of our prospective labours, that thinking, however it is to be analysed, is in itself a delightful occupation, and that there is no enemy to thinking so deadly as a false simplicity. Travelling, whether in the mental or the physical world, is a joy, and it is good to know that, in the mental world at least, there are vast countries still very imperfectly explored.

The view expressed by Brentano has been held very generally, and developed by many writers. Among these we may take as an example his Austrian successor Meinong.[1] According to him there are three elements involved in the thought of an object. These three he calls the act, the content and the object. The act is the same in any two cases of the same kind of consciousness; for instance, if I think of Smith or think of Brown, the act of thinking, in itself, is exactly similar on both occasions. But the content of my thought, the particular event that is happening in my mind, is different when I think of Smith and when I think of Brown. The content, Meinong argues, must not be confounded with the object, since the content must exist in my mind at the moment when I have the thought, whereas the object need not do so. The object may be something past or future; it may be physical, not mental; it may be something abstract, like equality for example; it may be something imaginary, like a golden mountain; or it may even be something self-contradictory, like a round square. But in all these cases, so he contends, the content exists when the thought exists, and is what distinguishes it, as an occurrence, from other thoughts.

[1] See, e.g. his article: " Ueber Gegenstände höherer Ordnung und deren Verhältniss zur inneren Wahrnehmung," *Zeitschrift für Psychologie und Physiologie der Sinnesorgane*, vol. xxi, pp. 182–272 (1899), especially pp. 185–8.

To make this theory concrete, let us suppose that you are thinking of St. Paul's. Then, according to Meinong, we have to distinguish three elements which are necessarily combined in constituting the one thought. First, there is the act of thinking, which would be just the same whatever you were thinking about. Then there is what makes the character of the thought as contrasted with other thoughts ; this is the content. And finally there is St. Paul's, which is the object of your thought. There must be a difference between the content of a thought and what it is about, since the thought is here and now, whereas what it is about may not be ; hence it is clear that the thought is not identical with St. Paul's. This seems to show that we must distinguish between content and object. But if Meinong is right, there can be no thought without an object : the connection of the two is essential. The object might exist without the thought, but not the thought without the object : the three elements of act, content and object are all required to constitute the one single occurrence called " thinking of St. Paul's."

The above analysis of a thought, though I believe it to be mistaken, is very useful as affording a schema in terms of which other theories can be stated. In the remainder of the present lecture I shall state in outline the view which I advocate, and show how various other views out of which mine has grown result from modifications of the threefold analysis into act, content and object.

The first criticism I have to make is that the *act* seems unnecessary and fictitious. The occurrence of the content of a thought constitutes the occurrence of the thought. Empirically, I cannot discover anything corresponding to the supposed act ; and theoretically I cannot see that it is indispensable. We say : " *I* think so-and-so," and this word " I " suggests that thinking is the act of a person. Meinong's " act " is the ghost of the subject, or what once was the full-blooded soul. It is supposed that thoughts cannot just come and go, but need a person to think them. Now, of course it is true that thoughts can be collected into bundles, so that one bundle is my thoughts, another is your thoughts, and a third is the thoughts of Mr. Jones. But I think the person is not an ingredient in the single thought : he is rather constituted by relations of the thoughts to each other and to the body. This is a large question, which need not, in its entirety, concern us at present. All that I am concerned with for the moment is that the grammatical forms " I think," " you think," and " Mr. Jones thinks," are misleading if regarded as indicating an analysis of a single thought. It would be better to say " it thinks in me," like " it rains here " ; or better still, " there is a thought in me." This is simply on the ground that what Meinong calls the act in thinking is not empirically discoverable, or logically deducible from what we can observe.

The next point of criticism concerns the relation of content and object. The reference of thoughts to objects is not, I believe, the simple direct essential thing that Brentano and Meinong represent it as being. It seems to me to be derivative, and to consist largely in *beliefs* : beliefs that what constitutes the thought is connected with various other elements which together make up the object. You have, say, an image of St. Paul's, or merely the word " St. Paul's " in your head. You believe, however vaguely and dimly, that this is connected with what you would see if you went to St. Paul's, or what you would feel if you touched its walls ; it is further connected with what other people see and feel, with services and the Dean and Chapter and Sir Christopher Wren. These things are not mere thoughts of yours, but your thought stands in a relation to them of which you are more or less aware. The awareness of this relation is a further thought, and constitutes your feeling that the original thought had an " object." But in pure imagination you can get very similar thoughts without these accompanying beliefs ; and in this case your thoughts do not have objects or seem to have them. Thus in such instances you have content without object. On the other hand, in seeing or hearing it would be less misleading to say that you have object without content, since what you see or hear is actually part of the physical world, though not matter in the sense of physics. Thus the whole question of the relation of mental occurrences to objects grows very complicated, and cannot be settled by regarding reference to objects as of the essence of thoughts. All the above remarks are merely preliminary, and will be expanded later.

Speaking in popular and unphilosophical terms, we may say that the content of a thought is supposed to be something in your head when you think the thought, while the object is usually something in the outer world. It is held that knowledge of the outer world is constituted by the relation to the object, while the fact that knowledge is different from what it knows is due to the fact that knowledge comes by way of contents. We can begin to state the difference between realism and idealism in terms of this opposition of contents and objects. Speaking quite roughly and approximately, we may say that

idealism tends to suppress the object, while realism tends
to suppress the content. Idealism, accordingly, says
that nothing can be known except thoughts, and all
the reality that we know is mental ; while realism maintains that we know objects directly, in sensation certainly,
and perhaps also in memory and thought. Idealism does
not say that nothing can be known beyond the present
thought, but it maintains that the context of vague
belief, which we spoke of in connection with the thought
of St. Paul's, only takes you to other thoughts, never to
anything radically different from thoughts. The difficulty
of this view is in regard to sensation, where it seems as
if we came into direct contact with the outer world. But
the Berkeleian way of meeting this difficulty is so familiar
that I need not enlarge upon it now. I shall return to
it in a later lecture, and will only observe, for the present,
that there seem to me no valid grounds for regarding
what we see and hear as not part of the physical world.

Realists, on the other hand, as a rule, suppress the content, and maintain that a thought consists either of act
and object alone, or of object alone. I have been in the
past a realist, and I remain a realist as regards sensation,
but not as regards memory or thought. I will try to
explain what seem to me to be the reasons for and
against various kinds of realism.

Modern idealism professes to be by no means confined
to the present thought or the present thinker in regard
to its knowledge ; indeed, it contends that the world is
so organic, so dove-tailed, that from any one portion the
whole can be inferred, as the complete skeleton of an
extinct animal can be inferred from one bone. But the
logic by which this supposed organic nature of the world
is nominally demonstrated appears to realists, as it does

to me, to be faulty. They argue that, if we cannot know the physical world directly, we cannot really know anything outside our own minds : the rest of the world may be merely our dream. This is a dreary view, and they therefore seek ways of escaping from it. Accordingly they maintain that in knowledge we are in direct contact with objects, which may be, and usually are, outside our own minds. No doubt they are prompted to this view, in the first place, by bias, namely, by the desire to think that they can know of the existence of a world outside themselves. But we have to consider, not what led them to desire the view, but whether their arguments for it are valid.

There are two different kinds of realism, according as we make a thought consist of act and object, or of object alone. Their difficulties are different, but neither seems tenable all through. Take, for the sake of definiteness, the remembering of a past event. The remembering occurs now, and is therefore necessarily not identical with the past event. So long as we retain the act, this need cause no difficulty. The act of remembering occurs now, and has on this view a certain essential relation to the past event which it remembers. There is no *logical* objection to this theory, but there is the objection, which we spoke of earlier, that the act seems mythical, and is not to be found by observation. If, on the other hand, we try to constitute memory without the act, we are driven to a content, since we must have something that happens *now*, as opposed to the event which happened in the past. Thus, when we reject the act, which I think we must, we are driven to a theory of memory which is more akin to idealism. These arguments, however, do not apply to sensation. It is especially sensation, I think, which is

considered by those realists who retain only the object.[1]
Their views, which are chiefly held in America, are in
large measure derived from William James, and before
going further it will be well to consider the revolutionary
doctrine which he advocated. I believe this doctrine
contains important new truth, and what I shall have to
say will be in a considerable measure inspired by it.

William James's view was first set forth in an essay
called " Does ' consciousness ' exist ? "[2] In this essay
he explains how what used to be the soul has gradually
been refined down to the " transcendental ego," which,
he says, " attenuates itself to a thoroughly ghostly condition, being only a name for the fact that the ' content ' of
experience *is known*. It loses personal form and activity—
these passing over to the content—and becomes a bare
Bewusstheit or Bewusstsein überhaupt, of which in
its own right absolutely nothing can be said. I believe
(he continues) that ' consciousness,' when once it
has evaporated to this estate of pure diaphaneity, is
on the point of disappearing altogether. It is the name
of a nonentity, and has no right to a place among first
principles. Those who still cling to it are clinging to a
mere echo, the faint rumour left behind by the disappearing ' soul ' upon the air of philosophy " (p. 2).

He explains that this is no sudden change in his
opinions. " For twenty years past," he says, " I have
mistrusted ' consciousness ' as an entity ; for seven or

[1] This is explicitly the case with Mach's *Analysis of Sensations*,
a book of fundamental importance in the present connection.
(Translation of fifth German edition, Open Court Co., 1914. First
German edition, 1886.)

[2] *Journal of Philosophy, Psychology and Scientific Methods*,
vol. i, 1904. Reprinted in *Essays in Radical Empiricism* (Longmans, Green & Co., 1912), pp. 1–38, to which references in what
follows refer

eight years past I have suggested its non-existence to my students, and tried to give them its pragmatic equivalent in realities of experience. It seems to me that the hour is ripe for it to be openly and universally discarded " (p. 3).

His next concern is to explain away the air of paradox, for James was never wilfully paradoxical. " Undeniably," he says, " ' thoughts ' do exist." " I mean only to deny that the word stands for an entity, but to insist most emphatically that it does stand for a function. There is, I mean, no aboriginal stuff or quality of being, contrasted with that of which material objects are made, out of which our thoughts of them are made ; but there is a function in experience which thoughts perform, and for the performance of which this quality of being is invoked. That function is *knowing* " (pp. 3-4).

James's view is that the raw material out of which the world is built up is not of two sorts, one matter and the other mind, but that it is arranged in different patterns by its inter-relations, and that some arrangements may be called mental, while others may be called physical.

" My thesis is," he says, " that if we start with the supposition that there is only one primal stuff or material in the world, a stuff of which everything is composed, and if we call that stuff ' pure experience,' then knowing can easily be explained as a particular sort of relation towards one another into which portions of pure experience may enter. The relation itself is a part of pure experience ; one of its ' terms ' becomes the subject or bearer of the knowledge, the knower, the other becomes the object known " (p. 4).

After mentioning the duality of subject and object, which is supposed to constitute consciousness, he proceeds in italics : " *Experience, I believe, has no such*

*inner duplicity ; and the separation of it into consciousness
and content comes, not by way of subtraction, but by way
of addition* " (p. 9).

He illustrates his meaning by the analogy of paint
as it appears in a paint-shop and as it appears in a
picture : in the one case it is just " saleable matter,"
while in the other it " performs a spiritual function. Just
so, I maintain (he continues), does a given undivided
portion of experience, taken in one context of associates,
play the part of a knower, of a state of mind, of
' consciousness ' ; while in a different context the
same undivided bit of experience plays the part of a
thing known, of an objective ' content.' In a word,
in one group it figures as a thought, in another group
as a thing " (pp. 9–10).

He does not believe in the supposed immediate certainty of thought. " Let the case be what it may in
others," he says, " I am as confident as I am of anything
that, in myself, the stream of thinking (which I recognize emphatically as a phenomenon) is only a careless
name for what, when scrutinized, reveals itself to consist chiefly of the stream of my breathing. The ' I
think ' which Kant said must be able to accompany
all my objects, is the ' I breathe ' which actually does
accompany them " (pp. 36–37).

The same view of " consciousness " is set forth in
the succeeding essay, " A World of Pure Experience "
(*ib.*, pp. 39–91). The use of the phrase " pure experience "
in both essays points to a lingering influence of idealism.
" Experience," like " consciousness," must be a product,
not part of the primary stuff of the world. It must
be possible, if James is right in his main contentions,
that roughly the same stuff, differently arranged, would

not give rise to anything that could be called "experience." This word has been dropped by the American realists, among whom we may mention specially Professor R. B. Perry of Harvard and Mr. Edwin B. Holt. The interests of this school are in general philosophy and the philosophy of the sciences, rather than in psychology ; they have derived a strong impulsion from James, but have more interest than he had in logic and mathematics and the abstract part of philosophy. They speak of "neutral" entities as the stuff out of which both mind and matter are constructed. Thus Holt says : "If the terms and propositions of logic must be substantialized, they are all strictly of one substance, for which perhaps the least dangerous name is neutral-stuff. The relation of neutral-stuff to matter and mind we shall have presently to consider at considerable length." [1]

My own belief—for which the reasons will appear in subsequent lectures—is that James is right in rejecting consciousness as an entity, and that the American realists are partly right, though not wholly, in considering that both mind and matter are composed of a neutral-stuff which, in isolation, is neither mental nor material. I should admit this view as regards sensations : what is heard or seen belongs equally to psychology and to physics. But I should say that images belong only to the mental world, while those occurrences (if any) which do not form part of any "experience" belong only to the physical world. There are, it seems to me, *prima facie* different kinds of causal laws, one belonging to physics and the other to psychology. The law of gravitation, for example, is a physical law, while the law of association

[1] *The Concept of Consciousness* (Geo. Allen & Co., 1914), p. 52.

is a psychological law. Sensations are subject to both kinds of laws, and are therefore truly "neutral" in Holt's sense. But entities subject only to physical laws, or only to psychological laws, are not neutral, and may be called respectively purely material and purely mental. Even those, however, which are purely mental will not have that intrinsic reference to objects which Brentano assigns to them and which constitutes the essence of "consciousness" as ordinarily understood. But it is now time to pass on to other modern tendencies, also hostile to "consciousness."

There is a psychological school called "Behaviourists," of whom the protagonist is Professor John B. Watson,[1] formerly of the Johns Hopkins University. To them also, on the whole, belongs Professor John Dewey, who, with James and Dr. Schiller, was one of the three founders of pragmatism. The view of the "behaviourists" is that nothing can be known except by external observation. They deny altogether that there is a separate source of knowledge called "introspection," by which we can know things about ourselves which we could never observe in others. They do not by any means deny that all sorts of things *may* go on in our minds : they only say that such things, if they occur, are not susceptible of scientific observation, and do not therefore concern psychology as a science. Psychology as a science, they say, is only concerned with *behaviour*, i.e. with what we *do* ; this alone, they contend, can be accurately observed. Whether we think meanwhile, they tell us, cannot be known ; in their observation of the behaviour of human beings, they have not so far found any evidence

[1] See especially his *Behavior : an Introduction to Comparative Psychology*, New York, 1914.

of thought. True, we talk a great deal, and imagine that in so doing we are showing that we can think ; but behaviourists say that the talk they have to listen to can be explained without supposing that people think. Where you might expect a chapter on "thought pro-cesses" you come instead upon a chapter on "The Language Habit." It is humiliating to find how terribly adequate this hypothesis turns out to be.

Behaviourism has not, however, sprung from observing the folly of men. It is the wisdom of animals that has suggested the view. It has always been a common topic of popular discussion whether animals "think." On this topic people are prepared to take sides without having the vaguest idea what they mean by "thinking." Those who desired to investigate such questions were led to observe the behaviour of animals, in the hope that their behaviour would throw some light on their mental faculties. At first sight, it might seem that this is so. People say that a dog "knows" its name because it comes when it is called, and that it "remembers" its master, because it looks sad in his absence, but wags its tail and barks when he returns. That the dog behaves in this way is matter of observa-tion, but that it "knows" or "remembers" anything is an inference, and in fact a very doubtful one. The more such inferences are examined, the more precarious they are seen to be. Hence the study of animal behaviour has been gradually led to abandon all attempt at mental interpretation. And it can hardly be doubted that, in many cases of complicated behaviour very well adapted to its ends, there can be no prevision of those ends. The first time a bird builds a nest, we can hardly suppose it knows that there will be eggs to be laid in it, or that it will sit on the eggs, or that they will hatch into young birds. It does what it does at each stage because instinct gives it an impulse to do just that, not because it foresees and desires the result of its actions.[1]

Careful observers of animals, being anxious to avoid precarious inferences, have gradually discovered more and more how to give an account of the actions of animals without assuming what we call " consciousness." It has seemed to the behaviourists that similar methods can be applied to human behaviour, without assuming anything not open to external observation. Let us give a crude illustration, too crude for the authors in question, but capable of affording a rough insight into their meaning. Suppose two children in a school, both of whom are asked " What is six times nine ? " One says fifty-four, the other says fifty-six. The one, we say, " knows " what six times nine is, the other does not. But all that we can observe is a certain language-habit. The one child has acquired the habit of saying " six times nine is fifty-four " ; the other has not. There is no more need of " thought " in this than there is when a horse turns into his accustomed stable ; there are merely more numerous and complicated habits. There is obviously an observable fact called " knowing " such-and-such a thing ; examinations are experiments for discovering such facts. But all that is observed or discovered is a certain set of habits in the use of words. The thoughts (if any) in the mind of the examinee are of no interest to the

---

[1] An interesting discussion of the question whether instinctive actions, when first performed, involve any prevision, however vague, will be found in Lloyd Morgan's *Instinct and Experience* (Methuen, 1912), chap. ii.

examiner ; nor has the examiner any reason to suppose even the most successful examinee capable of even the smallest amount of thought.

Thus what is called " knowing," in the sense in which we can ascertain what other people " know," is a phenomenon exemplified in their physical behaviour, including spoken and written words. There is no reason—so Watson argues—to suppose that their knowledge *is* anything beyond the habits shown in this behaviour : the inference that other people have something non-physical called " mind " or " thought " is therefore unwarranted.

So far, there is nothing particularly repugnant to our prejudices in the conclusions of the behaviourists. We are all willing to admit that other people are thoughtless. But when it comes to ourselves, we feel convinced that we can actually perceive our own thinking. " Cogito, ergo sum " would be regarded by most people as having a true premiss. This, however, the behaviourist denies. He maintains that our knowledge of ourselves is no different in kind from our knowledge of other people. We may see *more*, because our own body is easier to observe than that of other people ; but we do not see anything radically unlike what we see of others. Introspection, as a separate source of knowledge, is entirely denied by psychologists of this school. I shall discuss this question at length in a later lecture ; for the present I will only observe that it is by no means simple, and that, though I believe the behaviourists somewhat overstate their case, yet there is an important element of truth in their contention, since the things which we can discover by introspection do not seem to differ in any very fundamental way from the things which we discover by external observation.

So far, we have been principally concerned with knowing. But it might well be maintained that desiring is what is really most characteristic of mind. Human beings are constantly engaged in achieving some end : they feel pleasure in success and pain in failure. In a purely material world, it may be said, there would be no opposition of pleasant and unpleasant, good and bad, what is desired and what is feared. A man's acts are governed by purposes. He decides, let us suppose, to go to a certain place, whereupon he proceeds to the station, takes his ticket and enters the train. If the usual route is blocked by an accident, he goes by some other route. All that he does is determined—or so it seems—by the end he has in view, by what lies in front of him, rather than by what lies behind. With dead matter, this is not the case. A stone at the top of a hill may start rolling, but it shows no pertinacity in trying to get to the bottom. Any ledge or obstacle will stop it, and it will exhibit no signs of discontent if this happens. It is not attracted by the pleasantness of the valley, as a sheep or cow might be, but propelled by the steepness of the hill at the place where it is. In all this we have characteristic differences between the behaviour of animals and the behaviour of matter as studied by physics.

Desire, like knowledge, is, of course, in one sense an observable phenomenon. An elephant will eat a bun, but not a mutton chop ; a duck will go into the water, but a hen will not. But when we think of our own desires, most people believe that we can know them by an immediate self-knowledge which does not depend upon observation of our actions. Yet if this were the case, it would be odd that people are so often mistaken as to what they desire. It is matter of common observation that "so-and-so does not know his own motives," or that "A is envious of B and malicious about him, but quite unconscious of being so." Such people are called self-deceivers, and are supposed to have had to go through some more or less elaborate process of concealing from themselves what would otherwise have been obvious. I believe that this is an entire mistake. I believe that the discovery of our own motives can only be made by the same process by which we discover other people's, namely, the process of observing our actions and inferring the desire which could prompt them. A desire is "conscious" when we have told ourselves that we have it. A hungry man may say to himself: "Oh, I do want my lunch." Then his desire is "conscious." But it only differs from an "unconscious" desire by the presence of appropriate words, which is by no means a fundamental difference.

The belief that a motive is normally conscious makes it easier to be mistaken as to our own motives than as to other people's. When some desire that we should be ashamed of is attributed to us, we notice that we have never had it consciously, in the sense of saying to ourselves, "I wish that would happen." We therefore look for some other interpretation of our actions, and regard our friends as very unjust when they refuse to be convinced by our repudiation of what we hold to be a calumny. Moral considerations greatly increase the difficulty of clear thinking in this matter. It is commonly argued that people are not to blame for unconscious motives, but only for conscious ones. In order, therefore, to be wholly virtuous it is only necessary to repeat virtuous formulas. We say: "I desire to be kind to my friends, honourable in business, philanthropic towards the poor, public-spirited in politics." So long as we refuse to allow ourselves, even in the watches of the night, to avow any contrary desires, we may be bullies at home, shady in the City, skinflints in paying wages and profiteers in dealing with the public ; yet, if only conscious motives are to count in moral valuation, we shall remain model characters. This is an agreeable doctrine, and it is not surprising that men are unwilling to abandon it. But moral considerations are the worst enemies of the scientific spirit and we must dismiss them from our minds if we wish to arrive at truth.

I believe—as I shall try to prove in a later lecture —that desire, like force in mechanics, is of the nature of a convenient fiction for describing shortly certain laws of behaviour. A hungry animal is restless until it finds food ; then it becomes quiescent. The thing which will bring a restless condition to an end is said to be what is desired. But only experience can show what will have this sedative effect, and it is easy to make mistakes. We feel dissatisfaction, and think that such-and-such a thing would remove it ; but in thinking this, we are theorizing, not observing a patent fact. Our theorizing is often mistaken, and when it is mistaken there is a difference between what we think we desire and what in fact will bring satisfaction. This is such a common phenomenon that any theory of desire which fails to accout for it must be wrong.

What have been called " unconscious " desires have been brought very much to the fore in recent years by psycho-analysis. Psycho-analysis, as every one knows, is primarily a method of understanding hysteria and

certain forms of insanity [1] ; but it has been found that
there is much in the lives of ordinary men and women
which bears a humiliating resemblance to the delusions
of the insane. The connection of dreams, irrational
beliefs and foolish actions with unconscious wishes has
been brought to light, though with some exaggeration,
by Freud and Jung and their followers. As regards
the nature of these unconscious wishes, it seems to me
—though as a layman I speak with diffidence—that
many psycho-analysts are unduly narrow ; no doubt the
wishes they emphasize exist, but others, e.g. for honour
and power, are equally operative and equally liable to
concealment. This, however, does not affect the value of
their general theories from the point of view of theoretic
psychology, and it is from this point of view that their
results are important for the analysis of mind.

What, I think, is clearly established, is that a man's
actions and beliefs may be wholly dominated by a desire
of which he is quite unconscious, and which he indig-
nantly repudiates when it is suggested to him. Such
a desire is generally, in morbid cases, of a sort which
the patient would consider wicked ; if he had to admit

[1] There is a wide field of "unconscious" phenomena which
does not depend upon psycho-analytic theories. Such occurrences
as automatic writing lead Dr. Morton Prince to say : " As I view
this question of the subconscious, far too much weight is given
to the point of awareness or not awareness of our conscious processes. As a matter of fact, we find entirely identical phenomena,
that is, identical in every respect but one—that of awareness—
in which sometimes we are aware of these conscious phenomena
and sometimes not " (p. 87 of *Subconscious Phenomena*, by various
authors, Rebman). Dr. Morton Price conceives that there may be
" consciousness " without " awareness." But this is a difficult
view, and one which makes some definition of " consciousness "
imperative. For my part, I cannot see how to separate consciousness from awareness.

that he had the desire, he would loathe himself. Yet it is so strong that it must force an outlet for itself ; hence it becomes necessary to entertain whole systems of false beliefs in order to hide the nature of what is desired. The resulting delusions in very many cases disappear if the hysteric or lunatic can be made to face the facts about himself. The consequence of this is that the treatment of many forms of insanity has grown more psychological and less physiological than it used to be. Instead of looking for a physical defect in the brain, those who treat delusions look for the repressed desire which has found this contorted mode of expression. For those who do not wish to plunge into the somewhat repulsive and often rather wild theories of psycho-analytic pioneers, it will be worth while to read a little book by Dr. Bernard Hart on *The Psychology of Insanity*.[1] On this question of the mental as opposed to the physiological study of the causes of insanity, Dr. Hart says :

" The psychological conception [of insanity] is based on the view that mental processes can be directly studied without any reference to the accompanying changes which are presumed to take place in the brain, and that insanity may therefore be properly attacked from the standpoint of psychology " (p. 9).

This illustrates a point which I am anxious to make clear from the outset. Any attempt to classify modern views, such as I propose to advocate, from the old standpoint of materialism and idealism, is only misleading. In certain respects, the views which I shall be setting forth approximate to materialism ; in certain others, they approximate to its opposite. On this question of

---

[1] Cambridge, 1912 ; 2nd edition, 1914. The following references are to the second edition.

the study of delusions, the practical effect of the modern theories, as Dr. Hart points out, is emancipation from the materialist method. On the other hand, as he also points out (pp. 38–9), imbecility and dementia still have to be considered physiologically, as caused by defects in the brain. There is no inconsistency in this. If, as we maintain, mind and matter are neither of them the actual stuff of reality, but different convenient groupings of an underlying material, then, clearly, the question whether, in regard to a given phenomenon, we are to seek a physical or a mental cause, is merely one to be decided by trial. Metaphysicians have argued endlessly as to the interaction of mind and matter. The followers of Descartes held that mind and matter are so different as to make any action of the one on the other impossible. When I will to move my arm, they said, it is not my will that operates on my arm, but God, who, by His omnipotence, moves my arm whenever I want it moved. The modern doctrine of psycho-physical parallelism is not appreciably different from this theory of the Cartesian school. Psycho-physical parallelism is the theory that mental and physical events each have causes in their own sphere, but run on side by side owing to the fact that every state of the brain coexists with a definite state of the mind, and vice versa. This view of the reciprocal causal independence of mind and matter has no basis except in metaphysical theory.[1] For us, there is no necessity to make any such assumption, which is very difficult to harmonize with obvious facts. I receive a letter inviting me to dinner : the letter is a

---

[1] It would seem, however, that Dr. Hart accepts this theory as a methodological precept. See his contribution to *Subconscious Phenomena* (quoted above), especially pp. 121–2.

physical fact, but my apprehension of its meaning is mental. Here we have an effect of matter on mind. In consequence of my apprehension of the meaning of the letter, I go to the right place at the right time ; here we have an effect of mind on matter. I shall try to persuade you, in the course of these lectures, that matter is not so material and mind not so mental as is generally supposed. When we are speaking of matter, it will seem as if we were inclining to idealism ; when we are speaking of mind, it will seem as if we were inclining to materialism. Neither is the truth. Our world is to be constructed out of what the American realists call "neutral" entities, which have neither the hardness and indestructibility of matter, nor the reference to objects which is supposed to characterize mind.

There is, it is true, one objection which might be felt, not indeed to the action of matter on mind, but to the action of mind on matter. The laws of physics, it may be urged, are apparently adequate to explain everything that happens to matter, even when it is matter in a man's brain. This, however, is only a hypothesis, not an established theory. There is no cogent empirical reason for supposing that the laws determining the motions of living bodies are exactly the same as those that apply to dead matter. Sometimes, of course, they are clearly the same. When a man falls from a precipice or slips on a piece of orange peel, his body behaves as if it were devoid of life. These are the occasions that make Bergson laugh. But when a man's bodily movements are what we call "voluntary," they are, at any rate *prima facie*, very different in their laws from the movements of what is devoid of life. I do not wish to say dogmatically that the difference is irreducible ; I think it highly probable that it is not. I say only that the study of the behaviour of living bodies, in the present state of our knowledge, is distinct from physics. The study of gases was originally quite distinct from that of rigid bodies, and would never have advanced to its present state if it had not been independently pursued. Nowadays both the gas and the rigid body are manufactured out of a more primitive and universal kind of matter. In like manner, as a question of methodology, the laws of living bodies are to be studied, in the first place, without any undue haste to subordinate them to the laws of physics. Boyle's law and the rest had to be discovered before the kinetic theory of gases became possible. But in psychology we are hardly yet at the stage of Boyle's law. Meanwhile we need not be held up by the bogey of the universal rigid exactness of physics. This is, as yet, a mere hypothesis, to be tested empirically without any preconceptions. It may be true, or it may not. So far, that is all we can say.

Returning from this digression to our main topic, namely, the criticism of " consciousness," we observe that Freud and his followers, though they have demonstrated beyond dispute the immense importance of " unconscious " desires in determining our actions and beliefs, have not attempted the task of telling us what an " unconscious " desire actually is, and have thus invested their doctrine with an air of mystery and mythology which forms a large part of its popular attractiveness. They speak always as though it were more normal for a desire to be conscious, and as though a positive cause had to be assigned for its being unconscious. Thus " the unconscious " becomes a sort of underground prisoner, living in a dungeon, breaking in at long intervals upon our daylight respectability with dark groans and maledictions and strange atavistic lusts. The ordinary reader, almost inevitably, thinks of this underground person as another consciousness, prevented by what Freud calls the " censor " from making his voice heard in company, except on rare and dreadful occasions when he shouts so loud that every one hears him and there is a scandal. Most of us like the idea that we could be desperately wicked if only we let ourselves go. For this reason, the Freudian " unconscious " has been a consolation to many quiet and well-behaved persons.

I do not think the truth is quite so picturesque as this. I believe an " unconscious " desire is merely a causal law of our behaviour,[1] namely, that we remain restlessly active until a certain state of affairs is realized, when we achieve temporary equilibrium If we know beforehand what this state of affairs is, our desire is conscious ; if not, unconscious. The unconscious desire is not something actually existing, but merely a tendency to a certain behaviour ; it has exactly the same status as a force in dynamics. The unconscious desire is in no way mysterious ; it is the natural primitive form of desire, from which the other has developed through our habit of observing and theorizing (often wrongly). It is not necessary to suppose, as Freud seems to do, that every unconscious wish was once conscious, and was then, in his terminology, " repressed " because we disapproved of it. On the contrary, we shall suppose that, although Freudian " repression " undoubtedly occurs and is important, it is not the usual reason for unconsciousness of our wishes. The usual reason is merely that wishes are all, to begin with, unconscious,

[1] Cf. Hart, *The Psychology of Insanity*, p. 19.

and only become known when they are actively noticed. Usually, from laziness, people do not notice, but accept the theory of human nature which they find current, and attribute to themselves whatever wishes this theory would lead them to expect. We used to be full of virtuous wishes, but since Freud our wishes have become, in the words of the Prophet Jeremiah, "deceitful above all things and desperately wicked." Both these views, in most of those who have held them, are the product of theory rather than observation, for observation requires effort, whereas repeating phrases does not.

The interpretation of unconscious wishes which I have been advocating has been set forth briefly by Professor John B. Watson in an article called "The Psychology of Wish Fulfilment," which appeared in *The Scientific Monthly* in November, 1916. Two quotations will serve to show his point of view :

" The Freudians (he says) have made more or less of a ' metaphysical entity ' out of the censor. They suppose that when wishes are repressed they are repressed into the ' unconscious,' and that this mysterious censor stands at the trapdoor lying between the conscious and the unconscious. Many of us do not believe in a world of the unconscious (a few of us even have grave doubts about the usefulness of the term consciousness), hence we try to explain censorship along ordinary biological lines. We believe that one group of habits can ' down ' another group of habits—or instincts. In this case our ordinary system of habits—those which we call expressive of our ' real selves '—inhibit or quench (keep inactive or partially inactive) those habits and instinctive tendencies which belong largely in the past " (p. 483).

Again, after speaking of the frustration of some impulses which is involved in acquiring the habits of a civilized adult, he continues :

" It is among these frustrated impulses that I would find the biological basis of the unfulfilled wish. Such ' wishes ' need never have been ' conscious,' and *need never have been suppressed into Freud's realm of the unconscious.* It may be inferred from this that there is no particular reason for applying the term ' wish ' to such tendencies " (p. 485).

One of the merits of the general analysis of mind which we shall be concerned with in the following lectures is that it removes the atmosphere of mystery from the phenomena brought to light by the psycho-analysts. Mystery is delightful, but unscientific, since it depends upon ignorance. Man has developed out of the animals, and there is no serious gap between him and the amœba. Something closely analogous to knowledge and desire, as regards its effects on behaviour, exists among animals, even where what we call " consciousness " is hard to believe in ; something equally analogous exists in ourselves in cases where no trace of " consciousness " can be found. It is therefore natural to suppose that, whatever may be the correct definition of " consciousness," " consciousness " is not the essence of life or mind. In the following lectures, accordingly, this term will disappear until we have dealt with words, when it will re-emerge as mainly a trivial and unimportant outcome of linguistic habits.

LECTURE II

INSTINCT AND HABIT

In attempting to understand the elements out of which mental phenomena are compounded, it is of the greatest importance to remember that from the protozoa to man there is nowhere a very wide gap either in structure or in behaviour. From this fact it is a highly probable inference that there is also nowhere a very wide mental gap. It is, of course, *possible* that there may be, at certain stages in evolution, elements which are entirely new from the standpoint of analysis, though in their nascent form they have little influence on behaviour and no very marked correlatives in structure. But the hypothesis of continuity in mental development is clearly preferable if no psychological facts make it impossible. We shall find, if I am not mistaken, that there are no facts which refute the hypothesis of mental continuity, and that, on the other hand, this hypothesis affords a useful test of suggested theories as to the nature of mind.

The hypothesis of mental continuity throughout organic evolution may be used in two different ways. On the one hand, it may be held that we have more knowledge of our own minds than those of animals, and that we should use this knowledge to infer the existence of something similar to our own mental processes in animals and even in plants. On the other hand, it may be held that animals and plants present simpler phenomena, more easily analysed than those of human minds ; on this ground it may be urged that explanations which are adequate in the case of animals ought not to be lightly rejected in the case of man. The practical effects of these two views are diametrically opposite : the first leads us to level up animal intelligence with what we believe ourselves to know about our own intelligence, while the second leads us to attempt a levelling down of our own intelligence to something not too remote from what we can observe in animals. It is therefore important to consider the relative justification of the two ways of applying the principle of continuity.

It is clear that the question turns upon another, namely, which can we know best, the psychology of animals or that of human beings ? If we can know most about animals, we shall use this knowledge as a basis for inference about human beings ; if we can know most about human beings, we shall adopt the opposite procedure. And the question whether we can know most about the psychology of human beings or about that of animals turns upon yet another, namely : Is introspection or external observation the surer method in psychology ? This is a question which I propose to discuss at length in Lecture VI ; I shall therefore content myself now with a statement of the conclusions to be arrived at.

We know a great many things concerning ourselves which we cannot know nearly so directly concerning animals or even other people. We know when we have a toothache, what we are thinking of, what dreams we have when we are asleep, and a host of other occurrences which we only know about others when they tell us of them, or otherwise make them inferable by their behaviour. Thus, so far as knowledge of detached facts is concerned, the advantage is on the side of self-knowledge as against external observation.

But when we come to the analysis and scientific understanding of the facts, the advantages on the side of self-knowledge become far less clear. We know, for example, that we have desires and beliefs, but we do not know what constitutes a desire or a belief. The phenomena are so familiar that it is difficult to realize how little we really know about them. We see in animals, and to a lesser extent in plants, behaviour more or less similar to that which, in us, is prompted by desires and beliefs, and we find that, as we descend in the scale of evolution, behaviour becomes simpler, more easily reducible to rule, more scientifically analysable and predictable. And just because we are not misled by familiarity we find it easier to be cautious in interpreting behaviour when we are dealing with phenomena remote from those of our own minds. Moreover, introspection, as psychoanalysis has demonstrated, is extraordinarily fallible even in cases where we feel a high degree of certainty. The net result seems to be that, though self-knowledge has a definite and important contribution to make to psychology, it is exceedingly misleading unless it is constantly checked and controlled by the test of external observation, and by the theories which such observation suggests when applied to animal behaviour. On the whole, therefore, there is probably more to be learnt about human psychology from animals than about animal psychology from human beings ; but this conclusion is one of degree, and must not be pressed beyond a point.

It is only bodily phenomena that can be directly observed

in animals, or even, strictly speaking, in other human beings. We can observe such things as their movements, their physiological processes, and the sounds they emit. Such things as desires and beliefs, which seem obvious to introspection, are not visible directly to external observation. Accordingly, if we begin our study of psychology by external observation, we must not begin by assuming such things as desires and beliefs, but only such things as external observation can reveal, which will be characteristics of the movements and physiological processes of animals. Some animals, for example, always run away from light and hide themselves in dark places. If you pick up a mossy stone which is lightly embedded in the earth, you will see a number of small animals scuttling away from the unwonted daylight and seeking again the darkness of which you have deprived them. Such animals are sensitive to light, in the sense that their movements are affected by it; but it would be rash to infer that they have sensations in any way analogous to our sensations of sight. Such inferences, which go beyond the observable facts, are to be avoided with the utmost care.

It is customary to divide human movements into three classes, voluntary, reflex and mechanical. We may illustrate the distinction by a quotation from William James (*Psychology*, i, 12) :

" If I hear the conductor calling ' all aboard ' as I enter the depot, my heart first stops, then palpitates, and my legs respond to the air-waves falling on my tympanum by quickening their movements. If I stumble as I run, the sensation of falling provokes a movement of the hands towards the direction of the fall, the effect of which is to shield the body from too sudden a shock.

If a cinder enter my eye, its lids close forcibly and a copious flow of tears tends to wash it out.

" These three responses to a sensational stimulus differ, however, in many respects. The closure of the eye and the lachrymation are quite involuntary, and so is the disturbance of the heart. Such involuntary responses we know as ' reflex ' acts. The motion of the arms to break the shock of falling may also be called reflex, since it occurs too quickly to be deliberately intended. Whether it be instinctive or whether it result from the pedestrian education of childhood may be doubtful ; it is, at any rate, less automatic than the previous acts, for a man might by conscious effort learn to perform it more skilfully, or even to suppress it altogether. Actions of this kind, with which instinct and volition enter upon equal terms, have been called ' semi-reflex.' The act of running towards the train, on the other hand, has no instinctive element about it. It is purely the result of education, and is preceded by a consciousness of the purpose to be attained and a distinct mandate of the will. It is a ' voluntary act.' Thus the animal's reflex and voluntary performances shade into each other gradually, being connected by acts which may often occur automatically, but may also be modified by conscious intelligence.

" An outside observer, unable to perceive the accompanying consciousness, might be wholly at a loss to discriminate between the automatic acts and those which volition escorted. But if the criterion of mind's existence be the choice of the proper means for the attainment of a supposed end, all the acts alike seem to be inspired by intelligence, for *appropriateness* characterizes them all alike."

There is one movement, among those that James mentions at first, which is not subsequently classified, namely, the stumbling. This is the kind of movement which may be called " mechanical " ; it is evidently of a different kind from either reflex or voluntary movements, and more akin to the movements of dead matter. We may define a movement of an animal's body as " mechanical " when it proceeds as if only dead matter were involved. For example, if you fall over a cliff, you move under the influence of gravitation, and your centre of gravity describes just as correct a parabola as if you were already dead. Mechanical movements have not the characteristic of appropriateness, unless by accident, as when a drunken man falls into a waterbutt and is sobered. But reflex and voluntary movements are not *always* appropriate, unless in some very recondite sense. A moth flying into a lamp is not acting sensibly ; no more is a man who is in such a hurry to get his ticket that he cannot remember the name of his destination. Appropriateness is a complicated and merely approximate idea, and for the present we shall do well to dismiss it from our thoughts.

As James states, there is no difference, from the point of view of the outside observer, between voluntary and reflex movements. The physiologist can discover that both depend upon the nervous system, and he may find that the movements which we call voluntary depend upon higher centres in the brain than those that are reflex. But he cannot discover anything as to the presence or absence of " will " or " consciousness," for these things can only be seen from within, if at all. For the present, we wish to place ourselves resolutely in the position of outside observers ; we will therefore ignore the distinction between voluntary and reflex movements. We will call the two together " vital " movements. We may then distinguish " vital " from mechanical movements by the fact that vital movements depend for their causation upon the special properties of the nervous system, while mechanical movements depend only upon the properties which animal bodies share with matter in general.

There is need for some care if the distinction between mechanical and vital movements is to be made precise. It is quite likely that, if we knew more about animal bodies, we could deduce all their movements from the laws of chemistry and physics. It is already fairly easy to see how chemistry reduces to physics, i.e. how the differences between different chemical elements can be accounted for by differences of physical structure, the constituents of the structure being electrons which are exactly alike in all kinds of matter. We only know in part how to reduce physiology to chemistry, but we know enough to make it likely that the reduction is possible. If we suppose it effected, what would become of the difference between vital and mechanical movements?

Some analogies will make the difference clear. A shock to a mass of dynamite produces quite different effects from an equal shock to a mass of steel : in the one case there is a vast explosion, while in the other case there is hardly any noticeable disturbance. Similarly, you may sometimes find on a mountain-side a large rock poised so delicately that a touch will set it crashing down into the valley, while the rocks all round are so firm that only a considerable force can dislodge them. What is analogous in these two cases is the existence of a great store of energy in unstable equilibrium ready to burst into violent motion by the addition of a very slight disturbance. Similarly, it requires only a very slight expenditure of energy to send a post-card with the words " All is discovered ; fly ! " but the effect in generating kinetic energy is said to be amazing. A human body, like a mass of dynamite, contains a store of energy in unstable equilibrium, ready to be directed in this direction or that by a disturbance which is physically very small, such as a spoken word. In all such cases the reduction of behaviour to physical laws can only be effected by entering into great minuteness ; so long as we confine ourselves to the observation of comparatively large masses, the way in which the equilibrium will be upset cannot be determined. Physicists distinguish between macroscopic and microscopic equations : the former determine the visible movements of bodies of ordinary size, the latter the minute occurrences in the smallest parts. It is only the microscopic equations that are supposed to be the same for all sorts of matter. The macroscopic equations result from a process of averaging out, and may be different in different cases. So, in our instance, the laws of macroscopic phenomena are different for mechanical and vital movements, though the laws of microscopic phenomena may be the same.

We may say, speaking somewhat roughly, that a stimulus applied to the nervous system, like a spark to dynamite, is able to take advantage of the stored energy in unstable equilibrium, and thus to produce movements out of proportion to the proximate cause. Movements produced in this way are vital movements, while mechanical movements are those in which the stored energy of a living body is not involved. Similarly dynamite may be exploded, thereby displaying its characteristic properties, or may (with due precautions) be carted about like any other mineral. The explosion is analogous to vital movements, the carting about to mechanical movements.

Mechanical movements are of no interest to the psychologist, and it has only been necessary to define them in order to be able to exclude them. When a psychologist studies behaviour, it is only vital movements that concern him. We shall, therefore, proceed to ignore mechanical movements, and study only the properties of the remainder.

The next point is to distinguish between movements that are instinctive and movements that are acquired by experience. This distinction also is to some extent one of degree. Professor Lloyd Morgan gives the following definition of " instinctive behaviour " :

" That which is, on its first occurrence, independent of prior experience ; which tends to the well-being of the individual and the preservation of the race ; which is similarly performed by all members of the same more or less restricted group of animals ; and which may be subject to subsequent modification under the guidance of experience." [1]

This definition is framed for the purposes of biology, and is in some respects unsuited to the needs of psychology. Though perhaps unavoidable, allusion to " the same more or less restricted group of animals " makes it impossible to judge what is instinctive in the behaviour of an isolated individual. Moreover, " the well-being of the individual and the preservation of the race " is only a usual characteristic, not a universal one, of the sort of movements that, from our point of view, are to be called instinctive ; instances of harmful instincts will be given

[1] *Instinct and Experience* (Methuen, 1912) p. 5

shortly. The essential point of the definition, from our point of view, is that an instinctive movement is independent of prior experience.

We may say that an "instinctive" movement is a vital movement performed by an animal the first time that it finds itself in a novel situation ; or, more correctly, one which it would perform if the situation were novel.[1] The instincts of an animal are different at different periods of its growth, and this fact may cause changes of behaviour which are not due to learning. The maturing and seasonal fluctuation of the sex-instinct affords a good illustration. When the sex-instinct first matures, the behaviour of an animal in the presence of a mate is different from its previous behaviour in similar circumstances, but is not learnt, since it is just the same if the animal has never previously been in the presence of a mate.

On the other hand, a movement is " learnt," or embodies a " habit," if it is due to previous experience of similar situations, and is not what it would be if the animal had had no such experience.

There are various complications which blur the sharpness of this distinction in practice. To begin with, many instincts mature gradually, and while they are immature an animal may act in a fumbling manner which is very difficult to distinguish from learning. James (*Psychology*, ii, 407) maintains that children walk by instinct, and that the awkwardness of their first attempts is only due to the fact that the instinct has not yet ripened. He hopes that "some scientific widower, left alone with

---

[1] Though this can only be decided by comparison with other members of the species, and thus exposes us to the need of comparison which we thought an objection to Professor Lloyd Morgan's definition.

his offspring at the critical moment, may ere long test this suggestion on the living subject." However this may be, he quotes evidence to show that " birds do not *learn* to fly," but fly by instinct when they reach the appropriate age (*ib.*, p. 406). In the second place, instinct often gives only a rough outline of the sort of thing to do, in which case learning is necessary in order to acquire certainty and precision in action. In the third place, even in the clearest cases of acquired habit, such as speaking, some instinct is required to set in motion the process of learning. In the case of speaking, the chief instinct involved is commonly supposed to be that of imitation, but this may be questioned. (See Thorndike's *Animal Intelligence*, p. 253 ff.)

In spite of these qualifications, the broad distinction between instinct and habit is undeniable. To take extreme cases, every animal at birth can take food by instinct, before it has had opportunity to learn ; on the other hand, no one can ride a bicycle by instinct, though, after learning, the necessary movements become just as automatic as if they were instinctive.

The process of learning, which consists in the acquisition of habits, has been much studied in various animals.[1] For example : you put a hungry animal, say a cat, in a cage which has a door that can be opened by lifting a latch ; outside the cage you put food. The cat at first dashes all round the cage, making frantic efforts to force a way out. At last, by accident, the latch is lifted, and the cat pounces on the food. Next day you repeat the experiment, and you find that the cat gets out much more quickly than the first time, although it still makes

[1] The scientific study of this subject may almost be said to begin with Thorndike's *Animal Intelligence* (Macmillan, 1911).

some random movements. The third day it gets out still more quickly, and before long it goes straight to the latch and lifts it at once. Or you make a model of the Hampton Court maze, and put a rat in the middle, assaulted by the smell of food on the outside. The rat starts running down the passages, and is constantly stopped by blind alleys, but at last, by persistent attempts, it gets out. You repeat this experiment day after day ; you measure the time taken by the rat in reaching the food ; you find that the time rapidly diminishes, and that after a while the rat ceases to make any wrong turnings. It is by essentially similar processes that we learn speaking, writing, mathematics, or the government of an empire.

Professor Watson (*Behavior*, pp. 262-3) has an ingenious theory as to the way in which habit arises out of random movements. I think there is a reason why his theory cannot be regarded as alone sufficient, but it seems not unlikely that it is partly correct. Suppose, for the sake of simplicity, that there are just ten random movements which may be made by the animal—say, ten paths down which it may go—and that only one of these leads to food, or whatever else represents success in the case in question. Then the successful movement always occurs during the animal's attempts, whereas each of the others, on the average, occurs in only half the attempts. Thus the tendency to repeat a previous performance (which is easily explicable without the intervention of " consciousness ") leads to a greater emphasis on the successful movement than on any other, and in time causes it alone to be performed. The objection to this view, if taken as the sole explanation, is that on improvement ought to set in till after the *second* trial, whereas experiment shows that already at the second attempt the animal does better than the first time. Something further is, therefore, required to account for the genesis of habit from random movements ; but I see no reason to suppose that what is further required involves " consciousness."

Mr. Thorndike (*op. cit.*, p. 244) formulates two " pro visional laws of acquired behaviour or learning," as follows :

" The Law of Effect is that : Of several responses made to the same situation, those which are accompanied or closely followed by satisfaction to the animal will, other things being equal, be more firmly connected with the situation, so that, when it recurs, they will be more likely to recur ; those which are accompanied or closely followed by discomfort to the animal will, other things being equal, have their connections with that situation weakened, so that, when it recurs, they will be less likely to occur. The greater the satisfaction or discomfort, the greater the strengthening or weakening of the bond.

" The Law of Exercise is that : Any response to a situation will, other things being equal, be more strongly connected with the situation in proportion to the number of times it has been connected with that situation and to the average vigour and duration of the connections."

With the explanation to be presently given of the meaning of " satisfaction " and " discomfort," there seems every reason to accept these two laws.

What is true of animals, as regards instinct and habit, is equally true of men. But the higher we rise in the evolutionary scale, broadly speaking, the greater becomes the power of learning, and the fewer are the occasions when pure instinct is exhibited unmodified in adult life.

This applies with great force to man, so much so that some have thought instinct less important in the life of man than in that of animals. This, however, would be a mistake. Learning is only possible when instinct supplies the driving-force. The animals in cages, which gradually learn to get out, perform random movements at first, which are purely instinctive. But for these random movements, they would never acquire the experience which afterwards enables them to produce the right movement. (This is partly questioned by Hobhouse [1] —wrongly, I think.) Similarly, children learning to talk make all sorts of sounds, until one day the right sound comes by accident. It is clear that the original making of random sounds, without which speech would never be learnt, is instinctive. I think we may say the same of all the habits and aptitudes that we acquire: in all of them there has been present throughout some instinctive activity, prompting at first rather inefficient movements, but supplying the driving force while more and more effective methods are being acquired. A cat which is hungry smells fish, and goes to the larder. This is a thoroughly efficient method when there is fish in the larder, and it is often successfully practised by children. But in later life it is found that merely going to the larder does not cause fish to be there; after a series of random movements it is found that this result is to be caused by going to the City in the morning and coming back in the evening. No one would have guessed *a priori* that this movement of a middle-aged man's body would cause fish to come out of the sea into his larder, but experience shows that it does, and the middle-aged man therefore continues to go to the City,

[1] *Mind in Evolution* (Macmillan, 1915), pp. 236–237.

just as the cat in the cage continues to lift the latch when it has once found it. Of course, in actual fact, human learning is rendered easier, though psychologically more complex, through language; but at bottom language does not alter the essential character of learning, or of the part played by instinct in promoting learning. Language, however, is a subject upon which I do not wish to speak until a later lecture.

The popular conception of instinct errs by imagining it to be infallible and preternaturally wise, as well as incapable of modification. This is a complete delusion. Instinct, as a rule, is very rough and ready, able to achieve its result under ordinary circumstances, but easily misled by anything unusual. Chicks follow their mother by instinct, but when they are quite young they will follow with equal readiness any moving object remotely resembling their mother, or even a human being (James, *Psychology*, ii, 396). Bergson, quoting Fabre, has made play with the supposed extraordinary accuracy of the solitary wasp Ammophila, which lays its eggs in a caterpillar. On this subject I will quote from Drever's *Instinct in Man*, p. 92:

"According to Fabre's observations, which Bergson accepts, the Ammophila stings its prey *exactly* and *unerringly* in *each* of the nervous centres. The result is that the caterpillar is paralyzed, but not immediately killed, the advantage of this being that the larva cannot be injured by any movement of the caterpillar, upon which the egg is deposited, and is provided with fresh meat when the time comes.

"Now Dr. and Mrs. Peckham have shown that the sting of the wasp is *not unerring*, as Fabre alleges, that the number of stings is *not constant*, that sometimes the caterpillar is *not paralyzed*, and sometimes it *is killed outright*, and that *the different circumstances do not apparently make any difference to the larva*, which is not injured by slight movements of the caterpillar, nor by consuming food decomposed rather than fresh caterpillar."

This illustrates how love of the marvellous may mislead even so careful an observer as Fabre and so eminent a philosopher as Bergson.

In the same chapter of Dr. Drever's book there are some interesting examples of the mistakes made by instinct. I will quote one as a sample :

" The larva of the Lomechusa beetle eats the young of the ants, in whose nest it is reared. Nevertheless, the ants tend the Lomechusa larvæ with the same care they bestow on their own young. Not only so, but they apparently discover that the methods of feeding, which suit their own larvæ, would prove fatal to the guests, and accordingly they change their whole system of nursing " (*loc. cit.*, p. 106).

Semon (*Die Mneme*, pp. 207-9) gives a good illustration of an instinct growing wiser through experience. He relates how hunters attract stags by imitating the sounds of other members of their species, male or female, but find that the older a stag becomes the more difficult it is to deceive him, and the more accurate the imitation has to be.

The literature of instinct is vast, and illustrations might be multiplied indefinitely. The main points as regards instinct, which need to be emphasized as against the popular conceptions of it, are :

(1) That instinct requires no prevision of the biological end which it serves ;

(2) That instinct is only adapted to achieve this end in the usual circumstances of the animal in question, and has no more precision than is necessary for success *as a rule* ;

(3) That processes initiated by instinct often come to be performed better after experience ;

(4) That instinct supplies the impulses to experimental movements which are required for the process of learning ;

(5) That instincts in their nascent stages are easily modifiable, and capable of being attached to various sorts of objects.

All the above characteristics of instinct can be established by purely external observation, except the fact that instinct does not require prevision. This, though not strictly capable of being *proved* by observation, is irresistibly suggested by the most obvious phenomena. Who can believe, for example, that a new-born baby is aware of the necessity of food for preserving life ? Or that insects, in laying eggs, are concerned for the preservation of their species ? The essence of instinct, one might say, is that it provides a mechanism for acting without foresight in a manner which is usually advantageous biologically. It is partly for this reason that it is so important to understand the fundamental position of instinct in prompting both animal and human behaviour.

LECTURE III

DESIRE AND FEELING

DESIRE is a subject upon which, if I am not mistaken, true views can only be arrived at by an almost complete reversal of the ordinary unreflecting opinion. It is natural to regard desire as in its essence an attitude towards something which is imagined, not actual ; this something is called the *end* or *object* of the desire, and is said to be the *purpose* of any action resulting from the desire. We think of the content of the desire as being just like the content of a belief, while the attitude taken up towards the content is different. According to this theory, when we say : " I hope it will rain," or " I expect it will rain," we express, in the first case, a desire, and in the second, a belief, with an identical content, namely, the image of rain. It would be easy to say that, just as belief is one kind of feeling in relation to this content, so desire is another kind. According to this view, what comes first in desire is something imagined, with a specific feeling related to it, namely, that specific feeling which we call " desiring " it. The discomfort associated with un-satisfied desire, and the actions which aim at satisfying desire, are, in this view, both of them effects of the desire. I think it is fair to say that this is a view against which common sense would not rebel ; nevertheless, I believe it to be radically mistaken. It cannot be refuted logically, but various facts can be adduced which make it gradually less simple and plausible, until at last it turns out to be easier to abandon it wholly and look at the matter in a totally different way.

The first set of facts to be adduced against the common-sense view of desire are those studied by psycho-analysis. In all human beings, but most markedly in those suffering from hysteria and certain forms of insanity, we find what are called "unconscious" desires, which are commonly regarded as showing self-deception. Most psycho-analysts pay little attention to the analysis of desire, being interested in discovering by observation what it is that people desire, rather than in discovering what actually constitutes desire. I think the strangeness of what they report would be greatly diminished if it were expressed in the language of a behaviourist theory of desire, rather than in the language of every-day beliefs. The general description of the sort of phenomena that bear on our present question is as follows : A person states that his desires are so-and-so, and that it is these desires that inspire his actions ; but the outside observer perceives that his actions are such as to realize quite different ends from those which he avows, and that these different ends are such as he might be expected to desire. Generally they are less virtuous than his professed desires, and are therefore less agreeable to profess than these are. It is accordingly supposed that they really exist as desires for ends, but in a subconscious part of the mind, which the patient refuses to admit into conscious-ness for fear of having to think ill of himself. There are no doubt many cases to which such a supposition is applicable without obvious artificiality. But the deeper the Freudians delve into the underground regions of instinct, the further they travel from anything resembling conscious desire, and the less possible it becomes to believe that only positive self-deception conceals from us that we really wish for things which are abhorrent to our explicit life.

In the cases in question we have a conflict between the outside observer and the patient's consciousness. The whole tendency of psycho-analysis is to trust the outside observer rather than the testimony of introspection. I believe this tendency to be entirely right, but to demand a re-statement of what constitutes desire, exhibiting it as a causal law of our actions, not as something actually existing in our minds.

But let us first get a clearer statement of the essential characteristic of the phenomena.

A person, we find, states that he desires a certain end A, and that he is acting with a view to achieving it. We observe, however, that his actions are such as are likely to achieve a quite different end B, and that B is the sort of end that often seems to be aimed at by animals and savages, though civilized people are supposed to have discarded it. We sometimes find also a whole set of false beliefs, of such a kind as to persuade the patient that his actions are really a means to A, when in fact they are a means to B. For example, we have an impulse to inflict pain upon those whom we hate ; we therefore believe that they are wicked, and that punishment will reform them. This belief enables us to act upon the impulse to inflict pain, while believing that we are acting upon the desire to lead sinners to repentance. It is for this reason that the criminal law has been in all ages more severe than it would have been if the impulse to ameliorate the criminal had been what really inspired it. It seems simple to explain such a state of affairs as due to " self-deception," but this explanation is often mythical. Most people, in thinking about punishment, have had no more need to hide their vindictive impulses from themselves than they have had to hide the exponential theorem. Our impulses are not patent to a casual observation, but are only to be discovered by a scientific study of our actions, in the course of which we must regard ourselves as objectively as we should the motions of the planets or the chemical reactions of a new element.

The study of animals reinforces this conclusion, and is in many ways the best preparation for the analysis of desire. In animals we are not troubled by the disturbing influence of ethical considerations. In dealing with human beings, we are perpetually distracted by being told that such-and-such a view is gloomy or cynical or pessimistic : ages of human conceit have built up such a vast myth as to our wisdom and virtue that any intrusion of the mere scientific desire to know the facts is instantly resented by those who cling to comfortable illusions. But no one cares whether animals are virtuous or not, and no one is under the delusion that they are rational. Moreover, we do not expect them to be so " conscious," and are prepared to admit that their instincts prompt useful actions without any prevision of the ends which they achieve. For all these reasons, there is much in the analysis of mind which is more easily discovered by the study of animals than by the observation of human beings.

We all think that, by watching the behaviour of animals, we can discover more or less what they desire.

If this is the case—and I fully agree that it is—desire must be capable of being exhibited in actions, for it is only the actions of animals that we can observe. They *may* have minds in which all sorts of things take place, but we can know nothing about their minds except by means of inferences from their actions ; and the more such inferences are examined, the more dubious they appear. It would seem, therefore, that actions alone must be the test of the desires of animals. From this it is an easy step to the conclusion that an animal's desire is nothing but a characteristic of a certain series of actions, namely, those which would be commonly regarded as inspired by the desire in question. And when it has been shown that this view affords a satisfactory account of animal desires, it is not difficult to see that the same explanation is applicable to the desires of human beings.

We judge easily from the behaviour of an animal of a familiar kind whether it is hungry or thirsty, or pleased or displeased, or inquisitive or terrified. The verification of our judgment, so far as verification is possible, must be derived from the immediately succeeding actions of the animal. Most people would say that they infer first something about the animal's state of mind—whether it is hungry or thirsty and so on—and thence derive their expectations as to its subsequent conduct. But this détour through the animal's supposed mind is wholly unnecessary. We can say simply : The animal's behaviour during the last minute has had those characteristics which distinguish what is called "hunger," and it is likely that its actions during the next minute will be similar in this respect, unless it finds food, or is interrupted by a stronger impulse, such as fear. An animal which is hungry is restless, it goes to the places where food is often to be found, it sniffs with its nose or peers with its eyes or otherwise increases the sensitiveness of its sense-organs ; as soon as it is near enough to food for its sense-organs to be affected, it goes to it with all speed and proceeds to eat ; after which, if the quantity of food has been sufficient, its whole demeanour changes : it may very likely lie down and go to sleep. These things and others like them are observable phenomena distinguishing a hungry animal from one which is not hungry. The characteristic mark by which we recognize a series of actions which display hunger is not the animal's mental state, which we cannot observe, but something in its bodily behaviour ; it is this observable trait in the bodily behaviour that I am proposing to call " hunger," not some possibly mythical and certainly unknowable ingredient of the animal's mind.

Generalizing what occurs in the case of hunger, we may say that what we call a desire in an animal is always displayed in a cycle of actions having certain fairly well-marked characteristics. There is first a state of activity, consisting, with qualifications to be mentioned presently, of movements likely to have a certain result ; these movements, unless interrupted, continue until the result is achieved, after which there is usually a period of comparative quiescence. A cycle of actions of this sort has marks by which it is broadly distinguished from the motions of dead matter. The most notable of these marks are—(1) the appropriateness of the actions for the realization of a certain result ; (2) the continuance of action until that result has been achieved. Neither of these can be pressed beyond a point. Either may be (a) to some extent present in dead matter, and (b) to a considerable extent absent in animals, while vegetables are intermediate, and display only a much fainter form of the behaviour which leads us to attribute desire to animals. (*a*) One might say rivers " desire " the sea : water, roughly speaking, remains in restless motion until it reaches either the sea or a place from which it cannot issue without going uphill, and therefore we might say that this is what it wishes while it is flowing. We do not say so, because we can account for the behaviour of water by the laws of physics ; and if we knew more about animals, we might equally cease to attribute desires to them, since we might find physical and chemical reactions sufficient to account for their behaviour. (*b*) Many of the movements of animals do not exhibit the characteristics of the cycles which seem to embody desire. There are first of all the movements which are " mechanical," such as slipping and falling, where ordinary physical forces operate upon the animal's body almost as if it were dead matter. An animal which falls over a cliff may make a number of desperate struggles while it is in the air, but its centre of gravity will move exactly as it would if the animal were dead. In this case, if the animal is killed at the end of the fall, we have, at first sight, just the characteristics of a cycle of actions embodying desire, namely, restless movement until the ground is reached, and then quiescence. Nevertheless, we feel no temptation to say that the animal desired what occurred, partly because of the obviously mechanical nature of the whole occurrence, partly because, when an animal survives a fall, it tends not to repeat the experience. There may be other reasons also, but of them I do not wish to speak yet. Besides mechanical movements, there are interrupted movements, as when a bird, on its way to eat your best peas, is frightened away

by the boy whom you are employing for that purpose.
If interruptions are frequent and completion of cycles
rare, the characteristics by which cycles are observed
may become so blurred as to be almost unrecognizable.
The result of these various considerations is that the
differences between animals and dead matter, when
we confine ourselves to external unscientific observation
of integral behaviour, are a matter of degree and not
very precise. It is for this reason that it has always been
possible for fanciful people to maintain that even stocks
and stones have some vague kind of soul. The evidence
that animals have souls is so very shaky that, if it is
assumed to be conclusive, one might just as well go a
step further and extend the argument by analogy to
all matter. Nevertheless, in spite of vagueness and
doubtful cases, the existence of cycles in the behaviour
of animals is a broad characteristic by which they are
prima facie distinguished from ordinary matter ; and
I think it is this characteristic which leads us to attribute
desires to animals, since it makes their behaviour resemble
what we do when (as we say) we are acting from desire.

I shall adopt the following definitions for describing
the behaviour of animals :

A " behaviour-cycle " is a series of voluntary or reflex
movements of an animal, tending to cause a certain
result, and continuing until that result is caused, unless
they are interrupted by death, accident, or some new
behaviour-cycle. (Here " accident " may be defined as
the intervention of purely physical laws causing mechanical
movements.)

The " purpose " of a behaviour-cycle is the result
which brings it to an end, normally by a condition of
temporary quiescence—provided there is no interruption.

An animal is said to " desire " the purpose of a behaviour-cycle while the behaviour-cycle is in progress.

I believe these definitions to be adequate also to human purposes and desires, but for the present I am only occupied with animals and with what can be learnt by external observation. I am very anxious that no ideas should be attached to the words " purpose " and " desire " beyond those involved in the above definitions.

We have not so far considered what is the nature of the initial stimulus to a behaviour-cycle. Yet it is here that the usual view of desire seems on the strongest ground. The hungry animal goes on making movements until it gets food ; it seems natural, therefore, to suppose that the idea of food is present throughout the process, and that the thought of the end to be achieved sets the whole process in motion. Such a view, however, is obviously untenable in many cases, especially where instinct is concerned. Take, for example, reproduction and the rearing of the young. Birds mate, build a nest, lay eggs in it, sit on the eggs, feed the young birds, and care for them until they are fully grown. It is totally impossible to suppose that this series of actions, which constitutes one behaviour-cycle, is inspired by any prevision of the end, at any rate the first time it is performed.[1] We must suppose that the stimulus to the performance of each act is an impulsion from behind, not an attraction from the future. The bird does what it does, at each stage, because it has an impulse to that particular action, not because it perceives that the whole cycle of actions will contribute to the preservation of the species. The same considerations apply to other

[1] For evidence as to birds' nests, cf. Semon, *Die Mneme*, pp. 209, 210

instincts. A hungry animal feels restless, and is led by instinctive impulses to perform the movements which give it nourishment ; but the act of seeking food is not sufficient evidence from which to conclude that the animal has the thought of food in its " mind."

Coming now to human beings, and to what we know about our own actions, it seems clear that what, with us, sets a behaviour-cycle in motion is some sensation of the sort which we call disagreeable. Take the case of hunger : we have first an uncomfortable feeling inside, producing a disinclination to sit still, a sensitiveness to savoury smells, and an attraction towards any food that there may be in our neighbourhood. At any moment during this process we may become aware that we are hungry, in the sense of saying to ourselves, " I am hungry " ; but we may have been acting with reference to food for some time before this moment. While we are talking or reading, we may eat in complete unconsciousness ; but we perform the actions of eating just as we should if we were conscious, and they cease when our hunger is appeased. What we call " consciousness " seems to be a mere spectator of the process ; even when it issues orders, they are usually, like those of a wise parent, just such as would have been obeyed even if they had not been given. This view may seem at first exaggerated, but the more our so-called volitions and their causes are examined, the more it is forced upon us. The part played by words in all this is complicated, and a potent source of confusions ; I shall return to it later. For the present, I am still concerned with primitive desire, as it exists in man, but in the form in which man shows his affinity to his animal ancestors.

Conscious desire is made up partly of what is essential to desire, partly of beliefs as to what we want. It is important to be clear as to the part which does not consist of beliefs.

The primitive non-cognitive element in desire seems to be a push, not a pull, an impulsion away from the actual, rather than an attraction towards the ideal. Certain sensations and other mental occurrences have a property which we call discomfort; these cause such bodily movements as are likely to lead to their cessation. When the discomfort ceases, or even when it appreciably diminishes, we have sensations possessing a property which we call *pleasure*. Pleasurable sensations either stimulate no action at all, or at most stimulate such action as is likely to prolong them. I shall return shortly to the consideration of what discomfort and pleasure are in themselves; for the present, it is their connection with action and desire that concerns us. Abandoning momentarily the standpoint of behaviourism, we may presume that hungry animals experience sensations involving discomfort, and stimulating such movements as seem likely to bring them to the food which is outside the cages. When they have reached the food and eaten it, their discomfort ceases and their sensations become pleasurable. It *seems*, mistakenly, as if the animals had had this situation in mind throughout, when in fact they have been continually pushed by discomfort. And when an animal is reflective, like some men, it comes to think that it had the final situation in mind throughout; sometimes it comes to know what situation will bring satisfaction, so that in fact the discomfort does bring the thought of what will allay it. Nevertheless the sensation involving discomfort remains the prime mover.

This brings us to the question of the nature of discomfort and pleasure. Since Kant it has been customary to recognize three great divisions of mental phenomena, which are typified by knowledge, desire and feeling, where " feeling " is used to mean pleasure and discomfort. Of course, " knowledge " is too definite a word : the states of mind concerned are grouped together as " cognitive," and are to embrace not only beliefs, but perceptions, doubts, and the understanding of concepts. " Desire," also, is narrower than what is intended : for example, *will* is to be included in this category, and in fact everything that involves any kind of striving, or " conation " as it is technically called. I do not myself believe that there is any value in this threefold division of the contents of mind. I believe that sensations (including images) supply all the " stuff " of the mind, and that everything else can be analysed into groups of sensations related in various ways, or characteristics of sensations or of groups of sensations. As regards belief, I shall give grounds for this view in later lectures. As regards desires, I have given some grounds in this lecture. For the present, it is pleasure and discomfort that concern us.

There are broadly three theories that might be held in regard to them. We may regard them as separate existing items in those who experience them, or we may regard them as intrinsic qualities of sensations and other mental occurrences, or we may regard them as mere names for the causal characteristics of the occurrences which are uncomfortable or pleasant. The first of these theories, namely, that which regards discomfort and pleasure as actual contents in those who experience them, has, I think, nothing conclusive to be said in its favour.[1]

[1] Various arguments in its favour are advanced by A. Wohlgemuth, " On the feelings and their neural correlate, with an examination of the nature of pain," *British Journal of Psychology*, viii, 4

It is suggested chiefly by an ambiguity in the word
"pain," which has misled many people, including
Berkeley, whom it supplied with one of his arguments
for subjective idealism. We may use "pain" as the
opposite of "pleasure," and "painful" as the opposite
of "pleasant," or we may use "pain" to mean a certain
sort of sensation, on a level with the sensations of heat
and cold and touch. The latter use of the word has
prevailed in psychological literature, and it is now no
longer used as the opposite of "pleasure." Dr. H. Head,
in a recent publication, has stated this distinction as
follows : [1]

"It is necessary at the outset to distinguish clearly
between 'discomfort' and 'pain.' Pain is a distinct
sensory quality equivalent to heat and cold, and its
intensity can be roughly graded according to the force
expended in stimulation. Discomfort, on the other
hand, is that feeling-tone which is directly opposed to
pleasure. It may accompany sensations not in themselves
essentially painful, as for instance that produced by
tickling the sole of the foot. The reaction produced
by repeated pricking contains both these elements ; for
it evokes that sensory quality known as pain, accompanied
by a disagreeable feeling-tone, which we have called
discomfort. On the other hand, excessive pressure,
except when applied directly over some nerve-trunk,
tends to excite more discomfort than pain."

The confusion between discomfort and pain has made

(1917).   But as these arguments are largely a *reductio ad absurdum*
of other theories, among which that which I am advocating is not
included, I cannot regard them as establishing their contention.

[1] "Sensation and the Cerebral Cortex," *Brain*, vol. xli, part ii
(September, 1918), p. 90.   Cf. also Wohlgemuth, *loc. cit.*, pp. 437,
450.

people regard discomfort as a more substantial thing than it is, and this in turn has reacted upon the view taken of pleasure, since discomfort and pleasure are evidently on a level in this respect. As soon as discomfort is clearly distinguished from the sensation of pain, it becomes more natural to regard discomfort and pleasure as properties of mental occurrences than to regard them as separate mental occurrences on their own account. I shall therefore dismiss the view that they are separate mental occurrences, and regard them as properties of such experiences as would be called respectively uncomfortable and pleasant.

It remains to be examined whether they are actual qualities of such occurrences, or are merely differences as to causal properties. I do not myself see any way of deciding this question ; either view seems equally capable of accounting for the facts. If this is true, it is safer to avoid the assumption that there are such intrinsic qualities of mental occurrences as are in question, and to assume only the causal differences which are undeniable. Without condemning the intrinsic theory, we can define discomfort and pleasure as consisting in causal properties, and say only what will hold on either of the two theories. Following this course, we shall say :

"Discomfort " is a property of a sensation or other mental occurrence, consisting in the fact that the occurrence in question stimulates voluntary or reflex movements tending to produce some more or less definite change involving the cessation of the occurrence.

" Pleasure " is a property of a sensation or other mental occurrence, consisting in the fact that the occurrence in question either does not stimulate any voluntary or reflex movement, or, if it does, stimulates only such as tend to prolong the occurrence in question.[1]

" Conscious " desire, which we have now to consider, consists of desire in the sense hitherto discussed, together with a true belief as to its " purpose," i.e. as to the state of affairs that will bring quiescence with cessation of the discomfort. If our theory of desire is correct, a belief as to its purpose may very well be erroneous, since only experience can show what causes a discomfort to cease. When the experience needed is common and simple, as in the case of hunger, a mistake is not very probable. But in other cases—e.g erotic desire in those who have had little or no experience of its satisfaction— mistakes are to be expected, and do in fact very often occur. The practice of inhibiting impulses, which is to a great extent necessary to civilized life, makes mistakes easier, by preventing experience of the actions to which a desire would otherwise lead, and by often causing the inhibited impulses themselves to be unnoticed or quickly forgotten. The perfectly natural mistakes which thus arise constitute a large proportion of what is, mistakenly in part, called self-deception, and attributed by Freud to the " censor."

But there is a further point which needs emphasizing, namely, that a belief that something is desired has often a tendency to cause the very desire that is believed in. It is this fact that makes the effect of " consciousness " on desire so complicated.

When we believe that we desire a certain state of affairs, that often tends to cause a real desire for it. This is due partly to the influence of words upon our emotions, in rhetoric for example, and partly to the general fact

[1] Cf. Thorndike, *op. cit.*, p. 245.

that discomfort normally belongs to the belief that we
desire such-and-such a thing that we do not possess.
Thus what was originally a false opinion as to the object
of a desire acquires a certain truth : the false opinion
generates a secondary subsidiary desire, which nevertheless becomes real. Let us take an illustration. Suppose
you have been jilted in a way which wounds your vanity.
Your natural impulsive desire will be of the sort expressed
in Donne's poem :

> When by thy scorn, O Murderess, I am dead,

in which he explains how he will haunt the poor lady
as a ghost, and prevent her from enjoying a moment's
peace. But two things stand in the way of your expressing yourself so naturally : on the one hand, your vanity,
which will not acknowledge how hard you are hit ; on
the other hand, your conviction that you are a civilized
and humane person, who could not possibly indulge so
crude a desire as revenge. You will therefore experience
a restlessness which will at first seem quite aimless, but
will finally resolve itself in a conscious desire to change
your profession, or go round the world, or conceal your
identity and live in Putney, like Arnold Bennett's hero.
Although the prime cause of this desire is a false judgment as to your previous unconscious desire, yet the new
conscious desire has its own derivative genuineness, and
may influence your actions to the extent of sending you
round the world. The initial mistake, however, will have
effects of two kinds. First, in uncontrolled moments,
under the influence of sleepiness or drink or delirium,
you will say things calculated to injure the faithless
deceiver. Secondly, you will find travel disappointing,
and the East less fascinating than you had hoped—unless,

some day, you hear that the wicked one has in turn been jilted. If this happens, you will believe that you feel sincere sympathy, but you will suddenly be much more delighted than before with the beauties of tropical islands or the wonders of Chinese art. A secondary desire, derived from a false judgment as to a primary desire, has its own power of influencing action, and is therefore a real desire according to our definition. But it has not the same power as a primary desire of bringing thorough satisfaction when it is realized ; so long as the primary desire remains unsatisfied, restlessness continues in spite of the secondary desire's success. Hence arises a belief in the vanity of human wishes : the vain wishes are those that are secondary, but mistaken beliefs prevent us from realizing that they are secondary.

What may, with some propriety, be called self-deception arises through the operation of desires for beliefs. We desire many things which it is not in our power to achieve : that we should be universally popular and admired, that our work should be the wonder of the age, and that the universe should be so ordered as to bring ultimate happiness to all, though not to our enemies until they have repented and been purified by suffering. Such desires are too large to be achieved through our own efforts. But it is found that a considerable portion of the satisfaction which these things would bring us if they were realized is to be achieved by the much easier operation of believing that they are or will be realized. This desire for beliefs, as opposed to desire for the actual facts, is a particular case of secondary desire, and, like all secondary desire, its satisfaction does not lead to a complete cessation of the initial discomfort. Nevertheless, desire for beliefs, as opposed to desire for facts, is exceedingly potent both

Individually and socially. According to the form of belief desired, it is called vanity, optimism, or religion. Those who have sufficient power usually imprison or put to death any one who tries to shake their faith in their own excellence or in that of the universe ; it is for this reason that seditious libel and blasphemy have always been, and still are, criminal offences.

It is very largely through desires for beliefs that the primitive nature of desire has become so hidden, and that the part played by consciousness has been so confusing and so exaggerated.

We may now summarize our analysis of desire and feeling.

A mental occurrence of any kind—sensation, image, belief, or emotion—may be a cause of a series of actions, continuing, unless interrupted, until some more or less definite state of affairs is realized. Such a series of actions we call a " behaviour-cycle." The degree of definiteness may vary greatly : hunger requires only food in general, whereas the sight of a particular piece of food raises a desire which requires the eating of that piece of food. The property of causing such a cycle of occurrences is called " discomfort " ; the property of the mental occurrences in which the cycle ends is called " pleasure." The actions constituting the cycle must not be purely mechanical, i.e. they must be bodily movements in whose causation the special properties of nervous tissue are involved. The cycle ends in a condition of quiescence, or of such action as tends only to preserve the *status quo*. The state of affairs in which this condition of quiescence is achieved is called the " purpose " of the cycle, and the initial mental occurrence involving discomfort is called a " desire " for the state of affairs that brings quiescence.

A desire is called " conscious " when it is accompanied by a true belief as to the state of affairs that will bring quiescence ; otherwise it is called "unconscious." All primitive desire is unconscious, and in human beings beliefs as to the purposes of desires are often mistaken. These mistaken beliefs generate secondary desires, which cause various interesting complications in the psychology of human desire, without fundamentally altering the character which it shares with animal desire.

LECTURE IV

INFLUENCE OF PAST HISTORY ON PRESENT OCCURRENCES IN LIVING ORGANISMS

In this lecture we shall be concerned with a very general characteristic which broadly, though not absolutely, distinguishes the behaviour of living organisms from that of dead matter. The characteristic in question is this :

The response of an organism to a given stimulus is very often dependent upon the past history of the organism, and not merely upon the stimulus and the *hitherto discoverable* present state of the organism.

This characteristic is embodied in the saying " a burnt child fears the fire." The burn may have left no visible traces, yet it modifies the reaction of the child in the presence of fire. It is customary to assume that, in such cases, the past operates by modifying the structure of the brain, not directly. I have no wish to suggest that this hypothesis is false ; I wish only to point out that it is a hypothesis. At the end of the present lecture I shall examine the grounds in its favour. If we confine ourselves to facts which have been actually observed, we must say that past occurrences, in addition to the present stimulus and the present ascertainable condition of the organism, enter into the causation of the response.

The characteristic is not wholly confined to living organisms. For example, magnetized steel looks just like steel which has not been magnetized, but its behaviour is in some ways different. In the case of dead matter, however, such phenomena are less frequent and important than in the case of living organisms, and it is far less difficult to invent satisfactory hypotheses as to the microscopic changes of structure which mediate between the past occurrence and the present changed response. In the case of living organisms, practically everything that is distinctive both of their physical and of their mental behaviour is bound up with this persistent influence of the past. Further, speaking broadly, the change in response is usually of a kind that is biologically advantageous to the organism

Following a suggestion derived from Semon (*Die Mneme*, Leipzig, 1904; 2nd edition, 1908, English translation, Allen & Unwin, 1921; *Die mnemischen Empfindungen*, Leipzig, 1909), we will give the name of " mnemic phenomena " to those responses of an organism which, so far as hitherto observed facts are concerned, can only be brought under causal laws by including past occurrences in the history of the organism as part of the causes of the present response. I do not mean merely—what would always be the case—that past occurrences are part of a *chain* of causes leading to the present event. I mean that, in attempting to state the *proximate* cause of the present event, some past event or events must be included, unless we take refuge in hypothetical modifications of brain structure. For example : you smell peat-smoke, and you recall some occasion when you smelt it before. The cause of your recollection, so far as hitherto observable phenomena are concerned, consists both of the peat-smoke (present stimulus) and of the former occasion (past experience). The same stimulus will not produce the same recollection in another man who did not share your former experience, although the former experience left no *observable* traces in the structure of the brain. According to the maxim "same cause, same effect," we cannot therefore regard the peat-smoke alone as the cause of your recollection, since it does not have the same effect in other cases. The cause of your recollection must be both the peat-smoke and the past occurrence. Accordingly your recollection is an instance of what we are calling "mnemic phenomena."

Before going further, it will be well to give illustrations of different classes of mnemic phenomena.

(a) *Acquired Habits.*—In Lecture II we saw how animals can learn by experience how to get out of cages or mazes, or perform other actions which are useful to them but not provided for by their instincts alone. A cat which is put into a cage of which it has had experience behaves differently from the way in which it behaved at first. We can easily invent hypotheses, which are quite likely to be true, as to connections in the brain caused by past experience, and themselves causing the different response. But the observable fact is that the stimulus of being in the cage produces differing results with repetition, and that the ascertainable cause of the cat's behaviour is not merely the cage and its own ascertainable organization, but also its past history in regard to the cage. From our present point of view, the matter is independent of the question whether the cat's behaviour is due to some mental fact called "knowledge," or displays a merely bodily habit. Our habitual knowledge is not always in our minds, but is called up by the appropriate stimuli. If we are asked "What is the capital of France?" we answer " Paris," because of past experience ; the past experience is as essential as the present question in the causation of our response. Thus all our habitual knowledge consists of acquired habits, and comes under the head of mnemic phenomena.

(b) *Images.*—I shall have much to say about images in a later lecture ; for the present I am merely concerned with them in so far as they are " copies " of past sensations. When you hear New York spoken of, some image probably comes into your mind, either of the place itself (if you have been there), or of some picture of it (if you have not). The image is due to your past experience, as well as to the present stimulus of the words " New York." Similarly, the images you have in dreams are all dependent upon your past experience, as well as upon the present stimulus to dreaming. It is generally believed that all images, in their simpler parts, are copies of sensations ; if so, their mnemic character is evident. This is important, not only on its own account, but also because, as we shall see later, images play an essential part in what is called " thinking."

(c) *Association.*—The broad fact of association, on the mental side, is that when we experience something which we have experienced before, it tends to call up the context of the former experience. The smell of peat-smoke recalling a former scene is an instance which we discussed a moment ago. This is obviously a mnemic phenomenon. There is also a more purely physical association, which is indistinguishable from physical habit. This is the kind studied by Mr. Thorndike in animals, where a certain simulus is associated with a certain act. This is the sort which is taught to soldiers in dr lling, for example. In such a case there need not be anything mental, but merely a habit of the body. There is no essential distinction between association and habit, and the observations which we made concerning habit as a mnemic phenomenon are equally applicable to association.

(d) *Non-sensational Elements in Perception.*—When we perceive any object of a familiar kind, much of what appears subjectively to be immediately given is really derived from past experience. When we see an object, say a penny, we seem to be aware of its " real " shape : we have the impression of something circular, not of something elliptical. In learning to draw, it is necessary to acquire the art of representing things according to the sensation, not according to the perception. And the visual appearance is filled out with feeling of what the object would be like to touch, and so on. This filling out and supplying of the " real " shape and so on consists of the most usual correlates of the sensational core in our perception. It may happen that, in the particular case, the real correlates are unusual ; for example, if what we are seeing is a carpet made to look like tiles. If so, the non-sensational part of our perception will be illusory, i.e. it will supply qualities which the object in question does not in fact have. But as a rule objects do have the qualities added by perception, which is to be expected, since experience of what is usual is the cause of the addition. If our experience had been different, we should not fill out sensation in the same way, except in so far as the filling out is instinctive, not acquired. It would seem that, in man, all that makes up space-perception, including the correlation of sight and touch and so on, is almost entirely acquired. In that case there is a large mnemic element in all the common perceptions by means of which we handle common objects. And, to take another kind of instance, imagine what our astonishment would be if we were to hear a cat bark or a dog mew. This emotion would be dependent upon past experience, and would therefore be a mnemic phenomenon according to the definition.

(e) *Memory as Knowledge.*—The kind of memory of which I am now speaking is definite knowledge of some past event in one's own experience. From time to time we remember things that have happened to us, because something in the present reminds us of them. Exactly the same present fact would not call up the same memory if our past experience had been different. Thus our remembering is caused by—

(1) The present stimulus,
(2) The past occurrence.

It is therefore a mnemic phenomenon according to our definition. A definition of " mnemic phenomena " which did not include memory would, of course, be a bad one. The point of the definition is not that it includes memory, but that it includes it as one of a class of phenomena which embrace all that is characteristic in the subject-matter of psychology.

(f) *Experience.*—The word " experience " is often used very vaguely. James, as we saw, uses it to cover the whole primal stuff of the world, but this usage seems objectionable, since, in a purely physical world, things would happen without there being any experience. It is only mnemic phenomena that embody experience. We may say that an animal "experiences" an occurrence when this occurrence modifies the animal's subsequent behaviour, i.e. when it is the mnemic portion of the cause of future occurrences in the animal's life. The burnt child that fears the fire has " experienced " the fire, whereas a stick that has been thrown on and taken off again has not " experienced " anything, since it offers no more resistance than before to being thrown on. The essence of " experience " is the modification of behaviour produced by what is experienced. We might, in fact, define one chain of experience, or one biography, as a series of occurrences linked by mnemic causation. I think it is this characteristic, more than any other, that distinguishes sciences dealing with living organisms from physics.

The best writer on mnemic phenomena known to me is Richard Semon, the fundamental part of whose theory I shall endeavour to summarize before going further :

When an organism, either animal or plant, is subjected to a stimulus, producing in it some state of excitement, the removal of the stimulus allows it to return to a condition of equilibrium. But the new state of equilibrium is different from the old, as may be seen by the changed capacity for reaction. The state of equilibrium before the stimulus may be called the " primary indifference-state " ; that after the cessation of the stimulus, the " secondary indifference-state." We define the " engraphic effect " of a stimulus as the effect in making a difference between the primary and secondary indifference-states, and this difference itself we define as the " engram " due to the stimulus. " Mnemic phenomena " are defined as those due to engrams ; in animals, they are specially associated with the nervous system, but not exclusively, even in man.

When two stimuli occur together, one of them occurring afterwards, may call out the reaction for the other also. We call this an " ekphoric influence," and stimuli having this character are called " ekphoric stimuli." In such a case we call the engrams of the two stimuli "associated." All simultaneously generated engrams are associated ; there is also association of successively aroused engrams, though this is reducible to simultaneous association. In fact, it is not an isolated stimulus that leaves an engram, but the totality of the stimuli at any moment ; consequently any portion of this totality tends, if it recurs, to arouse the whole reaction which was aroused before. Semon holds that engrams can be inherited, and that an animal's innate habits may be due to the experience of its ancestors ; on this subject he refers to Samuel Butler.

Semon formulates two " mnemic principles." The first, or " Law of Engraphy," is as follows : " All simultaneous excitements in an organism form a connected simultaneous excitement-complex, which as such works engraphically, i.e. leaves behind a connected engram-complex, which in so far forms a whole " (*Die mnemischen Empfindungen*, p. 146). The second mnemic principle, or " Law of Ekphory," is as follows : " The partial return of the energetic situation which formerly worked engraphically operates ekphorically on a simultaneous engram-complex " (*ib.*, p. 173). These two laws together represent in part a hypothesis (the engram), and in part an observable fact. The observable fact is that, when a certain complex of stimuli has originally caused a certain complex of reactions, the recurrence of part of the stimuli tends to cause the recurrence of the whole of the reactions.

Semon's applications of his fundamental ideas in various directions are interesting and ingenious. Some of them

will concern us later, but for the present it is the fundamental character of mnemic phenomena that is in question.

Concerning the nature of an engram, Semon confesses
that at present it is impossible to say more than that it
must consist in some material alteration in the body of
the organism (*Die mnemischen Empfindungen*, p. 376). It
is, in fact, hypothetical, invoked for theoretical uses, and
not an outcome of direct observation. No doubt physiology, especially the disturbances of memory through
lesions in the brain, affords grounds for this hypothesis ; nevertheless it does remain a hypothesis, the
validity of which will be discussed at the end of this
lecture.

I am inclined to think that, in the present state of
physiology, the introduction of the engram does not
serve to simplify the account of mnemic phenomena
We can, I think, formulate the known laws of such phenomena in terms, wholly, of observable facts, by recognizing
provisionally what we may call " mnemic causation."
By this I mean that kind of causation of which I spoke
at the beginning of this lecture, that kind, namely, in
which the proximate cause consists not merely of a present event, but of this together with a past event. I
do not wish to urge that this form of causation is ultimate, but that, in the present state of our knowledge, it
affords a simplification, and enables us to state laws of
behaviour in less hypothetical terms than we should
otherwise have to employ.

The clearest instance of what I mean is recollection
of a past event. What we observe is that certain present
stimuli lead us to recollect certain occurrences, but that at
times when we are not recollecting them, there is nothing
discoverable in our minds that could be called memory

of them. Memories, as mental facts, arise from time to time, but do not, so far as we can see, exist in any shape while they are " latent." In fact, when we say that they are " latent," we mean merely that they will exist under certain circumstances. If, then, there is to be some standing difference between the person who can remember a certain fact and the person who cannot, that standing difference must be, not in anything mental, but in the brain. It is quite probable that there is such a difference in the brain, but its nature is unknown and it remains hypothetical. Everything that has, so far, been made matter of observation as regards this question can be put together in the statement : When a certain complex of sensations has occurred to a man, the recurrence of part of the complex tends to arouse the recollection of the whole. In like manner, we can collect all mnemic phenomena in living organisms under a single law, which contains what is hitherto verifiable in Semon's two laws. This single law is :

If a complex stimulus A has caused a complex reaction B in an organism, the occurrence of a part of A on a future occasion tends to cause the whole reaction B.

This law would need to be supplemented by some account of the influence of frequency, and so on ; but it seems to contain the essential characteristic of mnemic phenomena, without admixture of anything hypothetical.

Whenever the effect resulting from a stimulus to an organism differs according to the past history of the organism, without our being able actually to detect any relevant difference in its present structure, we will speak of " mnemic causation," provided we can discover laws embodying the influence of the past. In ordinary physical causation, as it appears to common sense, we have approximate uniformities of sequence, such as "lightning is followed by thunder," "drunkenness is followed by headache," and so on.   None of these sequences are theoretically invariable, since something may intervene to disturb them.   In order to obtain invariable physical laws, we have to proceed to differential equations, showing the direction of change at each moment, not the integral change after a finite interval, however short.   But for the purposes of daily life many sequences are to all intents and purposes invariable.   With the behaviour of human beings, however, this is by no means the case. If you say to an Englishman, "You have a smut on your nose," he will proceed to remove it, but there will be no such effect if you say the same thing to a Frenchman who knows no English.   The effect of words upon the hearer is a mnemic phenomena, since it depends upon the past experience which gave him understanding of the words.   If there are to be purely psychological causal laws, taking no account of the brain and the rest of the body, they will have to be of the form, not " X now causes Y now," but—

"A, B, C, . . . in the past, together with X now, cause Y now."   For it cannot be successfully maintained that our understanding of a word, for example, is an actual existent content of the mind at times when we are not thinking of the word.   It is merely what may be called a "disposition," i.e. it is capable of being aroused whenever we hear the word or happen to think of it. A "disposition" is not something actual, but merely the mnemic portion of a mnemic causal law.

In such a law as " A, B, C, . . . in the past, together with X now, cause Y now," we will call A, B, C, . . . the mnemic cause, X the occasion or stimulus, and Y the reaction. All cases in which experience influences behaviour are instances of mnemic causation.

Believers in psycho-physical parallelism hold that psychology can theoretically be freed entirely from all dependence on physiology or physics. That is to say, they believe that every psychical event has a psychical cause and a physical concomitant. If there is to be parallelism, it is easy to prove by mathematical logic that the causation in physical and psychical matters must be of the same sort, and it is impossible that mnemic causation should exist in psychology but not in physics. But if psychology is to be independent of physiology, and if physiology can be reduced to physics, it would seem that mnemic causation is essential in psychology. Otherwise we shall be compelled to believe that all our knowledge, all our store of images and memories, all our mental habits, are at all times existing in some latent mental form, and are not merely aroused by the stimuli which lead to their display. This is a very difficult hypothesis. It seems to me that if, as a matter of method rather than metaphysics, we desire to obtain as much independence for psychology as is practically feasible, we shall do better to accept mnemic causation in psychology *pro tem.* and therefore reject parallelism, since there is no good ground for admitting mnemic causation in physics.

It is perhaps worth while to observe that mnemic causation is what led Bergson to deny that there is causation at all in the psychical sphere. He points out, very truly, that the same stimulus, repeated, does not have the same consequences, and he argues that this is contrary to the maxim, "same cause, same effect." It is only necessary, however, to take account of past occurrences and include them with the cause, in order to re-establish the maxim, and the possibility of psychological causal laws. The metaphysical conception of a cause lingers in our manner of viewing causal laws : we want to be able to *feel* a connection between cause and effect, and to be able to imagine the cause as " operating." This makes us unwilling to regard causal laws as *merely* observed uniformities of sequence ; yet that is all that science has to offer. To ask *why* such-and-such a kind of sequence occurs is either to ask a meaningless question, or to demand some more general kind of sequence which includes the one in question. The widest empirical laws of sequence known at any time can only be " explained " in the sense of being subsumed by later discoveries under wider laws ; but these wider laws, until they in turn are subsumed, will remain brute facts, resting solely upon observation, not upon some supposed inherent rationality.

There is therefore no *a priori* objection to a causal law in which part of the cause has ceased to exist. To argue against such a law on the ground that what is past cannot operate now, is to introduce the old metaphysical notion of cause, for which science can find no place. The only reason that could be validly alleged against mnemic causation would be that, in fact, all the phenomena can be explained without it. They are explained without it by Semon's " engram," or by any theory which regards the results of experience as embodied in modifications of the brain and nerves. But they are not explained, unless with extreme artificiality, by any theory which regards the latent effects of experience as psychical rather than physical. Those who desire to make psychology as far as possible independent of physiology would do well, it seems to me, if they adopted mnemic causation. For my part, however, I have no such desire, and I shall therefore endeavour to state the grounds which occur to me in favour of some such view as that of the " engram."

One of the first points to be urged is that mnemic phenomena are just as much to be found in physiology as in psychology. They are even to be found in plants, as Sir Francis Darwin pointed out (cf. Semon, *Die Mneme*, 2nd edition, p. 28 *n*.). Habit is a characteristic of the body at least as much as of the mind. We should, therefore, be compelled to allow the intrusion of mnemic causation, if admitted at all, into non-psychological regions, which ought, one feels, to be subject only to causation of the ordinary physical sort. The fact is that a great deal of what, at first sight, distinguishes psychology from physics is found, on examination, to be common to psychology and physiology ; this whole question of the influence of experience is a case in point. Now it is possible, of course, to take the view advocated by Professor J. S. Haldane, who contends that physiology is not theoretically reducible to physics and chemistry.[1] But the weight of opinion among physiologists appears to be against him on this point ; and we ought certainly to require very strong evidence before admitting any such breach of continuity as between living and dead matter. The argument from the existence of mnemic phenomena in physiology must therefore be allowed a certain weight against the hypothesis that mnemic causation is ultimate.

The argument from the connection of brain-lesions with loss of memory is not so strong as it looks, though

[1] See his *The New Physiology and Other Addresses*, Griffin, 1919; also the symposium, " Are Physical, Biological and Psychological Categories Irreducible ? " in *Life and Finite Individuality*, edited for the Aristotelian Society, with an Introduction. By H. Wildon Carr, Williams & Norgate, 1918.

it has also some weight.   What we know is that memory, and mnemic phenomena generally, can be disturbed or destroyed by changes in the brain.   This certainly proves that the brain plays an essential part in the causation of memory, but does not prove that a certain state of the brain is, by itself, a sufficient condition for the existence of memory.   Yet it is this last that has to be proved. The theory of the engram, or any similar theory, has to maintain that, given a body and brain in a suitable state, a man will have a certain memory, without the need of any further conditions.   What is known, however, is only that he will not have memories if his body and brain are not in a suitable state.   That is to say, the appropriate state of body and brain is proved to be necessary for memory, but not to be sufficient.   So far, therefore, as our definite knowledge goes, memory may require for its causation a past occurrence as well as a certain present state of the brain.

In order to prove conclusively that mnemic phenomena arise whenever certain physiological conditions are fulfilled, we ought to be able actually to see differences between the brain of a man who speaks English and that of a man who speaks French, between the brain of a man who has seen New York and can recall it, and that of a man who has never seen that city.   It may be that the time will come when this will be possible, but at present we are very far removed from it.   At present, there is, so far as I am aware, no good evidence that every difference between the knowledge possessed by A and that possessed by B is paralleled by some difference in their brains.   We may believe that this is the case, but if we do, our belief is based upon analogies and general scientific maxims, not upon any foundation of detailed observation.   I am myself inclined, as a working hypothesis, to adopt the belief in question, and to hold that past experience only affects present behaviour through modifications of physiological structure. But the evidence seems not quite conclusive, so that I do not think we ought to forget the other hypothesis, or to reject entirely the possibility that mnemic causation may be the ultimate explanation of mnemic phenomena. I say this, not because I think it *likely* that mnemic causation is ultimate, but merely because I think it *possible*, and because it often turns out important to the progress of science to remember hypotheses which have previously seemed improbable.

LECTURE V

PSYCHOLOGICAL AND PHYSICAL CAUSAL LAWS

THE traditional conception of cause and effect is one which modern science shows to be fundamentally erroneous, and requiring to be replaced by a quite different notion, that of *laws of change*. In the traditional conception, a particular event A caused a particular event B, and by this it was implied that, given any event B, some earlier event A could be discovered which had a relation to it, such that—

(1) Whenever A occurred, it was followed by B ;

(2) In this sequence, there was something " necessary," not a mere *de facto* occurrence of A first and then B.

The second point is illustrated by the old discussion as to whether it can be said that day causes night, on the ground that day is always followed by night. The orthodox answer was that day could not be called the cause of night, because it would not be followed by night if the earth's rotation were to cease, or rather to grow so slow that one complete rotation would take a year. A cause, it was held, must be such that under no conceivable circumstances could it fail to be followed by its effect.

As a matter of fact, such sequences as were sought by believers in the traditional form of causation have not so far been found in nature. Everything in nature is apparently in a state of continuous change,[1] so that what we call one " event " turns out to be really a process. If this event is to cause another event, the two will have to be contiguous in time ; for if there is any interval between them, something may happen during that interval to prevent the expected effect. Cause and effect, therefore, will have to be temporally contiguous processes. It is difficult to believe, at any rate where physical laws are concerned, that the earlier part of the process which is the cause can make any difference to the effect, so long as the later part of the process which is the cause remains unchanged. Suppose, for example, that a man dies of arsenic poisoning, we say that his taking arsenic was the cause of death. But clearly the process by which he acquired the arsenic is irrelevant : everything that happened before he swallowed it may be ignored, since it cannot alter the effect except in so far as it alters his condition at the moment of taking the dose. But we may go further : swallowing arsenic is not really the proximate cause of death, since a man might be shot through the head immediately after taking the dose, and then it would not be of arsenic that he would die. The arsenic produces certain physiological changes, which take a finite time before they end in death. The earlier parts of these changes can be ruled out in the same way as we can rule out the process by which the arsenic was

[1] The theory of quanta suggests that the continuity is only apparent. If so, we shall be able theoretically to reach events which are not processes. But in what is directly observable there is still apparent continuity, which justifies the above remarks for the present.

acquired. Proceeding in this way, we can shorten the process which we are calling the cause more and more. Similarly we shall have to shorten the effect. It may happen that immediately after the man's death his body is blown to pieces by a bomb. We cannot say what will happen after the man's death, through merely knowing that he has died as the result of arsenic poisoning. Thus, if we are to take the cause as one event and the effect as another, both must be shortened indefinitely. The result is that we merely have, as the embodiment of our causal law, a certain direction of change at each moment. Hence we are brought to differential equations as embodying causal laws. A physical law does not say " A will be followed by B," but tells us what acceleration a particle will have under given circumstances, i.e. it tells us how the particle's motion is changing at each moment, not where the particle will be at some future moment.

Laws embodied in differential equations may possibly be exact, but cannot be known to be so. All that we can know empirically is approximate and liable to exceptions ; the exact laws that are assumed in physics are known to be somewhere near the truth, but are not known to be true just as they stand. The laws that we actually know empirically have the form of the traditional causal laws, except that they are not to be regarded as universal or necessary. " Taking arsenic is followed by death " is a good empirical generalization ; it may have exceptions, but they will be rare. As against the professedly exact laws of physics, such empirical generalizations have the advantage that they deal with observable phenomena. We cannot observe infinitesimals, whether in time or space ; we do not even know whether time and space are infinitely divisible. Therefore rough empirical generalizations have a definite place in science, in spite of not being exact or universal. They are the data for more exact laws, and the grounds for believing that they are *usually* true are stronger than the grounds for believing that the more exact laws are *always* true.

Science starts, therefore, from generalizations of the form, " A is usually followed by B." This is the nearest approach that can be made to a causal law of the traditional sort. It may happen in any particular instance that A is *always* followed by B, but we cannot know this, since we cannot foresee all the perfectly possible circumstances that might make the sequence fail, or know that none of them will actually occur. If, however, we know of a very large number of cases in which A is followed by B, and few or none in which the sequence fails, we shall in *practice* be justified in saying "A causes B," provided we do not attach to the notion of cause any of the metaphysical superstitions that have gathered about the word.

There is another point, besides lack of universality and necessity, which it is important to realize as regards causes in the above sense, and that is the lack of uniqueness. It is generally assumed that, given any event, there is some one phenomenon which is *the* cause of the event in question. This seems to be a mere mistake. Cause, in the only sense in which it can be practically applied, means " nearly invariable antecedent." We cannot in practice obtain an antecedent which is *quite* invariable, for this would require us to take account of the whole universe, since something not taken account of may prevent the expected effect. We cannot distinguish, among nearly invariable antecedents, one as *the* cause, and the others as merely its concomitants : the attempt to do this depends upon a notion of cause which is derived from will, and will (as we shall see later) is not at all the sort of thing that it is generally supposed to be, nor is there any reason to think that in the physical world there is anything even remotely analogous to what will is supposed to be. If we could find one antecedent, and only one, that was *quite* invariable, we could call that one *the* cause without introducing any notion derived from mistaken ideas about will. But in fact we cannot find any antecedent that we know to be quite invariable, and we can find many that are nearly so. For example, men leave a factory for dinner when the hooter sounds at twelve o'clock. You may say the hooter is *the* cause of their leaving. But innumerable other hooters in other factories, which also always sound at twelve o'clock, have just as good a right to be called the cause. Thus every event has many nearly invariable antecedents, and therefore many antecedents which may be called its cause.

The laws of traditional physics, in the form in which they deal with movements of matter or electricity, have an apparent simplicity which somewhat conceals the empirical character of what they assert. A piece of matter, as it is known empirically, is not a single existing thing, but a system of existing things. When several people simultaneously see the same table, they all see something different; therefore "the" table, which they are supposed all to see, must be either a hypothesis or a construction. "The" table is to be neutral as between different observers: it does not favour the aspect seen by one man at the expense of that seen by another. It was natural, though to my mind mistaken, to regard the "real" table as the common cause of all the appearances which the table presents (as we say) to different observers. But why should we suppose that there is some one common cause of all these appearances? As we have just seen, the notion of " cause " is not so reliable as to allow us to infer the existence of something that, by its very nature, can never be observed.

Instead of looking for an impartial source, we can secure neutrality by the equal representation of all parties. Instead of supposing that there is some unknown cause, the " real " table, behind the different sensations of those who are said to be looking at the table, we may take the whole set of these sensations (together possibly with certain other particulars) as actually *being* the table That is to say, the table which is neutral as between different observers (actual and possible) is the set of all those particulars which would naturally be called "aspects" of the table from different points of view. (This is a first approximation, modified later.)

It may be said : If there is no single existent which is the source of all these " aspects," how are they collected together? The answer is simple : Just as they would be if there were such a single existent. The supposed " real " table underlying its appearances is, in any case, not itself perceived, but inferred, and the question whether such-and-such a particular is an " aspect " of this table is only to be settled by the connection of the particular in question with the one or more particulars by which the table is defined. That is to say, even if we assume a " real " table, the particulars which are its aspects have to be collected together by their relations to each other, not to it, since it is merely inferred from them. We have only, therefore, to notice how they are collected together, and **we can** then keep the collection without assuming any

" real " table as distinct from the collection. When different people see what they call the same table, they see things which are not exactly the same, owing to difference of point of view, but which are sufficiently alike to be described in the same words, so long as no great accuracy or minuteness is sought. These closely similar particulars are collected together by their similarity primarily and, more correctly, by the fact that they are related to each other approximately according to the laws of perspective and of reflection and diffraction of light. I suggest, as a first approximation, that these particulars, together with such correlated others as are unperceived, jointly *are* the table ; and that a similar definition applies to all physical objects.[1]

In order to eliminate the reference to our perceptions, which introduces an irrelevant psychological suggestion, I will take a different illustration, namely, stellar photography. A photographic plate exposed on a clear night reproduces the appearance of the portion of the sky concerned, with more or fewer stars according to the power of the telescope that is being used. Each separate star which is photographed produces its separate effect on the plate, just as it would upon ourselves if we were looking at the sky. If we assume, as science normally does, the continuity of physical processes, we are forced to conclude that, at the place where the plate is, and at all places between it and a star which it photographs, *something* is happening which is specially connected with that star. In the days when the æther was less in doubt, we should have said that what was happening was a certain kind of transverse vibration in the æther.

[1] See *Our Knowledge of the External World* (Allen & Unwin), chaps. iii and iv.

But it is not necessary or desirable to be so explicit : all that we need say is that *something* happens which is specially connected with the star in question. It must be something specially connected with that star, since that star produces its own special effect upon the plate. Whatever it is must be the end of a process which starts from the star and radiates outwards, partly on general grounds of continuity, partly to account for the fact that light is transmitted with a certain definite velocity. We thus arrive at the conclusion that, if a certain star is visible at a certain place, or could be photographed by a sufficiently sensitive plate at that place, something is happening there which is specially connected with that star. Therefore in every place at all times a vast multitude of things must be happening, namely, at least one for every physical object which can be seen or photographed from that place. We can classify such happenings on either of two principles :

(1) We can collect together all the happenings in one place, as is done by photography so far as light is concerned ;

(2) We can collect together all the happenings, in different places, which are connected in the way that common sense regards as being due to their emanating from one object.

Thus, to return to the stars, we can collect together either—

(1) All the appearances of different stars in a given place, or,

(2) All the appearances of a given star in different places.

But when I speak of " appearances," I do so only for brevity: I do not mean anything that must " appear " to somebody, but only that happening, whatever it may be, which is connected, at the place in question, with a given physical object—according to the old ortho-dox theory, it would be a transverse vibration in the æther. Like the different appearances of the table to a number of simultaneous observers, the different particu-lars that belong to one physical object are to be collected together by continuity and inherent laws of correlation, not by their supposed causal connection with an unknown assumed existent called a piece of matter, which would be a mere unnecessary metaphysical thing in itself. A piece of matter, according to the definition that I propose, is, as a first approximation,[1] the collection of all those correlated particulars which would normally be regarded as its appearances or effects in different places. Some further elaborations are desirable, but we can ignore them for the present. I shall return to them at the end of this lecture.

According to the view that I am suggesting, a physical object or piece of matter is the collection of all those correlated particulars which would be regarded by common sense as its effects or appearances in different places. On the other hand, all the happenings in a given place represent what common sense would regard as the appearances of a number of different objects as viewed from that place. All the happenings in one place may be regarded as the view of the world from that place. I shall call the view of the world from a given place a " perspective." A photograph represents a perspective. On the other

[1] The exact definition of a piece of matter as a construction will be given later.

hand, if photographs of the stars were taken in all points throughout space, and in all such photographs a certain star, say Sirius, were picked out whenever it appeared, all the different appearances of Sirius, taken together, would represent Sirius. For the understanding of the difference between psychology and physics it is vital to understand these two ways of classifying particulars, namely :

(1) According to the place where they occur ;
(2) According to the system of correlated particulars in different places to which they belong, such system being defined as a physical object.

Given a system of particulars which is a physical object, I shall define that one of the system which is in a given place (if any) as the " appearance of that object in that place."

When the appearance of an object in a given place changes, it is found that one or other of two things occurs. The two possibilities may be illustrated by an example. You are in a room with a man, whom you see : you may cease to see him either by shutting your eyes or by his going out of the room. In the first case, his appearance to other people remains unchanged ; in the second, his appearance changes from all places. In the first case, you say that it is not he who has changed, but your eyes ; in the second, you say that he has changed. Generalizing, we distinguish—

(1) Cases in which only certain appearances of the object change, while others, and especially appearances from places very near to the object, do not change ;

(2) Cases where all, or almost all, the appearances of the object undergo a connected change.

In the first case, the change is attributed to the medium between the object and the place ; in the second, it is attributed to the object itself.[1]

It is the frequency of the latter kind of change, and the comparatively simple nature of the laws governing the simultaneous alterations of appearances in such cases, that have made it possible to treat a physical object as one thing, and to overlook the fact that it is a system of particulars. When a number of people at a theatre watch an actor, the changes in their several perspectives are so similar and so closely correlated that all are popularly regarded as identical with each other and with the changes of the actor himself. So long as all the changes in the appearances of a body are thus correlated there is no pressing *prima facie* need to break up the system of appearances, or to realize that the body in question is not really one thing but a set of correlated particulars. It is especially and primarily such changes that physics deals with, i.e. it deals primarily with processes in which the unity of a physical object need not be broken up because all its appearances change simultaneously according to the same law—or, if not all, at any rate all from places sufficiently near to the object, with increasing accuracy as we approach the object.

The changes in appearances of an object which are due to changes in the intervening medium will not affect, or will affect only very slightly, the appearances from

[1] The application of this distinction to motion raises complications due to relativity, but we may ignore these for our present purposes.

places close to the object. If the appearances from sufficiently neighbouring places are either wholly unchanged, or changed to a diminishing extent which has zero for its limit, it is usually found that the changes can be accounted for by changes in objects which are between the object in question and the places from which its appearance has changed appreciably. Thus physics is able to reduce the laws of most changes with which it deals to changes in physical objects, and to state most of its fundamental laws in terms of matter. It is only in those cases in which the unity of the system of appearances constituting a piece of matter has to be broken up, that the statement of what is happening cannot be made exclusively in terms of matter. The whole of psychology, we shall find, is included among such cases ; hence their importance for our purposes.

We can now begin to understand one of the fundamental differences between physics and psychology. Physics treats as a unit the whole system of appearances of a piece of matter, whereas psychology is interested in certain of these appearances themselves. Confining ourselves for the moment to the psychology of perceptions, we observe that perceptions are certain of the appearances of physical objects. From the point of view that we have been hitherto adopting, we might define them as the appearances of objects at places from which sense-organs and the suitable parts of the nervous system form part of the intervening medium. Just as a photographic plate receives a different impression of a cluster of stars when a telescope is part of the intervening medium, so a brain receives a different impression when an eye and an optic nerve are part of the intervening medium. An impression due to this sort of intervening medium is called a perception, and is interesting to psychology on its own account, not merely as one of the set of correlated particulars which is the physical object of which (as we say) we are having a perception.

We spoke earlier of two ways of classifying particulars. One way collects together the appearances commonly regarded as a given object from different places; this is, broadly speaking, the way of physics, leading to the construction of physical objects as sets of such appearances. The other way collects together the appearances of different objects from a given place, the result being what we call a perspective. In the particular case where the place concerned is a human brain, the perspective belonging to the place consists of all the perceptions of a certain man at a given time. Thus classification by perspectives is relevant to psychology, and is essential in defining what we mean by one mind.

I do not wish to suggest that the way in which I have been defining perceptions is the only possible way, or even the best way. It is the way that arose naturally out of our present topic. But when we approach psychology from a more introspective standpoint, we have to distinguish sensations and perceptions, if possible, from other mental occurrences, if any. We have also to consider the psychological effects of sensations, as opposed to their physical causes and correlates. These problems are quite distinct from those with which we have been concerned in the present lecture, and I shall not deal with them until a later stage.

It is clear that psychology is concerned essentially with actual particulars, not merely with systems of particulars. In this it differs from physics, which, broadly speaking, is concerned with the cases in which all the particulars which make up one physical object can be treated as a single causal unit, or rather the particulars which are sufficiently near to the object of which they are appearances can be so treated. The laws which physics seeks can, broadly speaking, be stated by treating such systems of particulars as causal units. The laws which psychology seeks cannot be so stated, since the particulars themselves are what interests the psychologist. This is one of the fundamental differences between physics and psychology ; and to make it clear has been the main purpose of this lecture.

I will conclude with an attempt to give a more precise definition of a piece of matter. The appearances of a piece of matter from different places change partly according to intrinsic laws (the laws of perspective, in the case of visual shape), partly according to the nature of the intervening medium—fog, blue spectacles, telescopes, microscopes, sense-organs, etc. As we approach nearer to the object, the effect of the intervening medium grows less. In a generalized sense, all the intrinsic laws of change of appearance may be called " laws of perspective." Given any appearance of an object, we can construct hypothetically a certain system of appearances to which the appearance in question would belong if the laws of perspective alone were concerned. If we construct this hypothetical system for each appearance of the object in turn, the system corresponding to a given appearance x will be independent of any distortion due to the medium beyond x, and will only embody such distortion as is due to the medium between x and the object. Thus, as the appearance by which our hypothetical system is defined is moved nearer and nearer to the object, the hypothetical system of appearances defined by its means embodies less and less of the effect of the medium. The different sets of appearances resulting from moving x nearer and nearer to the object will approach to a limiting set, and this limiting set will be that system of appearances which the object would present if the laws of perspective alone were operative and the medium exercised no distorting effect. This limiting set of appearances may be defined, for purposes of physics, as the piece of matter concerned.

LECTURE VI

INTROSPECTION

ONE of the main purposes of these lectures is to give grounds for the belief that the distinction between mind and matter is not so fundamental as is commonly supposed. In the preceding lecture I dealt in outline with the physical side of this problem. I attempted to show that what we call a material object is not itself a substance, but is a system of particulars analogous in their nature to sensations, and in fact often including actual sensations among their number. In this way the stuff of which physical objects are composed is brought into relation with the stuff of which part, at least, of our mental life is composed.

There is, however, a converse task which is equally necessary for our thesis, and that is, to show that the stuff of our mental life is devoid of many qualities which it is commonly supposed to have, and is not possessed of any attributes which make it incapable of forming part of the world of matter. In the present lecture I shall begin the arguments for this view.

Corresponding to the supposed duality of matter and mind, there are, in orthodox psychology, two ways of knowing what exists. One of these, the way of sensation and external perception, is supposed to furnish data for

our knowledge of matter, the other, called " introspection,"
is supposed to furnish data for knowledge of our mental
processes. To common sense, this distinction seems
clear and easy. When you see a friend coming along
the street, you acquire knowledge of an external, physical
fact ; when you realize that you are glad to meet him,
you acquire knowledge of a mental fact. Your dreams
and memories and thoughts, of which you are often
conscious, are mental facts, and the process by which you
become aware of them *seems* to be different from sensation. Kant calls it the " inner sense " ; sometimes it is
spoken of as " consciousness of self " ; but its commonest
name in modern English psychology is "introspection."
It is this supposed method of acquiring knowledge of our
mental processes that I wish to analyse and examine in
this lecture.

I will state at the outset the view which I shall aim at
establishing. I believe that the stuff of our mental life,
as opposed to its relations and structure, consists wholly
of sensations and images. Sensations are connected with
matter in the way that I tried to explain in Lecture V,
i.e. each is a member of a system which is a certain
physical object. Images, though they *usually* have
certain characteristics, especially lack of vividness, that
distinguish them from sensations, are not *invariably* so
distinguished, and cannot therefore be defined by these
characteristics. Images, as opposed to sensations, can
only be defined by their different causation : they are
caused by association with a sensation, not by a stimulus
external to the nervous system—or perhaps one should
say external to the brain, where the higher animals are
concerned. The occurrence of a sensation or image
does not in itself constitute knowledge but any sensation

or image may come to be known if the conditions are suitable. When a sensation—like the hearing of a clap of thunder—is normally correlated with closely similar sensations in our neighbours, we regard it as giving knowledge of the external world, since we regard the whole set of similar sensations as due to a common external cause. But images and bodily sensations are not so correlated. Bodily sensations can be brought into a correlation by physiology, and thus take their place ultimately among sources of knowledge of the physical world. But images cannot be made to fit in with the simultaneous sensations and images of others. Apart from their hypothetical causes in the brain, they have a causal connection with physical objects, through the fact that they are copies of past sensations ; but the physical objects with which they are thus connected are in the past, not in the present. These images remain private in a sense in which sensations are not. A sensation *seems* to give us knowledge of a present physical object, while an image does not, except when it amounts to a hallucination, and in this case the seeming is deceptive. Thus the whole context of the two occurrences is different. But in themselves they do not differ profoundly, and there is no reason to invoke two different ways of knowing for the one and for the other. Consequently introspection as a separate kind of knowledge disappears.

The criticism of introspection has been in the main the work of American psychologists. I will begin by summarizing an article which seems to me to afford a good specimen of their arguments, namely, " The Case against Introspection," by Knight Dunlap (*Psychological Review*, vol xix, No. 5, pp. 404–413, September, 1912). After a few historical quotations, he comes to two modern

defenders of introspection, Stout and James. He quotes
from Stout such statements as the following : " Psychical
states as such become objects only when we attend to them
in an introspective way. Otherwise they are not themselves objects, but only constituents of the process by
which objects are recognized " (*Manual*, 2nd edition,
p. 134. The word " recognized " in Dunlap's quotation
should be " cognized.") " The object itself can never
be identified with the present modification of the individual's consciousness by which it is cognized " (*ib.*
p. 60). This is to be true even when we are thinking
about modifications of our own consciousness ; such
modifications are to be always at least partially distinct
from the conscious experience in which we think of them.

At this point I wish to interrupt the account of Knight
Dunlap's article in order to make some observations on
my own account with reference to the above quotations
from Stout. In the first place, the conception of " psychical states " seems to me one which demands analysis
of a somewhat destructive character. This analysis I
shall give in later lectures as regards cognition ; I have
already given it as regards desire. In the second place,
the conception of " objects " depends upon a certain view
as to cognition which I believe to be wholly mistaken,
namely, the view which I discussed in my first lecture
in connection with Brentano. In this view a single
cognitive occurrence contains both content and object,
the content being essentially mental, while the object
is physical except in introspection and abstract thought.
I have already criticized this view, and will not dwell
upon it now, beyond saying that " the process by which
objects are cognized " appears to be a very slippery
phrase. When we " see a table," as common sense
would say, the table as a physical object is not the

"object" (in the psychological sense) of our perception. Our perception is made up of sensations, images and beliefs, but the supposed " object " is something inferential, externally related, not logically bound up with what is occurring in us. This question of the nature of the object also affects the view we take of self-consciousness. Obviously, a "conscious experience" is different from a physical object ; therefore it is natural to assume that a thought or perception whose object is a conscious experience must be different from a thought or perception whose object is a physical object. But if the relation to the object is inferential and external, as I maintain, the difference between two thoughts may bear very little relation to the difference between their objects. And to speak of "the present modification of the individual's consciousness by which an object is cognized" is to suggest that the cognition of objects is a far more direct process, far more intimately bound up with the objects, than I believe it to be. All these points will be amplified when we come to the analysis of knowledge, but it is necessary briefly to state them now in order to suggest the atmosphere in which our analysis of "introspection" is to be carried on.

Another point in which Stout's remarks seem to me to suggest what I regard as mistakes is his use of "consciousness." There is a view which is prevalent among psycho logists, to the effect that one can speak of "a conscious experience" in a curious dual sense, meaning, on the one hand, an experience which is conscious of something, and, on the other hand, an experience which has some intrinsic nature characteristic of what is called "consciousness." That is to say, a "conscious experience" is characterized on the one hand by relation to its object and on the other hand by being composed of a certain peculiar stuff, the stuff of "consciousness." And in many authors there is yet a third confusion : a " conscious experience," in this third sense, is an experience of which we are conscious. All these, it seems to me, need to be clearly separated. To say that one occurrence is " conscious " of another is, to my mind, to assert an external and rather remote relation between them. I might illustrate it by the relation of uncle and nephew : a man becomes an uncle through no effort of his own, merely through an occurrence elsewhere. Similarly, when you are said to be " conscious " of a table, the question whether this is really the case cannot be decided by examining only your state of mind : it is necessary also to ascertain whether your sensation is having those correlates which past experience causes you to assume, or whether the table happens, in this case, to be a mirage. And, as I explained in my first lecture, I do not believe that there is any " stuff " of consciousness, so that there is no intrinsic character by which a " conscious " experience could be distinguished from any other.

After these preliminaries, we can return to Knight Dunlap's article. His criticism of Stout turns on the difficulty of giving any empirical meaning to such notions as the " mind " or the " subject " ; he quotes from Stout the sentence : " The most important drawback is that the mind, in watching its own workings, must necessarily have its attention divided between two objects," and he concludes : " Without question, Stout is bringing in here illicitly the concept of a single observer, and his introspection does not provide for the observation of this observer ; for the process observed and the observer are distinct " (p. 407). The objections to any theory

which brings in the single observer were considered in
Lecture I, and were acknowledged to be cogent. In so
far, therefore, as Stout's theory of introspection rests
upon this assumption, we are compelled to reject it.
But it is perfectly possible to believe in introspection
without supposing that there is a single observer.

William James's theory of introspection, which Dunlap
next examines, does not assume a single observer. It
changed after the publication of his *Psychology*, in
consequence of his abandoning the dualism of thought
and things. Dunlap summarizes his theory as follows :

" The essential points in James's scheme of consciousness
are *subject, object,* and a *knowing* of the object by the subject.
The difference between James's scheme and other schemes
involving the same terms is that James considers subject
and object to be the same thing, but at different times
In order to satisfy this requirement James supposes a
realm of existence which he at first called 'states of
consciousness' or 'thoughts,' and later, ' pure experience,' the latter term including both the 'thoughts'
and the 'knowing.' This scheme, with all its magnifi-
cent artificiality, James held on to until the end, simply
dropping the term consciousness and the dualism between
the thought and an external reality " (p. 409).

He adds : " All that James's system really amounts
to is the acknowledgment that a succession of things
are known, and that they are known by something. This
is all any one can claim, except for the fact that the things
are known together, and that the knower for the different
items is one and the same " (*ib.*).

In this statement, to my mind, Dunlap concedes far
more than James did in his later theory. I see no reason
to suppose that " the knower for different items is one

and the same," and I am convinced that this proposition could not possibly be ascertained except by introspection of the sort that Dunlap rejects. The first of these points must wait until we come to the analysis of belief : the second must be considered now. Dunlap's view is that there is a dualism of subject and object, but that the subject can never become object, and therefore there is no awareness of an awareness. He says in discussing the view that introspection reveals the occurrence of knowledge : " There can be no denial of the existence of the thing (knowing) which is alleged to be known or observed in this sort of 'introspection.' The allegation that the knowing is observed is that which may be denied. Knowing there certainly is ; known, the knowing certainly is not " (p. 410). And again : " I am never aware of an awareness " (*ib.*). And on the next page : " It may sound paradoxical to say that one cannot observe the process (or relation) of observation, and yet may be certain that there is such a process : but there is really no inconsistency in the saying. How do I know that there is awareness ? By being aware of something. There is no meaning in the term 'awareness' which is not expressed in the statement 'I am aware of a colour (or what-not).' "

But the paradox cannot be so lightly disposed of. The statement "I am aware of a colour" is assumed by Knight Dunlap to be known to be true, but he does not explain how it comes to be known. The argument against him is not conclusive, since he may be able to show some valid way of inferring our awareness. But he does not suggest any such way. There is nothing odd in the hypothesis of beings which are aware of objects, but not of their own awareness ; it is, indeed, highly probable that young children and the higher animals are such beings. But such beings cannot make the statement " I am aware of a colour," which *we* can make. We have, therefore, some knowledge which they lack. It is necessary to Knight Dunlap's position to maintain that this additional knowledge is purely inferential, but he makes no attempt to show how the inference is possible. It may, of course, be possible, but I cannot see how. To my mind the fact (which he admits) that we know there is awareness, is *all but* decisive against his theory, and in favour of the view that we can be aware of an awareness.

Dunlap asserts (to return to James) that the real ground for James's original belief in introspection was his belief in two sorts of objects, namely, thoughts and things. He suggests that it was a mere inconsistency on James's part to adhere to introspection after abandoning the dualism of thoughts and things. I do not wholly agree with this view, but it is difficult to disentangle the difference as to introspection from the difference as to the nature of knowing. Dunlap suggests (p. 411) that what is called introspection really consists of awareness of " images," visceral sensations, and so on. This view, in essence, seems to me sound. But then I hold that knowing itself consists of such constituents suitably related, and that in being aware of them we are sometimes being aware of instances of knowing. For this reason, much as I agree with his view as to what are the objects of which there is awareness, I cannot wholly agree with his conclusion as to the impossibility of introspection.

The behaviourists have challenged introspection even more vigorously than Knight Dunlap, and have gone so far as to deny the existence of images. But I think that they have confused various things which are very commonly confused, and that it is necessary to make several distinctions before we can arrive at what is true and what false in the criticism of introspection.

I wish to distinguish three distinct questions, any one of which may be meant when we ask whether introspection is a source of knowledge. The three questions are as follows :

(1) Can we observe anything about ourselves which we cannot observe about other people, or is everything we can observe *public*, in the sense that another could also observe it if suitably placed ?

(2) Does everything that we can observe obey the laws of physics and form part of the physical world, or can we observe certain things that lie outside physics ?

(3) Can we observe anything which differs in its intrinsic nature from the constituents of the physical world, or is everything that we can observe composed of elements intrinsically similar to the constituents of what is called matter ?

Any one of these three questions may be used to define introspection. I should favour introspection in the sense of the first question, i.e. I think that some of the things we observe cannot, even theoretically, be observed by any one else. The second question, tentatively and for the present, I should answer in favour of introspection ; I think that images, in the actual condition of science, cannot be brought under the causal laws of physics, though perhaps ultimately they may be. The third question I should answer adversely to introspection : I think that observation shows us nothing that is not composed of sensations and images, and that images differ from sensations in their causal laws, not intrinsically. I shall deal with the three questions successively.

(1) *Publicity or privacy of what is observed.* Confining ourselves, for the moment, to sensations, we find that there are different degrees of publicity attaching to different sorts of sensations. If you feel a toothache when the other people in the room do not, you are in no way surprised ; but if you hear a clap of thunder when they do not, you begin to be alarmed as to your mental condition. Sight and hearing are the most public of the senses ; smell only a trifle less so ; touch, again, a trifle less, since two people can only touch the same spot successively, not simultaneously. Taste has a sort of semi-publicity, since people seem to experience similar taste-sensations when they eat similar foods ; but the publicity is incomplete, since two people cannot eat actually the same piece of food.

But when we pass on to bodily sensations—headache, toothache, hunger, thirst, the feeling of fatigue, and so on—we get quite away from publicity, into a region where other people can tell us what they feel, but we cannot directly observe their feeling. As a natural result of this state of affairs, it has come to be thought that the public senses give us knowledge of the outer world, while the private senses only give us knowledge as to our own bodies. As regards privacy, all images, of whatever sort, belong with the sensations which only give knowledge of our own bodies, i.e. each is only observable by one observer. This is the reason why images of sight and hearing are more obviously different from sensations of sight and hearing than images of bodily sensations are from bodily sensations ; and that is why the argument in favour of images is more conclusive in such cases as sight and hearing than in such cases as inner speech.

The whole distinction of privacy and publicity, however,

so long as we confine ourselves to sensations, is one of degree, not of kind. No two people, there is good empirical reason to think, ever have exactly similar sensations related to the same physical object at the same moment ; on the other hand, even the most private sensation has correlations which would theoretically enable another observer to infer it.

That no sensation is ever completely public, results from differences of point of view. Two people looking at the same table do not get the same sensation, because of perspective and the way the light falls. They get only correlated sensations. Two people listening to the same sound do not hear exactly the same thing, because one is nearer to the source of the sound than the other, one has better hearing than the other, and so on. Thus publicity in sensations consists, not in having *precisely* similar sensations, but in having more or less similar sensations correlated according to ascertainable laws. The sensations which strike us as public are those where the correlated sensations are very similar and the correlations are very easy to discover. But even the most private sensations have correlations with things that others can observe. The dentist does not observe your ache, but he can see the cavity which causes it, and could guess that you are suffering even if you did not tell him. This fact, however, cannot be used, as Watson would apparently wish, to extrude from science observations which are private to one observer, since it is by means of many such observations that correlations are established, e.g. between toothaches and cavities. Privacy, therefore does not by itself make a datum unamenable to scientific treatment. On this point, the argument against introspection must be rejected.

(2) *Does everything observable obey the laws of physics?*
We come now to the second ground of objection to introspection, namely, that its data do not obey the laws of
physics. This, though less emphasized, is, I think, an
objection which is really more strongly felt than the
objection of privacy. And we obtain a definition of introspection more in harmony with usage if we define it as observation of data not subject to physical laws than if we define
it by means of privacy. No one would regard a man as
introspective because he was conscious of having a stomach-
ache. Opponents of introspection do not mean to deny
the obvious fact that we can observe bodily sensations
which others cannot observe. For example, Knight
Dunlap contends that images are really muscular contractions,[1] and evidently regards our awareness of muscular
contractions as not coming under the head of introspection.
I think it will be found that the essential characteristic
of introspective data, in the sense which now concerns
us, has to do with *localization* : either they are not localized
at all, or they are localized, like visual images, in a place
already physically occupied by something which would
be inconsistent with them if they were regarded as part
of the physical world. If you have a visual image of
your friend sitting in a chair which in fact is empty,
you cannot locate the image in your body, because it
is visual, nor (as a physical phenomenon) in the chair,
because the chair, as a physical object, is empty. Thus
it seems to follow that the physical world does not include

---

[1] *Psychological Review*, 1916, " Thought-Content and Feeling,"
p. 59. See also *ib.*, 1912, " The Nature of Perceived Relations,"
where he says : " ' Introspection,' divested of its mythological
suggestion of the observing of consciousness, is really the observation of bodily sensations (sensibles) and feelings (feelables) "
(p. 427 *n.*).

all that we are aware of, and that images, which are introspective data, have to be regarded, for the present, as not obeying the laws of physics ; this is, I think, one of the chief reasons why an attempt is made to reject them. I shall try to show in Lecture VIII that the purely empirical reasons for accepting images are overwhelming. But we cannot be nearly so certain that they will not ultimately be brought under the laws of physics. Even if this should happen, however, they would still be distinguishable from sensations by their proximate causal laws, as gases remain distinguishable from solids.

(3) *Can we observe anything intrinsically different from sensations ?* We come now to our third question concerning introspection. It is commonly thought that by looking within we can observe all sorts of things that are radically different from the constituents of the physical world, e.g. thoughts, beliefs, desires, pleasures, pains and emotions. The difference between mind and matter is increased partly by emphasizing these supposed introspective data, partly by the supposition that matter is composed of atoms or electrons or whatever units physics may at the moment prefer. As against this latter supposition, I contend that the ultimate constituents of matter are not atoms or electrons, but sensations, and other things similar to sensations as regards extent and duration. As against the view that introspection reveals a mental world radically different from sensations, I propose to argue that thoughts, beliefs, desires, pleasures, pains and emotions are all built up out of sensations and images alone, and that there is reason to think that images do not differ from sensations in their intrinsic character. We thus effect a mutual *rapprochement* of mind and matter, and reduce the ultimate data of introspection (in our

second sense) to images alone. On this third view of the meaning of introspection, therefore, our decision is wholly against it.

There remain two points to be considered concerning introspection. The first is as to how far it is trustworthy; the second is as to whether, even granting that it reveals no radically different *stuff* from that revealed by what might be called external perception, it may not reveal different *relations*, and thus acquire almost as much importance as is traditionally assigned to it.

To begin with the trustworthiness of introspection. It is common among certain schools to regard the knowledge of our own mental processes as incomparably more certain than our knowledge of the "external" world; this view is to be found in the British philosophy which descends from Hume, and is present, somewhat veiled, in Kant and his followers. There seems no reason whatever to accept this view. Our spontaneous, unsophisticated beliefs, whether as to ourselves or as to the outer world, are always extremely rash and very liable to error. The acquisition of caution is equally necessary and equally difficult in both directions. Not only are we often unaware of entertaining a belief or desire which exists in us; we are often actually mistaken. The fallibility of introspection as regards what we desire is made evident by psycho-analysis; its fallibility as to what we know is easily demonstrated. An autobiography, when confronted by a careful editor with documentary evidence, is usually found to be full of obviously inadvertent errors. Any of us confronted by a forgotten letter written some years ago will be astonished to find how much more foolish our opinions were than we had remembered them as being. And as to the analysis of our mental operations

—believing, desiring, willing, or what not—introspection unaided gives very little help : it is necessary to construct hypotheses and test them by their consequences, just as we do in physical science. Introspection, therefore, though it is one among our sources of knowledge, is not, in isolation, in any degree more trustworthy than " external " perception.

I come now to our second question : Does introspection give us materials for the knowledge of relations other than those arrived at by reflecting upon external perception ? It might be contended that the essence of what is " mental " consists of relations, such as knowing for example, and that our knowledge concerning these essentially mental relations is entirely derived from introspection. If " knowing " were an unanalysable relation, this view would be incontrovertible, since clearly no such relation forms part of the subject matter of physics. But it would seem that " knowing " is really various relations, all of them complex. Therefore, until they have been analysed, our present question must remain unanswered   I shall return to it at the end of the present course of lectures.

LECTURE VII

THE DEFINITION OF PERCEPTION

In Lecture V we found reason to think that the ultimate constituents [1] of the world do not have the characteristics of either mind or matter as ordinarily understood : they are not solid persistent objects moving through space, nor are they fragments of " consciousness." But we found two ways of grouping particulars, one into " things " or " pieces of matter," the other into series of " perspectives," each series being what may be called a " biography." Before we can define either sensations or images, it is necessary to consider this twofold classification in somewhat greater detail, and to derive from it a definition of perception. It should be said that, in so far as the classification assumes the whole world of physics (including its unperceived portions), it contains hypothetical elements. But we will not linger on the grounds for admitting these, which belong to the philosophy of physics rather than of psychology.

The physical classification of particulars collects together

---

[1] When I speak of " ultimate constituents," I do not mean necessarily such as are theoretically incapable of analysis, but only such as, at present, we can see no means of analysing. I speak of such constituents as " particulars," or as " *relative* particulars " when I wish to emphasize the fact that they may be themselves complex.

all those that are aspects of one " thing." Given any one particular, it is found often (we do not say always) that there are a number of other particulars differing from this one in gradually increasing degrees. Those (or some of those) that differ from it only very slightly will be found to differ approximately according to certain laws which may be called, in a generalized sense, the laws of " perspective "; they include the ordinary laws of perspective as a special case. This approximation grows more and more nearly exact as the difference grows less ; in technical language, the laws of perspective account for the differences to the first order of small quantities, and other laws are only required to account for second-order differences. That is to say, as the difference diminishes, the part of the difference which is not according to the laws of perspective diminishes much more rapidly, and bears to the total difference a ratio which tends towards zero as both are made smaller and smaller. By this means we can theoretically collect together a number of particulars which may be defined as the "aspects" or "appearances" of one thing at one time. If the laws of perspective were sufficiently known, the connection between different aspects would be expressed in differential equations.

This gives us, so far, only those particulars which constitute one thing at one time. This set of particulars may be called a "momentary thing." To define that series of "momentary things" that constitutes the successive states of one thing is a problem involving the laws of dynamics. These give the laws governing the changes of aspects from one time to a slightly later time, with the same sort of differential approximation to exactness as we obtained for spatially neighbouring aspects through the laws of perspective. Thus a momentary thing is a set of particulars, while a thing (which may be identified with the whole history of the thing) is a series of such sets of particulars. The particulars in one set are collected together by the laws of perspective ; the successive sets are collected together by the laws of dynamics. This is the view of the world which is appropriate to traditional physics.

The definition of a " momentary thing " involves problems concerning time, since the particulars constituting a momentary thing will not be all simultaneous, but will travel outward from the thing with the velocity of light (in case the thing is *in vacuo*). There are complications connected with relativity, but for our present purpose they are not vital, and I shall ignore them.

Instead of first collecting together all the particulars constituting a momentary thing, and then forming the series of successive sets, we might have first collected together a series of successive aspects related by the laws of dynamics, and then have formed the set of such series related by the laws of perspective. To illustrate by the case of an actor on the stage : our first plan was to collect together all the aspects which he presents to different spectators at one time, and then to form the series of such sets. Our second plan is first to collect together all the aspects which he presents successively to a given spectator, and then to do the same thing for the other spectators, thus forming a set of series instead of a series of sets. The first plan tells us what he does ; the second the impressions he produces. This second way of classifying particulars is one which obviously has more relevance to psychology than the other. It is partly by this second method of classification that we obtain definitions of one "experience" or "biography" or "person." This method of classification is also essential to the definition of sensations and images, as I shall endeavour to prove later on. But we must first amplify the definition of perspectives and biographies.

In our illustration of the actor, we spoke, for the moment, as though each spectator's mind were wholly occupied by the one actor. If this were the case, it might be possible to define the biography of one spectator as a series of successive aspects of the actor related according to the laws of dynamics. But in fact this is not the case. We are at all times during our waking life receiving a variety of impressions, which are aspects of a variety of things. We have to consider what binds together two simultaneous sensations in one person, or, more generally, any two occurrences which form part of one experience. We might say, adhering to the standpoint of physics, that two aspects of different things belong to the same perspective when they are in the same place. But this would not really help us, since a "place" has not yet been defined. Can we define what is meant by saying that two aspects are "in the same place," without introducing anything beyond the laws of perspective and dynamics?

I do not feel sure whether it is possible to frame such a definition or not; accordingly I shall not assume that it is possible, but shall seek other characteristics by which a perspective or biography may be defined.

When (for example) we see one man and hear another speaking at the same time, what we see and what we hear have a relation which we can perceive, which makes the two together form, in some sense, one experience.

It is when this relation exists that two occurrences become associated. Semon's " engram " is formed by all that we experience at one time. He speaks of two parts of this total as having the relation of " Nebeneinander " (M. 118 ; M.E. 33 ff.), which is reminiscent of Herbart's " Zusammen." I think the relation may be called simply " simultaneity." It might be said that at any moment all sorts of things that are not part of my experience are happening in the world, and that therefore the relation we are seeking to define cannot be merely simultaneity. This, however, would be an error—the sort of error that the theory of relativity avoids. There is not one universal time, except by an elaborate construction ; there are only local times, each of which may be taken to be the time within one biography. Accordingly, if I am (say) hearing a sound, the only occurrences that are, in any simple sense, simultaneous with my sensation are events in my private world, i.e. in my biography. We may therefore define the " perspective " to which the sensation in question belongs as the set of particulars that are simultaneous with this sensation. And similarly we may define the " biography " to which the sensation belongs as the set of particulars that are earlier or later than, or simultaneous with, the given sensation. Moreover, the very same definitions can be applied to particulars which are not sensations. They are actually required for the theory of relativity, if we are to give a philosophical explanation of what is meant by " local time " in that theory The relations of simultaneity and succession are known to us in our own experience ; they may be analysable, but that does not affect their suitability for defining perspectives and biographies. Such time-relations as can be constructed between events in different biographies are of a different kind : they are not experienced, and are merely logical, being designed to afford convenient ways of stating the correlations between different biographies.

It is not only by time-relations that the parts of one biography are collected together in the case of living beings. In this case there are the mnemic phenomena which constitute the unity of one " experience," and transform mere occurrences into " experiences." I have already dwelt upon the importance of mnemic phenomena for psychology, and shall not enlarge upon them now, beyond observing that they are what transforms a biography (in our technical sense) into a life. It is they that give the continuity of a " person " or a " mind." But there is no reason to suppose that mnemic phenomena are associated with biographies except in the case of animals and plants.

Our twofold classification of particulars gives rise to the dualism of body and biography in regard to everything in the universe, and not only in regard to living things. This arises as follows. Every particular of the sort considered by physics is a member of two groups :

(1) The group of particulars constituting the other aspects of the same physical object ;
(2) The group of particulars that have direct time-relations to the given particular.

Each of these is associated with a place. When I look at a star, my sensation is :

(1) A member of the group of particulars which is the star, and which is associated with the place where the star is ;

(2) A member of the group of particulars which is
    my biography, and which is associated with
    the place where I am.[1]

The result is that every particular of the kind relevant
to physics is associated with *two* places ; e.g. my sensation of the star is associated with the place where I am
and with the place where the star is. This dualism has
nothing to do with any " mind " that I may be supposed
to possess ; it exists in exactly the same sense if I am
replaced by a photographic plate. We may call the two
places the active and passive places respectively.[2] Thus
in the case of a perception or photograph of a star, the
active place is the place where the star is, while the
passive place is the place where the percipient or photographic plate is.

We can thus, without departing from physics, collect
together all the particulars actively at a given place, or
all the particulars passively at a given place. In our
own case. the one group is our body (or our brain), while
the other is our mind, in so far as it consists of perceptions.
In the case of the photographic plate, the first group is
the plate as dealt with by physics, the second the aspect
of the heavens which it photographs. (For the sake of
schematic simplicity, I am ignoring various complications connected with time, which require some tedious
but perfectly feasible elaborations.) Thus what may be
called subjectivity in the point of view is not a distinctive
peculiarity of mind : it is present just as much in the

[1] I have explained elsewhere the manner in which space is constructed on this theory, and in which the position of a perspective
is brought into relation with the position of a physical object (*Our
Knowledge of the External World*, Lecture III, pp. 90, 91).

[2] I use these as mere names ; I do not want to introduce any
notion of " activity."

photographic plate. And the photographic plate has its biography as well as its "matter." But this biography is an affair of physics, and has none of the peculiar characteristics by which "mental" phenomena are distinguished, with the sole exception of subjectivity.

Adhering, for the moment, to the standpoint of physics, we may define a "perception" of an object as the appearance of the object from a place where there is a brain (or, in lower animals, some suitable nervous structure), with sense-organs and nerves forming part of the intervening medium. Such appearances of objects are distinguished from appearances in other places by certain peculiarities, namely :

(1) They give rise to mnemic phenomena ;
(2) They are themselves affected by mnemic phenomena.

That is to say, they may be remembered and associated or influence our habits, or give rise to images, etc., and they are themselves different from what they would have been if our past experience had been different— for example, the effect of a spoken sentence upon the hearer depends upon whether the hearer knows the language or not, which is a question of past experience. It is these two characteristics, both connected with mnemic phenomena, that distinguish perceptions from the appearances of objects in places where there is no living being.

Theoretically, though often not practically, we can, in our perception of an object, separate the part which is due to past experience from the part which proceeds without mnemic influences out of the character of the object. We may define as "sensation" that part which proceeds in this way, while the remainder, which is a mnemic phenomenon, will have to be added to the sensation to make up what is called the "perception." According to this definition, the sensation is a theoretical core in the actual experience ; the actual experience is the perception. It is obvious that there are grave difficulties in carrying out these definitions, but we will not linger over them. We have to pass, as soon as we can, from the physical standpoint, which we have been hitherto adopting, to the standpoint of psychology, in which we make more use of introspection in the first of the three senses discussed in the preceding lecture.

But before making the transition, there are two points which must be made clear. First : Everything outside my own personal biography is outside my experience ; therefore if anything can be known by me outside my biography, it can only be known in one of two ways :

(1) By inference from things within my biography, or
(2) By some *a priori* principle independent of experience.

I do not myself believe that anything approaching certainty is to be attained by either of these methods, and therefore whatever lies outside my personal biography must be regarded, theoretically, as hypothesis. The theoretical argument for adopting the hypothesis is that it simplifies the statement of the laws according to which events happen in our experience. But there is no very good ground for supposing that a simple law is more likely to be true than a complicated law, though there is good ground for assuming a simple law in scientific *practice*, as a working hypothesis, if it explains the facts as well as another which is less simple. Belief in the existence of things outside my own biography exists antecedently to evidence, and can only be destroyed, if at all, by a long course of philosophic doubt. For purposes of science, it is justified practically by the simplification which it introduces into the laws of physics. But from the standpoint of theoretical logic it must be regarded as a prejudice, not as a well-grounded theory. With this proviso, I propose to continue yielding to the prejudice.

The second point concerns the relating of our point of view to that which regards sensations as caused by stimuli external to the nervous system (or at least to the brain), and distinguishes images as " centrally excited," i.e. due to causes in the brain which cannot be traced back to anything affecting the sense-organs. It is clear that, if our analysis of physical objects has been valid, this way of defining sensations needs re-interpretation. It is also clear that we must be able to find such a new interpretation if our theory is to be admissible.

To make the matter clear, we will take the simplest possible illustration. Consider a certain star, and suppose for the moment that its size is negligible. That is to say, we will regard it as, for practical purposes, a luminous point. Let us further suppose that it exists only for a very brief time, say a second. Then, according to physics, what happens is that a spherical wave of light travels outward from the star through space, just as, when you drop a stone into a stagnant pond, ripples travel outward from the place where the stone hit the water. The wave of light travels with a certain very nearly constant velocity, roughly 300,000 kilometres per second. This velocity may be ascertained by sending a flash of light to a mirror, and observing how long it takes before the reflected flash reaches you, just as the velocity of sound may be ascertained by means of an echo.

What it is that happens when a wave of light reaches a given place we cannot tell, except in the sole case when the place in question is a brain connected with an eye which is turned in the right direction. In this one very special case we know what happens : we have the sensation called " seeing the star." In all other cases, though we know (more or less hypothetically) some of the correlations and abstract properties of the appearance of the star, we do not know the appearance itself. Now you may, for the sake of illustration, compare the different appearances of the star to the conjugation of a Greek verb, except that the number of its parts is really infinite, and not only apparently so to the despairing schoolboy. *In vacuo*, the parts are regular, and can be derived from the (imaginary) root according to the laws of grammar, i.e. of perspective. The star being situated in empty space, it may be defined, for purposes of physics, as consisting of all those appearances which it presents *in vacuo*, together with those which, according to the laws of perspective, it would present elsewhere if its appearances elsewhere were regular. This is merely the adaptation of the definition of matter which I gave in an earlier lecture. The appearance of a star at a certain place, if it is regular, does not require any cause or explanation beyond the existence of the star. Every regular appearance is an actual member of the system which is the star, and its causation is entirely internal to that system. We may express this by saying that a regular appearance is due to the star alone, and is actually part of the star, in the sense in which a man is part of the human race.

But presently the light of the star reaches our atmosphere. It begins to be refracted, and dimmed by mist, and its velocity is slightly diminished. At last it reaches a human eye, where a complicated process takes place, ending in a sensation which gives us our grounds for believing in all that has gone before. Now, the irregular appearances of the star are not, strictly speaking, members of the system which is the star, according to our definition of matter. The irregular appearances, however, are not merely irregular : they proceed according to laws which can be stated in terms of the matter through which the light has passed on its way. The sources of an irregular appearance are therefore twofold :

(1) The object which is appearing irregularly ;
(2) The intervening medium.

It should be observed that, while the conception of a regular appearance is perfectly precise, the conception of an irregular appearance is one capable of any degree of vagueness. When the distorting influence of the medium is sufficiently great, the resulting particular can no longer be regarded as an appearance of an object, but must be treated on its own account. This happens especially when the particular in question cannot be traced back to one object, but is a blend of two or more. This case is normal in perception : we see as one what the microscope or telescope reveals to be many different objects. The notion of perception is therefore not a precise one : we perceive things more or less, but always with a very considerable amount of vagueness and confusion.

In considering irregular appearances, there are certain very natural mistakes which must be avoided. In order that a particular may count as an irregular appearance of a certain object, it is not necessary that it should bear any resemblance to the regular appearances as regard its intrinsic qualities. All that is necessary is that it should be derivable from the regular appearances by the laws which express the distorting influence of the medium. When it is so derivable, the particular in question may be regarded as caused by the regular appearances, and therefore by the object itself, together with the modifications resulting from the medium. In other cases, the particular in question may, in the same sense, be regarded as caused by several objects together with the medium ; in this case, it may be called a confused appearance of several objects. If it happens to be in a brain, it may be called a confused perception of these objects. All actual perception is confused to a greater or less extent.

We can now interpret in terms of our theory the distinction between those mental occurrences which are said to have an external stimulus, and those which are said to be " centrally excited," i.e. to have no stimulus external to the brain. When a mental occurrence can be regarded as an appearance of an object external to the brain, however irregular, or even as a confused appearance of several such objects, then we may regard it as having for its stimulus the object or objects in question, or their appearances at the sense-organ concerned. When, on the other hand, a mental occurrence has not sufficient connection with objects external to the brain to be regarded as an appearance of such objects, then its physical causation (if any) will have to be sought in the brain. In the former case it can be called a perception ; in the latter it cannot be so called. But the distinction is one of degree, not of kind. Until this is realized, no satisfactory theory of perception, sensation, or imagination is possible.

LECTURE VIII

SENSATIONS AND IMAGES

THE dualism of mind and matter, if we have been right so far, cannot be allowed as metaphysically valid. Nevertheless, we seem to find a certain dualism, perhaps not ultimate, within the world as we observe it. The dualism is not primarily as to the stuff of the world, but as to causal laws. On this subject we may again quote William James. He points out that when, as we say, we merely " imagine " things, there are no such effects as would ensue if the things were what we call " real." He takes the case of imagining a fire :

" I make for myself an experience of blazing fire ; I place it near my body ; but it does not warm me in the least. I lay a stick upon it and the stick either burns or remains green, as I please. I call up water, and pour it on the fire, and absolutely no difference ensues. I account for all such facts by calling this whole train of experiences unreal, a mental train. Mental fire is what won't burn real sticks ; mental water is what won't necessarily (though of course it may) put out even a mental fire. . . . With ' real ' objects, on the contrary, consequences always accrue ; and thus the real experiences get sifted from the mental ones, the things from our thoughts of them, fanciful or true, and precipitated together as the stable part of the whole experience-chaos, under the name of the physical world." [1]

In this passage James speaks, by mere inadvertence, as though the phenomena which he is describing as " mental " had *no* effects. This is, of course, not the case : they have their effects, just as much as physical phenomena do, but their effects follow different laws. For example, dreams, as Freud has shown, are just as much subject to laws as are the motions of the planets. But the laws are different : in a dream you may be transported from one place to another in a moment, or one person may turn into another under your eyes. Such differences compel you to distinguish the world of dreams from the physical world.

If the two sorts of causal laws could be sharply distinguished, we could call an occurrence " physical " when it obeys causal laws appropriate to the physical world, and " mental " when it obeys causal laws appropriate to the mental world. Since the mental world and the physical world interact, there would be a boundary between the two : there would be events which would have physical causes and mental effects, while there would be others which would have mental causes and physical effects. Those that have physical causes and mental effects we should define as " sensations." Those that have mental causes and physical effects might perhaps be identified with what we call voluntary movements ; but they do not concern us at present.

These definitions would have all the precision that could be desired if the distinction between physical and psychological causation were clear and sharp. As a matter of fact, however, this distinction is, as yet, by

[1] *Essays in Radical Empiricism*, pp. 32-3

no means sharp. It is possible that, with fuller knowledge,
it will be found to be no more ultimate than the distinction
between the laws of gases and the laws of rigid bodies.
It also suffers from the fact that an event may be an
effect of several causes according to several causal laws :
we cannot, in general, point to anything unique as *the*
cause of such-and-such an event. And finally it is by
no means certain that the peculiar causal laws which
govern mental events are not really physiological. The
law of habit, which is one of the most distinctive, may be
fully explicable in terms of the peculiarities of nervous
tissue, and these peculiarities, in turn, may be explicable
by the laws of physics. It seems, therefore, that we
are driven to a different kind of definition. It is for
this reason that it was necessary to develop the definition
of perception. With this definition, we can define a
sensation as the non-mnemic elements in a perception.

When, following our definition, we try to decide what
elements in our experience are of the nature of sensations,
we find more difficulty than might have been expected.
Prima facie, everything is sensation that comes to us
through the senses : the sights we see, the sounds we
hear, the smells we smell, and so on ; also such things
as headache or the feeling of muscular strain. But in
actual fact so much interpretation, so much of habitual
correlation, is mixed with all such experiences, that the
core of pure sensation is only to be extracted by careful
investigation. To take a simple illustration : if you go
to the theatre in your own country, you seem to hear
equally well in the stalls or the dress circle ; in either
case you think you miss nothing. But if you go in a
foreign country where you have a fair knowledge of the
language, you will seem to have grown partially deaf,

and you will find it necessary to be much nearer the stage than you would need to be in your own country. The reason is that, in hearing our own language spoken, we quickly and unconsciously fill out what we really hear with inferences to what the man must be saying, and we never realize that we have not heard the words we have merely inferred. In a foreign language, these inferences are more difficult, and we are more dependent upon actual sensation. If we found ourselves in a foreign world, where tables looked like cushions and cushions like tables, we should similarly discover how much of what we think we see is really inference. Every fairly familiar sensation is to us a sign of the things that usually go with it, and many of these things will seem to form part of the sensation. I remember in the early days of motor-cars being with a friend when a tyre burst with a loud report. He thought it was a pistol, and supported his opinion by maintaining that he had seen the flash. But of course there had been no flash. Nowadays no one sees a flash when a tyre bursts.

In order, therefore, to arrive at what really is sensation in an occurrence which, at first sight, seems to contain nothing else, we have to pare away all that is due to habit or expectation or interpretation. This is a matter for the psychologist, and by no means an easy matter. For our purposes, it is not important to determine what exactly is the sensational core in any case; it is only important to notice that there certainly is a sensational core, since habit, expectation and interpretation are diversely aroused on diverse occasions, and the diversity is clearly due to differences in what is presented to the senses. When you open your newspaper in the morning, the actual sensations of seeing the print form a very minute part of what goes on in you, but they are the starting-point of all the rest, and it is through them that the newspaper is a means of information or mis-information. Thus, although it may be difficult to determine what exactly is sensation in any given experience, it is clear that there is sensation, unless, like Leibniz, we deny all action of the outer world upon us.

Sensations are obviously the source of our knowledge of the world, including our own body. It might seem natural to regard a sensation as itself a cognition, and until lately I did so regard it. When, say, I see a person I know coming towards me in the street, it *seems* as though the mere seeing were knowledge. It is of course undeniable that knowledge comes *through* the seeing, but I think it is a mistake to regard the mere seeing itself as knowledge. If we are so to regard it, we must distinguish the seeing from what is seen : we must say that, when we see a patch of colour of a certain shape, the patch of colour is one thing and our seeing of it is another. This view, however, demands the admission of the subject, or act, in the sense discussed in our first lecture. If there is a subject, it can have a relation to the patch of colour, namely, the sort of relation which we might call awareness. In that case the sensation, as a mental event, will consist of awareness of the colour, while the colour itself will remain wholly physical, and may be called the sense-datum, to distinguish it from the sensation. The subject, however, appears to be a logical fiction, like mathematical points and instants. It is introduced, not because observation reveals it, but because it is linguistically convenient and apparently demanded by grammar. Nominal entities of this sort may or may not exist, but there is no good ground for assuming that they do.

The functions that they appear to perform can always be performed by classes or series or other logical constructions, consisting of less dubious entities. If we are to avoid a perfectly gratuitous assumption, we must dispense with the subject as one of the actual ingredients of the world. But when we do this, the possibility of distinguishing the sensation from the sense-datum vanishes; at least I see no way of preserving the distinction. Accordingly the sensation that we have when we see a patch of colour simply *is* that patch of colour, an actual constituent of the physical world, and part of what physics is concerned with. A patch of colour is certainly not knowledge, and therefore we cannot say that pure sensation is cognitive. Through its psychological effects, it is the cause of cognitions, partly by being itself a sign of things that are correlated with it, as e.g. sensations of sight and touch are correlated, and partly by giving rise to images and memories after the sensation is faded. But in itself the pure sensation is not cognitive.

In the first lecture we considered the view of Brentano, that "we may define psychical phenomena by saying that they are phenomena which intentionally contain an object." We saw reasons to reject this view in general; we are now concerned to show that it must be rejected in the particular case of sensations. The kind of argument which formerly made me accept Brentano's view in this case was exceedingly simple. When I see a patch of colour, it seemed to me that the colour is not psychical, but physical, while my seeing is not physical, but psychical. Hence I concluded that the colour is something other than my seeing of the colour. This argument, to me historically, was directed against idealism : the emphatic part of it was the assertion that the colour is physical, not psychical. I shall not trouble you now with the grounds for holding as against Berkeley that the patch of colour is physical ; I have set them forth before, and I see no reason to modify them. But it does not follow that the patch of colour is not also psychical, unless we assume that the physical and the psychical cannot overlap, which I no longer consider a valid assumption. If we admit—as I think we should—that the patch of colour may be both physical and psychical, the reason for distinguishing the sense-datum from the sensation disappears, and we may say that the patch of colour and our sensation in seeing it are identical.

This is the view of William James, Professor Dewey, and the American realists. Perceptions, says Professor Dewey, are not *per se* cases of knowledge, but simply natural events with no more knowledge status than (say) a shower. " Let them [the realists] try the experiment of conceiving perceptions as pure natural events, not cases of awareness or apprehension, and they will be surprised to see how little they miss." [1] I think he is right in this, except in supposing that the realists will be surprised. Many of them already hold the view he is advocating, and others are very sympathetic to it. At any rate, it is the view which I shall adopt in these lectures.

The stuff of the world, so far as we have experience of it, consists, on the view that I am advocating, of innumerable transient particulars such as occur in seeing, hearing, etc., together with images more or less resembling these, of which I shall speak shortly. If physics is true, there are, besides the particulars that we experience,

[1] Dewey, *Essays in Experimental Logic*, pp. 253, 262.

others, probably equally (or almost equally) transient, which make up that part of the material world that does not come into the sort of contact with a living body that is required to turn it into a sensation. But this topic belongs to the philosophy of physics, and need not concern us in our present inquiry.

Sensations are what is common to the mental and physical worlds; they may be defined as the intersection of mind and matter. This is by no means a new view; it is advocated, not only by the American authors I have mentioned, but by Mach in his *Analysis of Sensations*, which was published in 1886. The essence of sensation, according to the view I am advocating, is its independence of past experience. It is a core in our actual experiences, never existing in isolation except possibly in very young infants. It is not itself knowledge, but it supplies the data for our knowledge of the physical world, including our own bodies.

There are some who believe that our mental life is built up out of sensations alone. This may be true; but in any case I think the only ingredients required in addition to sensations are *images*. What images are, and how they are to be defined, we have now to inquire.

The distinction between images and sensations might seem at first sight by no means difficult. When we shut our eyes and call up pictures of familiar scenes, we usually have no difficulty, so long as we remain awake, in discriminating between what we are imagining and what is really seen. If we imagine some piece of music that we know, we can go through it in our mind from beginning to end without any discoverable tendency to suppose that we are really hearing it. But although such cases are so clear that no confusion seems possible, there are

many others that are far more difficult, and the definition
of images is by no means an easy problem.

To begin with : we do not always know whether what
we are experiencing is a sensation or an image. The
things we see in dreams when our eyes are shut must
count as images, yet while we are dreaming they seem
like sensations. Hallucinations often begin as persistent
images, and only gradually acquire that influence over
belief that makes the patient regard them as sensations.
When we are listening for a faint sound—the striking of
a distant clock, or a horse's hoofs on the road—we
think we hear it many times before we really do, because
expectation brings us the image, and we mistake it for
sensation. The distinction between images and sensations
is, therefore, by no means always obvious to inspection.[1]

We may consider three different ways in which it has
been sought to distinguish images from sensations, namely :

(1) By the less degree of vividness in images ;
(2) By our absence of belief in their " physical
   reality " ;
(3) By the fact that their causes and effects are
   different from those of sensations.

I believe the third of these to be the only universally
applicable criterion. The other two are applicable in
very many cases, but cannot be used for purposes of
definition because they are liable to exceptions. Nevertheless, they both deserve to be carefully considered.

(1) Hume, who gives the names " impressions " and
" ideas " to what may, for present purposes, be identified with our " sensations " and " images," speaks of

---

[1] On the distinction between images and sensations, cf. Semon,
Die mnemischen Empfindungen, pp. 19 20.

impressions as " those perceptions which enter with most force and violence " while he defines ideas as " the faint images of these [i.e. of impressions] in thinking and reasoning ". His immediately following observations, however, show the inadequacy of his criteria of " force " and " faintness." He says :

" I believe it will not be very necessary to employ many words in explaining this distinction. Every one of himself will readily perceive the difference betwixt feeling and thinking. The common degrees of these are easily distinguished, though it is not impossible but in particular instances they may very nearly approach to each other. Thus in sleep, in a fever, in madness, or in any very violent emotions of soul, our ideas may approach to our impressions ; as, on the other hand, it sometimes happens, that our impressions are so faint and low that we cannot distinguish them from our ideas. But notwithstanding this near resemblance in a few instances, they are in general so very different, that no one can make a scruple to rank them under distinct heads, and assign to each a peculiar name to mark the difference" (*Treatise of Human Nature*, Part I, Section 1).

I think Hume is right in holding that they should be ranked under distinct heads, with a peculiar name for each. But by his own confession in the above passage, his criterion for distinguishing them is not always adequate. A definition is not sound if it only applies in cases where the difference is glaring : the essential purpose of a definition is to provide a mark which is applicable even in marginal cases—except, of course, when we are dealing with a conception, like, e.g. baldness, which is one of degree and has no sharp boundaries. But so far we have seen no reason to think that the difference between sensations and images is only one of degree.

Professor Stout, in his *Manual of Psychology*, after discussing various ways of distinguishing sensations and images, arrives at a view which is a modification of Hume's. He says (I quote from the second edition):

" Our conclusion is that at bottom the distinction between image and percept, as respectively faint and vivid states, is based on a difference of quality. The percept has an aggressiveness which does not belong to the image. It strikes the mind with varying degrees of force or liveliness according to the varying intensity of the stimulus. This degree of force or liveliness is part of what we ordinarily mean by the intensity of a sensation. But this constituent of the intensity of sensations is absent in mental imagery " (p. 419).

This view allows for the fact that sensations may reach any degree of faintness—e.g. in the case of a just visible star or a just audible sound—without becoming images, and that therefore mere faintness cannot be the characteristic mark of images. After explaining the sudden shock of a flash of lightning or a steam-whistle, Stout says that " no mere image ever does strike the mind in this manner " (p. 417). But I believe that this criterion fails in very much the same instances as those in which Hume's criterion fails in its original form. Macbeth speaks of—

> that suggestion
> Whose horrid image doth unfix my hair
> And make my seated heart knock at my ribs
> Against the use of nature.

The whistle of a steam-engine could hardly have a stronger effect than this. A very intense emotion will often bring with it—especially where some future action or some undecided issue is involved—powerful compelling images which may determine the whole course of life, sweeping aside all contrary solicitations to the will by their capacity for exclusively possessing the mind. And in all cases where images, originally recognized as such, gradually pass into hallucinations, there must be just that " force or liveliness " which is supposed to be always absent from images. The cases of dreams and fever-delirium are as hard to adjust to Professor Stout's modified criterion as to Hume's. I conclude therefore that the test of liveliness, however applicable in ordinary instances, cannot be used to define the differences between sensations and images.

(2) We might attempt to distinguish images from sensations by our absence of belief in the " physical reality " of images. When we are aware that what we are experiencing is an image, we do not give it the kind of belief that we should give to a sensation : we do not think that it has the same power of producing knowledge of the " external world." Images are " imaginary " ; in *some* sense they are " unreal." But this difference is hard to analyse or state correctly. What we call the " unreality " of images requires interpretation : it cannot mean what would be expressed by saying " there's no such thing." Images are just as truly part of the actual world as sensations are. All that we really mean by calling an image " unreal " is that it does not have the concomitants which it would have if it were a sensation. When we call up a visual image of a chair, we do not attempt to sit in it, because we know that, like Macbeth's dagger, it is not " sensible to feeling as to sight "—i.e. it does not have the correlations with tactile

sensations which it would have if it were a visual sensation and not merely a visual image. But this means that the so-called "unreality" of images consists merely in their not obeying the laws of physics, and thus brings us back to the causal distinction between images and sensations.

This view is confirmed by the fact that we only feel images to be "unreal" when we already know them to be images. Images cannot be defined by the *feeling* of unreality, because when we falsely believe an image to be a sensation, as in the case of dreams, it *feels* just as real as if it were a sensation. Our feeling of unreality results from our having already realized that we are dealing with an image, and cannot therefore be the definition of what we mean by an image. As soon as an image begins to deceive us as to its status, it also deceives us as to its correlations, which are what we mean by its "reality."

(3) This brings us to the third mode of distinguishing images from sensations, namely, by their causes and effects. I believe this to be the only valid ground of distinction. James, in the passage about the mental fire which won't burn real sticks, distinguishes images by their effects, but I think the more reliable distinction is by their causes. Professor Stout (*loc. cit.*, p. 127) says : "One characteristic mark of what we agree in calling sensation is its mode of production. It is caused by what we call a *stimulus*. A stimulus is always some condition external to the nervous system itself and operating upon it." I think that this is the correct view, and that the distinction between images and sensations can only be made by taking account of their causation. Sensations come through sense-organs, while images do

not. We cannot have visual sensations in the dark, or with our eyes shut, but we can very well have visual images under these circumstances. Accordingly images have been defined as " centrally excited sensations," i.e. sensations which have their physiological cause in the brain only, not also in the sense-organs and the nerves that run from the sense-organs to the brain. I think the phrase " centrally excited sensations " assumes more than is necessary, since it takes it for granted that an image must have a proximate physiological cause. This is probably true, but it is an hypothesis, and for our purposes an unnecessary one. It would seem to fit better with what we can immediately observe if we were to say that an image is occasioned, through association, by a sensation or another image, in other words that it has a mnemic cause—which does not prevent it from also having a physical cause. And I think it will be found that the causation of an image always proceeds according to mnemic laws, i.e. that it is governed by habit and past experience. If you listen to a man playing the pianola without looking at him, you will have images of his hands on the keys as if he were playing the piano ; if you suddenly look at him while you are absorbed in the music, you will experience a shock of surprise when you notice that his hands are not touching the notes. Your image of his hands is due to the many times that you have heard similar sounds and at the same time seen the player's hands on the piano. When habit and past experience play this part, we are in the region of mnemic as opposed to ordinary physical causation. And I think that, if we could regard as ultimately valid the difference between physical and mnemic causation, we could distinguish images from sensations as having mnemic causes, though they may also have physical causes. Sensations, on the other hand, will only have physical causes.

However this may be, the practically effective distinction between sensations and images is that in the causation of sensations, but not of images, the stimulation of nerves carrying an effect into the brain, usually from the surface of the body, plays an essential part. And this accounts for the fact that images and sensations cannot always be distinguished by their intrinsic nature.

Images also differ from sensations as regards their effects. Sensations, as a rule, have both physical and mental effects. As you watch the train you meant to catch leaving the station, there are both the successive positions of the train (physical effects) and the successive waves of fury and disappointment (mental effects). Images, on the contrary, though they *may* produce bodily movements, do so according to mnemic laws, not according to the laws of physics. All their effects, of whatever nature, follow mnemic laws. But this difference is less suitable for definition than the difference as to causes.

Professor Watson, as a logical carrying-out of his behaviourist theory, denies altogether that there are any observable phenomena such as images are supposed to be. He replaces them all by faint sensations, and especially by pronunciation of words *sotto voce*. When we " think " of a table (say), as opposed to seeing it, what happens, according to him, is usually that we are making small movements of the throat and tongue such as would lead to our uttering the word " table " if they were more pronounced. I shall consider his view again in connection with words ; for the present I am only concerned to combat his denial of images. This denial is set forth both in his book on *Behavior* and in an article called "Image and Affection in Behavior" in the *Journal of Philosophy, Psychology and Scientific Methods*, vol. x (July, 1913). It seems to me that in this matter he has been betrayed into denying plain facts in the interests of a theory, namely, the supposed impossibility of introspection. I dealt with the theory in Lecture VI; for the present I wish to reinforce the view that the facts are undeniable.

Images are of various sorts, according to the nature of the sensations which they copy. Images of bodily movements, such as we have when we imagine moving an arm or, on a smaller scale, pronouncing a word, might possibly be explained away on Professor Watson's lines, as really consisting in small incipient movements such as, if magnified and prolonged, would be the movements we are said to be imagining. Whether this is the case or not might even be decided experimentally. If there were a delicate instrument for recording small movements in the mouth and throat, we might place such an instrument in a person's mouth and then tell him to recite a poem to himself, as far as possible only in imagination. I should not be at all surprised if it were found that actual small movements take place while he is "mentally" saying over the verses. The point is important, because what is called "thought" consists mainly (though I think not wholly) of inner speech. If Professor Watson is right as regards inner speech, this whole region is transferred from imagination to sensation. But since the question is capable of experimental decision, it would be gratuitous rashness to offer an opinion while that decision is lacking.

But visual and auditory images are much more difficult to deal with in this way, because they lack the connection with physical events in the outer world which belongs to visual and auditory sensations. Suppose, for example, that I am sitting in my room, in which there is an empty arm-chair. I shut my eyes, and call up a visual image of a friend sitting in the arm-chair. If I thrust my image into the world of physics, it contradicts all the usual physical laws. My friend reached the chair without coming in at the door in the usual way ; subsequent inquiry will show that he was somewhere else at the moment. If regarded as a sensation, my image has all the marks of the supernatural. My image, therefore, is regarded as an event in me, not as having that position in the orderly happenings of the public world that belongs to sensations. By saying that it is an event in me, we leave it possible that it may be *physiologically* caused : its privacy may be only due to its connection with my body. But in any case it is not a public event, like an actual person walking in at the door and sitting down in my chair. And it cannot, like inner speech, be regarded as a *small* sensation, since it occupies just as large an area in my visual field as the actual sensation would do.

Professor Watson says : " I should throw out imagery altogether and attempt to show that all natural thought goes on in terms of sensori-motor processes in the larynx." This view seems to me flatly to contradict experience. If you try to persuade any uneducated person that she cannot call up a visual picture of a friend sitting in a chair, but can only use words describing what such an occurrence would be like, she will conclude that you are mad. (This statement is based upon experiment.) Galton, as every one knows, investigated visual imagery, and found that education tends to kill it : the Fellows of the Royal Society turned out to have much less of it than their wives. I see no reason to doubt his conclusion that the habit of abstract pursuits makes learned men much inferior to the average in power of visualizing, and much more exclusively occupied with words in their "thinking." And Professor Watson is a very learned man.

I shall henceforth assume that the existence of images is admitted, and that they are to be distinguished from sensations by their causes, as well as, in a lesser degree, by their effects. In their intrinsic nature, though they often differ from sensations by being more dim or vague or faint, yet they do not always or universally differ from sensations in any way that can be used for defining them. Their privacy need form no bar to the scientific study of them, any more than the privacy of bodily sensations does. Bodily sensations are admitted by even the most severe critics of introspection, although, like images, they can only be observed by one observer. It must be admitted, however, that the laws of the appearance and disappearance of images are little known and difficult to discover, because we are not assisted, as in the case of sensations, by our knowledge of the physical world.

There remains one very important point concerning images, which will occupy us much hereafter, and that is, their resemblance to previous sensations. They are said to be "copies" of sensations, always as regards the simple qualities that enter into them, though not always as regards the manner in which these are put together. It is generally believed that we cannot imagine a shade of colour that we have never seen, or a sound that we have never heard. On this subject Hume is the classic. He says, in the definitions already quoted :

" Those perceptions, which enter with most force and violence, we may name *impressions* ; and under this name I comprehend all our sensations, passions and emotions, as they make their first appearance in the soul. By *ideas* I mean the faint images of these in thinking and reasoning."

He next explains the difference between simple and complex ideas, and explains that a complex idea may occur without any similar complex impression. But as regards simple ideas, he states that " every simple idea has a simple impression, which resembles it, and every simple impression a correspondent idea." He goes on to enunciate the general principle " that all our simple ideas in their first appearance are derived from simple impressions, which are correspondent to them, and which they exactly represent" (*Treatise of Human Nature*, Part I, Section 1).

It is this fact, that images resemble antecedent sensations, which enables us to call them images " of " this or that. For the understanding of memory, and of knowledge generally, the recognizable resemblance of images and sensations is of fundamental importance.

There are difficulties in establishing Hume's principles, and doubts as to whether it is exactly true. Indeed, he himself signalized an exception immediately after stating his maxim. Nevertheless, it is impossible to doubt that in the main simple images are copies of similar simple sensations which have occurred earlier, and that the same is true of complex images in all cases of memory as opposed to mere imagination. Our power of acting with reference to what is sensibly absent is largely due to this characteristic of images, although, as education advances, images tend to be more and more replaced by words. We shall have much to say in the next two lectures on the subject of images as copies of sensations. What has been said now is merely by way of reminder that this is their most notable characteristic.

I am by no means confident that the distinction between images and sensations is ultimately valid, and I should be glad to be convinced that images can be reduced to sensations of a peculiar kind. I think it is clear, however, that, at any rate in the case of auditory and visual images, they do differ from ordinary auditory and visual sensations, and therefore form a recognizable class of occurrences, even if it should prove that they can be regarded as a sub-class of sensations. This is all that is necessary to validate the use of images to be made in the sequel.

LECTURE IX

MEMORY

MEMORY, which we are to consider to-day, introduces us to knowledge in one of its forms. The analysis of knowledge will occupy us until the end of the thirteenth lecture, and is the most difficult part of our whole enterprise.

I do not myself believe that the analysis of knowledge can be effected entirely by means of purely external observation, such as behaviourists employ. I shall discuss this question in later lectures. In the present lecture I shall attempt the analysis of memory-knowledge, both as an introduction to the problem of knowledge in general, and because memory, in some form, is presupposed in almost all other knowledge. Sensation, we decided, is not a form of knowledge. It might, however, have been expected that we should begin our discussion of knowledge with *perception*, i.e. with that integral experience of things in the environment, out of which sensation is extracted by psychological analysis. What is called perception differs from sensation by the fact that the sensational ingredients bring up habitual associates— images and expectations of their usual correlates—all of which are subjectively indistinguishable from the sensation. The *fact* of past experience is essential in producing this filling-out of sensation, but not the *recollection* of past experience. The non-sensational elements in perception can be wholly explained as the result of habit, produced by frequent correlations. Perception, according to our definition in Lecture VII, is no more a form of knowledge than sensation is, except in so far as it involves expectations. The purely psychological problems which it raises are not very difficult, though they have sometimes been rendered artificially obscure by unwillingness to admit the fallibility of the non-sensational elements of perception. On the other hand, memory raises many difficult and very important problems, which it is necessary to consider at the first possible moment.

One reason for treating memory at this early stage is that it seems to be involved in the fact that images are recognized as " copies " of past sensible experience. In the preceding lecture I alluded to Hume's principle " that all our simple ideas in their first appearance are derived from simple impressions, which are correspondent to them, and which they exactly represent." Whether or not this principle is liable to exceptions, everyone would agree that is has a broad measure of truth, though the word " exactly " might seem an overstatement, and it might seem more correct to say that ideas *approximately* represent impressions. Such modifications of Hume's principle, however, do not affect the problem which I wish to present for your consideration, namely : Why do we believe that images are, sometimes or always, approximately or exactly, copies of sensations ? What sort of evidence is there ? And what sort of evidence is logically possible ? The difficulty of this question arises through the fact that the sensation which an image is supposed to copy is in the past when the image exists, and can therefore only be known by memory, while, on the other hand, memory of past sensations seems only possible by means of present images. How, then, are we to find any way of comparing the present image and the past sensation ? The problem is just as acute if we say that images differ from their prototypes as if we say that they resemble them ; it is the very possibility of comparison that is hard to understand.[1] We think we can know that they are alike or different, but we cannot bring them together in one experience and compare them. To deal with this problem, we must have a theory of memory. In this way the whole status of images as " copies " is bound up with the analysis of memory.

In investigating memory-beliefs, there are certain points which must be borne in mind. In the first place, everything constituting a memory-belief is happening *now*, not in that past time to which the belief is said to refer. It is not logically necessary to the existence of a memory-belief that the event remembered should have occurred, or even that the past should have existed at all. There is no logical impossibility in the hypothesis that the world sprang into being five minutes ago, exactly as it then was, with a population that " remembered " a wholly unreal past. There is no logically necessary connection between events at different times ; therefore nothing that is happening now or will happen in the future can disprove the hypothesis that the world began

---

[1] How, for example, can we obtain such knowledge as the following : " If we look at, say, a red nose and perceive it, and after a little while *ekphore* its memory-image, we note immediately how unlike, in its likeness, this memory-image is to the original perception " (A. Wohlgemuth, " On the Feelings and their Neural Correlate with an Examination of the Nature of Pain," *Journal of Psychology*, vol. viii, part iv, June, 1917).

five minutes ago. Hence the occurrences which are *called* knowledge of the past are logically independent of the past ; they are wholly analysable into present contents, which might, theoretically, be just what they are even if no past had existed.

I am not suggesting that the non-existence of the past should be entertained as a serious hypothesis. Like all sceptical hypotheses, it is logically tenable, but uninteresting. All that I am doing is to use its logical tenability as a help in the analysis of what occurs when we remember.

In the second place, images without beliefs are insufficient to constitute memory ; and habits are still more insufficient. The behaviourist, who attempts to make psychology a record of behaviour, has to trust his memory in making the record. " Habit " is a concept involving the occurrence of similar events at different times ; if the behaviourist feels confident that there is such a phenomenon as habit, that can only be because he trusts his memory, when it assures him that there have been other times. And the same applies to images. If we are to know—as it is supposed we do—that images are " copies," accurate or inaccurate, of past events, something more than the mere occurrence of images must go to constitute this knowledge. For their mere occurrence, by itself, would not suggest any connection with anything that had happened before.

Can we constitute memory out of images together with suitable beliefs ? We may take it that memory-images, when they occur in true memory, are (*a*) known to be copies, (*b*) sometimes known to be imperfect copies (cf. footnote on previous page). How is it possible to know that a memory-image is an imperfect copy, without having a more accurate copy by which to replace it ? This would *seem* to suggest that we have a way of knowing the past which is independent of images, by means of which we can criticize image-memories. But I do not think such an inference is warranted.

What results, formally, from our knowledge of the past through images of which we recognize the inaccuracy, is that such images must have two characteristics by which we can arrange them in two series, of which one corresponds to the more or less remote period in the past to which they refer, and the other to our greater or less confidence in their accuracy. We will take the second of these points first.

Our confidence or lack of confidence in the accuracy of a memory-image must, in fundamental cases, be based upon a characteristic of the image itself, since we cannot evoke the past bodily and compare it with the present image. It might be suggested that vagueness is the required characteristic, but I do not think this is the case. We sometimes have images that are by no means peculiarly vague, which yet we do not trust—for example, under the influence of fatigue we may see a fri nd's face vividly and clearly, but horribly distorted. In such a case we distrust our image in spite of its being unusually clear. I think the characteristic by which we distinguish the images we trust is the feeling of *familiarity* that accompanies them. Some images, like some sensations, feel very familiar, while others feel strange. Familiarity is a feeling capable of degrees. In an image of a well-known face, for example, some parts may feel more familiar than others ; when this happens, we have more belief in the accuracy of the familiar parts than in that of the unfamiliar parts. I think it is by this means that we become critical of images, not by some imageless memory with which we compare them. I shall return to the consideration of familiarity shortly.

I come now to the other characteristic which memory-images must have in order to account for our knowledge of the past. They must have some characteristic which makes us regard them as referring to more or less remote portions of the past. That is to say if we suppose that A is the event remembered, B the remembering, and *t* the interval of time between A and B, there must be some characteristic of B which is capable of degrees, and which, in accurately dated memories, varies as *t* varies. It may increase as *t* increases, or diminish as *t* increases. The question which of these occurs is not of any importance for the theoretic serviceability of the characteristic in question.

In actual fact, there are doubtless various factors that concur in giving us the feeling of greater or less remoteness in some remembered event. There may be a specific feeling which could be called the feeling of "pastness," especially where immediate memory is concerned. But apart from this, there are other marks. One of these is context. A recent memory has, usually, more context than a more distant one. When a remembered event has a remembered context, this may occur in two ways, either (*a*) by successive images in the same order as their proto-types, or (*b*) by remembering a whole process simul-taneously, in the same way in which a present process may be apprehended, through akoluthic sensations which, by fading, acquire the mark of just-pastness in an increasing degree as they fade, and are thus placed in a series while all sensibly present. It will be context in this second sense, more specially, that will give us a sense of the nearness or remoteness of a remembered event.

There is, of course, a difference between knowing the temporal relation of a remembered event to the present, and knowing the time-order of two remembered events. Very often our knowledge of the temporal relation of a remembered event to the present is inferred from its temporal relations to other remembered events. It would seem that only rather recent events can be placed at all accurately by means of feelings giving their temporal relation to the present, but it is clear that such feelings must play an essential part in the process of dating remembered events.

We may say, then, that images are regarded by us as more or less accurate copies of past occurrences because they come to us with two sorts of feelings: (1) Those that may be called feelings of familiarity; (2) those that may be collected together as feelings giving a sense of pastness. The first lead us to trust our memories, the second to assign places to them in the time-order.

We have now to analyse the memory-belief, as opposed to the characteristics of images which lead us to base memory-beliefs upon them.

If we had retained the " subject " or " act " in knowledge, the whole problem of memory would have been comparatively simple. We could then have said that remembering is a direct relation between the present act or subject and the past occurrence remembered : the act of remembering is present, though its object is past. But the rejection of the subject renders some more complicated theory necessary. Remembering has to be a present occurrence in some way resembling, or related to, what is remembered. And it is difficult to find any ground, except a pragmatic one, for supposing that memory is not sheer delusion, if, as seems to be the case, there is not, apart from memory, any way of ascertaining that there really was a past occurrence having the required relation to our present remembering. What, if we followed Meinong's terminology, we should call the " object " in memory, i.e. the past event which we are said to be remembering, is unpleasantly remote from the " content," i.e. the present mental occurrence in remembering. There is an awkward gulf between the two, which raises difficulties for the theory of knowledge. But we must not falsify observation to avoid theoretical difficulties. For the present, therefore, let us forget these problems, and try to discover what actually occurs in memory.

Some points may be taken as fixed, and such as any theory of memory must arrive at. In this case, as in most others, what may be taken as certain in advance is rather vague. The study of any topic is like the continued observation of an object which is approaching us along a road : what is certain to begin with is the quite vague knowledge that there is *some* object on the road. If you attempt to be less vague, and to assert that the object is an elephant, or a man, or a mad dog, you run a risk of error ; but the purpose of continued observation is to enable you to arrive at such more precise knowledge. In like manner, in the study of memory, the certainties with which you begin are very vague, and the more precise propositions at which you try to arrive are less certain than the hazy data from which you set out. Nevertheless, in spite of the risk of error, precision is the goal at which we must aim.

The first of our vague but indubitable data is that there is knowledge of the past. We do not yet know with any precision what we mean by " knowledge," and we must admit that in any given instance our memory may be at fault. Nevertheless, whatever a sceptic might urge in theory, we cannot practically doubt that we got up this morning, that we did various things yesterday, that a great war has been taking place, and so on. How far our knowledge of the past is due to memory, and how far to other sources, is of course a matter to be investigated, but there can be no doubt that memory forms an indispensable part of our knowledge of the past.

The second datum is that we certainly have more capacity for knowing the past than for knowing the future. We know some things about the future, for example what eclipses there will be ; but this knowledge is a matter of elaborate calculation and inference, whereas some of our knowledge of the past comes to us without effort, in the same sort of immediate way in which we acquire knowledge of occurrences. in our present environment. We might provisionally, though perhaps not quite correctly, define " memory " as that way of knowing about the past which has no analogue in our knowledge of the future ; such a definition would at least serve to mark the problem with which we are concerned, though some expectations may deserve to rank with memory as regards immediacy.

A third point, perhaps not quite so certain as our previous two, is that the truth of memory cannot be wholly practical, as pragmatists wish all truth to be. It seems clear that some of the things I remember are trivial and without any visible importance for the future, but that my memory is true (or false) in virtue of a past event, not in virtue of any future consequences of my belief. The definition of truth as the correspondence between beliefs and facts seems peculiarly evident in the case of memory, as against not only the pragmatist definition but also the idealist definition by means of coherence. These considerations, however, are taking us away from psychology, to which we must now return.

It is important not to confuse the two forms of memory which Bergson distinguishes in the second chapter of his *Matter and Memory*, namely the sort that consists of habit, and the sort that consists of independent recollection. He gives the instance of learning a lesson by heart : when I know it by heart I am said to " remember " it, but this merely means that I have acquired certain habits ; on the other hand, my recollection of (say) the second time I read the lesson while I was learning it is the recollection of a unique event, which occurred only once. The recollection of a unique event cannot, so Bergson contends, be wholly constituted by habit, and is in fact something radically different from the memory which is habit. The recollection alone is true memory. This distinction is vital to the understanding of memory. But it is not so easy to carry out in practice as it is to draw in theory. Habit is a very intrusive feature of our mental life, and is often present where at first sight it seems not to be. There is, for example, a habit of remembering a unique event. When we have once described the event, the words we have used easily become habitual. We may even have used words to describe it to ourselves while it was happening ; in that case, the habit of these words may fulfil the function of Bergson's true memory, while in reality it is nothing but habit-memory. A gramophone, by the help of suitable records, might relate to us the incidents of its past ; and people are not so different from gramophones as they like to believe.

In spite, however, of a difficulty in distinguishing the two forms of memory in practice, there can be no doubt that both forms exist. I can set to work now to remember things I never remembered before, such as what I had to eat for breakfast this morning, and it can hardly be wholly habit that enables me to do this. It is this sort of occurrence that constitutes the essence of memory. Until we have analysed what happens in such a case as this, we have not succeeded in understanding memory.

The sort of memory with which we are here concerned is the sort which is a form of knowledge. Whether knowledge itself is reducible to habit is a question to which I shall return in a later lecture ; for the present I am only anxious to point out that, whatever the true analysis of knowledge may be, knowledge of past occurrences is not proved by behaviour which is due to past experience. The fact that a man can recite a poem does not show that he remembers any previous occasion on which he has recited or read it. Similarly, the performances of animals in getting out of cages or mazes to which they are accustomed do not prove that they remember having been in the same situation before. Arguments in favour of (for example) memory in plants are only arguments in favour of habit-memory, not of knowledge-memory. Samuel Butler's arguments in favour of the view that an animal remembers something of the lives of its ancestors[1] are, when examined, only arguments in favour of habit-memory. Semon's two books, mentioned in an earlier lecture, do not touch knowledge-memory at all closely. They give laws according to which images of past occurrences come into our minds, but do not discuss our belief that these images refer to past occurrences, which is what constitutes knowledge-memory. It is this that is of interest to theory of knowledge. I shall speak of it

[1] See his *Life and Habit* and *Unconscious Memory*

as "true" memory, to distinguish it from mere habit acquired through past experience.

Before considering true memory, it will be well to consider two things which are on the way towards memory, namely the feeling of familiarity and recognition.

We often feel that something in our sensible environment is familiar, without having any definite recollection of previous occasions on which we have seen it. We have this feeling normally in places where we have often been before—at home, or in well-known streets. Most people and animals find it essential to their happiness to spend a good deal of their time in familiar surroundings, which are especially comforting when any danger threatens. The feeling of familiarity has all sorts of degrees, down to the stage where we dimly feel that we have seen a person before. It is by no means always reliable; almost everybody has at some time experienced the well-known illusion that all that is happening now happened before at some time. There are occasions when familiarity does not attach itself to any definite object, when there is merely a vague feeling that *something* is familiar. This is illustrated by Turgenev's *Smoke*, where the hero is long puzzled by a haunting sense that something in his present is recalling something in his past, and at last traces it to the smell of heliotrope. Whenever the sense of familiarity occurs without a definite object, it leads us to search the environment until we are satisfied that we have found the appropriate object, which leads us to the judgment: "*This* is familiar." I think we may regard familiarity as a definite feeling, capable of existing without an object, but normally standing in a specific relation to some feature of the environment, the relation being that which we express in words by saying that the feature in question is familiar. The judgment that what is familiar has been experienced before is a product of reflection, and is no part of the feeling of familiarity, such as a horse may be supposed to have when he returns to his stable. Thus no knowledge as to the past is to be derived from the feeling of familiarity alone.

A further stage is *recognition*. This may be taken in two senses, the first when a thing not merely feels familiar, but we know it is such-and-such. We recognize our friend Jones, we know cats and dogs when we see them, and so on. Here we have a definite influence of past experience, but not necessarily any actual knowledge of the past. When we see a cat, we know it is a cat because of previous cats we have seen, but we do not, as a rule, recollect at the moment any particular occasion when we have seen a cat. Recognition in this sense does not necessarily involve more than a habit of association: the kind of object we are seeing at the moment is associated with the word "cat," or with an auditory image of purring, or whatever other characteristic we may happen to recognize in the cat of the moment. We are, of course, in fact able to judge, when we recognize an object, that we have seen it before, but this judgment is something over and above recognition in this first sense, and may very probably be impossible to animals that nevertheless have the experience of recognition in this first sense of the word.

There is, however, another sense of the word, in which we mean by recognition, not knowing the name of a thing or some other property of it, but knowing that we have seen it before. In this sense recognition does involve knowledge about the past. This knowledge is memory in one sense, though in another it is not. It does not involve a definite memory of a definite past event, but only the knowledge that something happening now is similar to something that happened before. It differs from the sense of familiarity by being cognitive; it is a belief or judgment, which the sense of familiarity is not. I do not wish to undertake the analysis of belief at present, since it will be the subject of the twelfth lecture; for the present I merely wish to emphasize the fact that recognition, in our second sense, consists in a belief, which we may express approximately in the words: " This has existed before."

There are, however, several points in which such an account of recognition is inadequate. To begin with, it might seem at first sight more correct to define recognition as " I have seen this before " than as " this has existed before." We recognize a thing (it may be urged) as having been in our experience before, whatever that may mean; we do not recognize it as merely having been in the world before. I am not sure that there is anything substantial in this point. The definition of " my experience " is difficult; broadly speaking, it is everything that is connected with what I am experiencing now by certain links, of which the various forms of memory are among the most important. Thus, if I recognize a thing, the occasion of its previous existence in virtue of which I recognize it forms part of " my experience " by *definition*: recognition will be one of the marks by which my experience is singled out from the rest of the world. Of course, the words " this has existed before " are a very inadequate translation of what actually happens when we form a judgment of recognition, but that is unavoidable: words are framed to express a level of thought which is by no

means primitive, and are quite incapable of expressing
such an elementary occurrence as recognition. I shall
return to what is virtually the same question in connection
with true memory, which raises exactly similar problems.

A second point is that, when we recognize something,
it was not in fact the very same thing, but only something
similar, that we experienced on a former occasion. Suppose the object in question is a friend's face. A person's
face is always changing, and is not exactly the same on
any two occasions. Common sense treats it as one face
with varying expressions ; but the varying expressions
actually exist, each at its proper time, while the one face
is merely a logical construction. We regard two objects
as the same, for common-sense purposes, when the reaction
they call for is practically the same. Two visual appearances, to both of which it is appropriate to say : " Hullo,
Jones ! " are treated as appearances of one identical
object, namely Jones. The name " Jones " is applicable
to both, and it is only reflection that shows us that many
diverse particulars are collected together to form the
meaning of the name " Jones." What we see on any
one occasion is not the whole series of particulars that
make up Jones, but only one of them (or a few in quick
succession). On another occasion we see another member
of the series, but it is sufficiently similar to count as the
same from the standpoint of common sense. Accordingly,
when we judge " I have seen *this* before," we judge falsely
if " this " is taken as applying to the actual constituent
of the world that we are seeing at the moment. The
word " this " must be interpreted vaguely so as to include
anything sufficiently like what we are seeing at the
moment. Here, again, we shall find a similar point as
regards true memory ; and in connection with true memory

we will consider the point again. It is sometimes suggested, by those who favour behaviourist views, that recognition consists in behaving in the same way when a stimulus is repeated as we behaved on the first occasion when it occurred. This seems to be the exact opposite of the truth. The essence of recognition is in the *difference* between a repeated stimulus and a new one. On the first occasion there is no recognition ; on the second occasion there is. In fact, recognition is another instance of the peculiarity of causal laws in psychology, namely, that the causal unit is not a single event, but two or more events. Habit is the great instance of this, but recognition is another. A stimulus occurring once has a certain effect ; occurring twice, it has the further effect of recognition. Thus the phenomenon of recognition has as its cause the *two* occasions when the stimulus has occurred ; either alone is insufficient. This complexity of causes in psychology might be connected with Bergson's arguments against repetition in the mental world. It does not prove that there are no causal laws in psychology, as Bergson suggests ; but it does prove that the causal laws of psychology are *prima facie* very different from those of physics. On the possibility of explaining away the difference as due.to the peculiarities of nervous tissue I have spoken before, but this possibility must not be forgotten if we are tempted to draw unwarranted metaphysical deductions.

True memory, which we must now endeavour to understand, consists of knowledge of past events, but not of all such knowledge. Some knowledge of past events, for example what we learn through reading history, is on a par with the knowledge we can acquire concerning the future : it is obtained by inference, not (so to speak)

spontaneously.   There is a similar distinction in our knowledge of the present : some of it is obtained through the
senses, some in more indirect ways.   I know that there
are at this moment a number of people in the streets of
New York, but I do not know this in the immediate way
in which I know of the people whom I see by looking
out of my window.   It is not easy to state precisely
wherein the difference between these two sorts of knowledge consists, but it is easy to feel the difference.   For
the moment, I shall not stop to analyse it, but shall content myself with saying that, in this respect, memory
resembles the knowledge derived from the senses.   It is
immediate, not inferred, not abstract ; it differs from
perception mainly by being referred to the past.

In regard to memory, as throughout the analysis of
knowledge, there are two very distinct problems, namely :
(1) as to the nature of the present occurrence in knowing ;
(2) as to the relation of this occurrence to what is known.
When we remember, the knowing is now, while what is
known is in the past.   Our two questions are, in the case
of memory

(1) What is the present occurrence when we remember ?

(2) What is the relation of this present occurrence
to the past event which is remembered ?

Of these two questions, only the first concerns the
psychologist ; the second belongs to theory of knowledge.
At the same time, if we accept the vague datum with
which we began, to the effect that, in some sense, there
is knowledge of the past, we shall have to find, if we can,
such an account of the present occurrence in remembering
as will make it not impossible for remembering to give

us knowledge of the past. For the present, however, we shall do well to forget the problems concerning theory of knowledge, and concentrate upon the purely psychological problem of memory.

Between memory-image and sensation there is an intermediate experience concerning the immediate past. For example, a sound that we have just heard is present to us in a way which differs both from the sensation while we are hearing the sound and from the memory-image of something heard days or weeks ago. James states that it is this way of apprehending the immediate past that is " the *original* of our experience of pastness, from whence we get the meaning of the term " (*Psychology*, i, p. 604). Everyone knows the experience of noticing (say) that the clock *has been* striking, when we did not notice it while it was striking. And when we hear a remark spoken, we are conscious of the earlier words while the later ones are being uttered, and this retention feels different from recollection of something definitely past. A sensation fades gradually, passing by continuous gradations to the status of an image. This retention of the immediate past in a condition intermediate between sensation and image may be called " immediate memory." Everything belonging to it is included with sensation in what is called the " specious present." The specious present includes elements at all stages on the journey from sensation to image. It is this fact that enables us to apprehend such things as movements, or the order of the words in a spoken sentence. Succession can occur within the specious present, of which we can distinguish some parts as earlier and others as later. It is to be supposed that the earliest parts are those that have faded most from their original force, while the latest parts are those that retain their full sensational character. At the beginning of a stimulus we have a sensation ; then a gradual transition ; and at the end an image. Sensations while they are fading are called " akoluthic " sensations.[1] When the process of fading is completed (which happens very quickly), we arrive at the image, which is capable of being revived on subsequent occasions with very little change. True memory, as opposed to " immediate memory," applies only to events sufficiently distant to have come to an end of the period of fading. Such events, if they are represented by anything present, can only be represented by images, not by those intermediate stages, between sensations and images, which occur during the period of fading.

Immediate memory is important both because it provides experience of succession, and because it bridges the gulf between sensations and the images which are their copies. But it is now time to resume the consideration of true memory.

Suppose you ask me what I ate for breakfast this morning. Suppose, further, that I have not thought about my breakfast in the meantime, and that I did not, while I was eating it, put into words what it consisted of. In this case my recollection will be true memory, not habit-memory. The process of remembering will consist of calling up images of my breakfast, which will come to me with a feeling of belief such as distinguishes memory-images from mere imagination-images. Or sometimes words may come without the intermediary of images ; but in this case equally the feeling of belief is essential.

Let us omit from our consideration, for the present, the memories in which words replace images. These are

[1] See Semon, *Die mnemischen Empfindungen*, chap. vi.

always, I think, really habit-memories, the memories that use images being the typical true memories.

Memory-images and imagination-images do not differ in their intrinsic qualities, so far as we can discover. They differ by the fact that the images that constitute memories, unlike those that constitute imagination, are accompanied by a feeling of belief which may be expressed in the words " this happened." The mere occurrence of images, without this feeling of belief, constitutes imagination ; it is the element of belief that is the distinctive thing in memory.[1]

There are, if I am not mistaken, at least three different kinds of belief-feeling, which we may call respectively memory, expectation and bare assent. In what I call bare assent, there is no time-element in the feeling of belief, though there may be in the content of what is believed. If I believe that Cæsar landed in Britain in B.C. 55, the time-determination lies, not in the feeling of belief, but in what is believed. I do not remember the occurrence, but have the same feeling towards it as towards the announcement of an eclipse next year. But when I have seen a flash of lightning and am waiting for the thunder, I have a belief-feeling analogous to memory, except that it refers to the future : I have an image of thunder, combined with a feeling which may be expressed in the words : " this will happen." So, in memory, the pastness lies, not in the content of what is believed, but in the nature of the belief-feeling. I might have just the same images and expect their realization ; I might entertain them without any belief, as in reading a novel ; or I might entertain them together with a time-determina-

[1] For belief of a specific kind, cf. Dorothy Wrinch "On the Nature of Memory," *Mind*, January, 1920.

tion, and give bare assent, as in reading history. I shall return to this subject in a later lecture, when we come to the analysis of belief. For the present, I wish to make it clear that a certain special kind of belief is the distinctive characteristic of memory.

The problem as to whether memory can be explained as habit or association requires to be considered afresh in connection with the causes of our remembering something. Let us take again the case of my being asked what I had for breakfast this morning. In this case the question leads to my setting to work to recollect. It is a little strange that the question should instruct me as to what it is that I am to recall. This has to do with understanding words, which will be the topic of the next lecture ; but something must be said about it now. Our understanding of the words " breakfast this morning " is a habit, in spite of the fact that on each fresh day they point to a different occasion. " This morning " does not, whenever it is used, mean the same thing, as " John " or " St. Paul's " does ; it means a different period of time on each different day. It follows that the habit which constitutes our understanding of the words " this morning " is not the habit of associating the words with a fixed object, but the habit of associating them with something having a fixed time-relation to our present. This morning has, to-day, the same time-relation to my present that yesterday morning had yesterday. In order to understand the phrase " this morning " it is necessary that we should have a way of feeling time-intervals, and that this feeling should give what is constant in the meaning of the words " this morning." This appreciation of time-intervals is, however, obviously a product of memory, not a presupposition of it. It will be better, therefore, if we wish to analyse the causation of memory by something not pre-supposing memory, to take some other instance than that of a question about " this morning."

Let us take the case of coming into a familiar room where something has been changed—say a new picture hung on the wall. We may at first have only a sense that *something* is unfamiliar, but presently we shall remember, and say " that picture was not on the wall before." In order to make the case definite, we will suppose that we were only in the room on one former occasion. In this case it seems fairly clear what happens. The other objects in the room are associated, through the former occasion, with a blank space of wall where now there is a picture. They call up an image of a blank wall, which clashes with perception of the picture. The image is associated with the belief-feeling which we found to be distinctive of memory, since it can neither be abolished nor harmonized with perception. If the room had remained unchanged, we might have had only the feeling of familiarity without the definite remembering ; it is the change that drives us from the present to memory of the past.

We may generalize this instance so as to cover the causes of many memories. Some present feature of the environment is associated, through past experiences, with something now absent ; this absent something comes before us as an image, and is contrasted with present sensation. In cases of this sort, habit (or association) explains why the present feature of the environment brings up the memory-image, but it does not explain the memory-belief. Perhaps a more complete analysis could explain the memory-belief also on lines of association and habit, but the causes of beliefs are obscure, and we cannot investigate them yet. For the present we must content ourselves with the fact that the memory-image can be explained by habit. As regards the memory-belief, we must, at least provisionally, accept Bergson's view that it cannot be brought under the head of habit, at any rate when it first occurs, i.e. when we remember something we never remembered before.

We must now consider somewhat more closely the content of a memory-belief. The memory-belief confers upon the memory-image something which we may call "meaning"; it makes us feel that the image points to an object which existed in the past. In order to deal with this topic we must consider the verbal expression of the memory-belief. We might be tempted to put the memory-belief into the words: "Something like this image occurred." But such words would be very far from an accurate translation of the simplest kind of memory-belief. "Something like this image" is a very complicated conception. In the simplest kind of memory we are not aware of the difference between an image and the sensation which it copies, which may be called its "prototype." When the image is before us, we judge rather "this occurred." The image is not distinguished from the object which existed in the past: the word "this" covers both, and enables us to have a memory-belief which does not introduce the complicated notion "something like this."

It might be objected that, if we judge "this occurred" when in fact "this" is a present image, we judge falsely, and the memory-belief, so interpreted, becomes deceptive. This, however, would be a mistake, produced by attempting to give to words a precision which they do not possess when used by unsophisticated people. It is true that the image is not absolutely identical with its prototype, and if the word " this " meant the image to the exclusion of everything else, the judgment " this occurred " would be false. But identity is a precise conception, and no word, in ordinary speech, stands for anything precise. Ordinary speech does not distinguish between identity and close similarity. A word always applies, not only to one particular, but to a group of associated particulars, which are not recognized as multiple in common thought or speech. Thus primitive memory, when it judges that " this occurred," is vague, but not false.

Vague identity, which is really close similarity, has been a source of many of the confusions by which philosophy has lived. Of a vague subject, such as a " this," which is both an image and its prototype, contradictory predicates are true simultaneously : this existed and does not exist, since it is a thing remembered, but also this exists and did not exist, since it is a present image. Hence Bergson's interpenetration of the present by the past, Hegelian continuity and identity-in-diversity, and a host of other notions which are thought to be profound because they are obscure and confused. The contradictions resulting from confounding image and prototype in memory force us to precision. But when we become precise, our remembering becomes different from that of ordinary life, and if we forget this we shall go wrong in the analysis of ordinary memory.

Vagueness and accuracy are important notions, which it is very necessary to understand. Both are a matter of degree. All thinking is vague to some extent, and complete accuracy is a theoretical ideal not practically attainable. To understand what is meant by accuracy, it will be well to consider first instruments of measurement, such as a balance or a thermometer. These are said to be accurate when they give different results for very slightly different stimuli.[1] A clinical thermometer is accurate when it enables us to detect very slight differences in the temperature of the blood. We may say generally that an instrument is accurate in proportion as it reacts differently to very slightly different stimuli. When a small difference of stimulus produces a great difference of reaction, the instrument is accurate ; in the contrary case it is not.

Exactly the same thing applies in defining accuracy of thought or perception. A musician will respond differently to very minute differences in playing which would be quite imperceptible to the ordinary mortal. A negro can see the difference between one negro and another : one is his friend, another his enemy. But to us such different responses are impossible : we can merely apply the word "negro" indiscriminately. Accuracy of response in regard to any particular kind of stimulus is improved by practice. Understanding a language is a case in point. Few Frenchmen can hear any difference between the sounds "hall" and "hole," which produce quite different impressions upon us. The two statements "the hall is full of water" and "the hole is full of water" call for different responses, and a hearing which cannot distinguish between them is inaccurate or vague in this respect.

Precision and vagueness in thought, as in perception, depend upon the degree of difference between responses to more or less similar stimuli. In the case of thought, the response does not follow immediately upon the sensational

[1] This is a necessary but not a sufficient condition. The subject of accuracy and vagueness will be considered again in Lecture XIII.

stimulus, but that makes no difference as regards our present question. Thus to revert to memory: A memory is "vague" when it is appropriate to many different occurrences: for instance, "I met a man" is vague, since any man would verify it. A memory is "precise" when the occurrences that would verify it are narrowly circumscribed: for instance, "I met Jones" is precise as compared to "I met a man." A memory is "accurate" when it is both precise and true, i.e. in the above instance, if it was Jones I met. It is precise even if it is false, provided some very definite occurrence would have been required to make it true.

It follows from what has been said that a vague thought has more likelihood of being true than a precise one. To try and hit an object with a vague thought is like trying to hit the bull's eye with a lump of putty: when the putty reaches the target, it flattens out all over it, and probably covers the bull's eye along with the rest. To try and hit an object with a precise thought is like trying to hit the bull's eye with a bullet. The advantage of the precise thought is that it distinguishes between the bull's eye and the rest of the target. For example, if the whole target is represented by the fungus family and the bull's eye by mushrooms, a vague thought which can only hit the target as a whole is not much use from a culinary point of view. And when I merely remember that I met a man, my memory may be very inadequate to my practical requirements, since it may make a great difference whether I met Brown or Jones. The memory "I met Jones" is relatively precise. It is accurate if I met Jones, inaccurate if I met Brown, but precise in either case as against the mere recollection that I met a man.

The distinction between accuracy and precision is however, not fundamental. We may omit precision from out thoughts and confine ourselves to the distinction between accuracy and vagueness. We may then set up the following definitions :

An instrument is "reliable" with respect to a given set of stimuli when to stimuli which are not relevantly different it gives always responses which are not relevantly different.

An instrument is a " measure " of a set of stimuli which are serially ordered when its responses, in all cases where they are relevantly different, are arranged in a series in the same order.

The " degree of accuracy " of an instrument which is a reliable measurer is the ratio of the difference of response to the difference of stimulus in cases where the difference of stimulus is small.[1] That is to say, if a small difference of stimulus produces a great difference of response, the instrument is very accurate ; in the contrary case, very inaccurate.

A mental response is called " vague " in proportion to its lack of accuracy, or rather precision.

These definitions will be found useful, not only in the case of memory, but in almost all questions concerned with knowledge.

It should be observed that vague beliefs, so far from being necessarily false, have a better chance of truth than precise ones, though their truth is less valuable than that of precise beliefs, since they do not distinguish between occurrences which may differ in important ways.

The whole of the above discussion of vagueness and

[1] Strictly speaking, the limit of this, i.e. the derivative of the response with respect to the stimulus.

accuracy was occasioned by the attempt to interpret the word " this " when we judge in verbal memory that " this occurred." The word " this," in such a judgment, is a vague word, equally applicable to the present memory-image and to the past occurrence which is its prototype. A vague word is not to be identified with a general word, though in practice the distinction may often be blurred. A word is general when it is understood to be applicable to a number of different objects in virtue of some common property. A word is vague when it is in fact applicable to a number of different objects because, in virtue of some common property, they have not appeared, to the person using the word, to be distinct. I emphatically do not mean that he has judged them to be identical, but merely that he has made the same response to them all and has not judged them to be different. We may compare a vague word to a jelly and a general word to a heap of shot. Vague words precede judgments of identity and difference ; both general and particular words are subsequent to such judgments. The word " this " in the primitive memory-belief is a vague word, not a general word ; it covers both the image and its prototype because the two are not distinguished.[1]

But we have not yet finished our analysis of the

[1] On the vague and the general cf. Ribot : *Evolution of General Ideas*, Open Court Co., 1899, p. 32 : " The sole permissible formula is this : Intelligence progresses from the indefinite to the definite. If ' indefinite ' is taken as synonymous with general, it may be said that the particular does not appear at the outset, but neither does the general in any exact sense : the vague would be more appropriate. In other words, no sooner has the intellect progressed beyond the moment of perception and of its immediate reproduction in memory, than the generic image makes its appearance, i.e. a state intermediate between the particular and the general, participating in the nature of the one and of the other—a confused simplification."

memory-belief. The tense in the belief that "this occurred" is provided by the nature of the belief-feeling involved in memory ; the word "this," as we have seen, has a vagueness which we have tried to describe. But we must still ask what we mean by "occurred." The image is, in one sense, occurring now ; and therefore we must find some other sense in which the past event occurred but the image does not occur.

There are two distinct questions to be asked : (1) What causes us to say that a thing occurs ?   (2) What are we feeling when we say this ?   As to the first question, in the crude use of the word, which is what concerns us, memory-images would not be said to occur ; they would not be noticed in themselves, but merely used as signs of the past event. Images are "merely imaginary" ; they have not, in crude thought, the sort of reality that belongs to outside bodies. Roughly speaking, "real" things would be those that can cause sensations, those that have correlations of the sort that constitute physical objects. A thing is said to be "real" or to "occur" when it fits into a context of such correlations. The prototype of our memory-image did fit into a physical context, while our memory-image does not. This causes us to feel that the prototype was "real," while the image is "imaginary."

‹ But the answer to our second question, namely as to what we are feeling when we say a thing "occurs" or is "real," must be somewhat different. We do not, unless we are unusually reflective, think about the presence or absence of correlations : we merely have different feelings which, intellectualized, may be represented as expectations of the presence or absence of correlations. A thing which "feels real" inspires us with hopes or fears, expectations

or curiosities, which are wholly absent when a thing
"feels imaginary." The feeling of reality is a feeling
akin to respect : it belongs *primarily* to whatever can do
things to us without our voluntary co-operation. This
feeling of reality, related to the memory-image, and
referred to the past by the specific kind of belief-feeling
that is characteristic of memory, seems to be what constitutes the act of remembering in its pure form.

We may now summarize our analysis of pure memory.
Memory demands (*a*) an image, (*b*) a belief in past
existence. The belief may be expressed in the words
" this existed."

The belief, like every other, may be analysed into
(1) the believing, (2) what is believed. The believing is
a specific feeling or sensation or complex of sensations,
different from expectation or bare assent in a way that
makes the belief refer to the past ; the reference to the
past lies in the belief-feeling, not in the content believed.
There is a relation between the belief-feeling and the
content, making the belief-feeling refer to the content,
and expressed by saying that the content is what is
believed.

The content believed may or may not be expressed in
words. Let us take first the case when it is not. In
that case, if we are merely remembering that something
of which we now have an image occurred, the content
consists of (*a*) the image, (*b*) the feeling, analogous to
respect, which we translate by saying that something is
" real " as opposed to " imaginary," (*c*) a relation between
the image and the feeling of reality, of the sort expressed
when we say that the feeling refers to the image. This
content does not contain in itself any time-determination :
the time-determination lies in the nature of the belief-

feeling, which is that called "remembering" or (better) "recollecting." It is only subsequent reflection upon this reference to the past that makes us realize the distinction between the image and the event recollected. When we have made this distinction, we can say that the image "means" the past event.

The content expressed in words is best represented by the words "the existence of this," since these words do not involve tense, which belongs to the belief-feeling, not to the content. Here "this" is a vague term, covering the memory-image and anything very like it, including its prototype. "Existence" expresses the feeling of a "reality" aroused primarily by whatever can have effects upon us without our voluntary co-operation. The word "of" in the phrase "the existence of this" represents the relation which subsists between the feeling of reality and the "this."

This analysis of memory is probably extremely faulty, but I do not know how to improve it.

NOTE.—When I speak of a *feeling* of belief, I use the word "feeling" in a popular sense, to cover a sensation or an image or a complex of sensations or images or both; I use this word because I do not wish to commit myself to any special analysis of the belief-feeling.

LECTURE X

WORDS AND MEANING

THE problem with which we shall be concerned in this lecture is the problem of determining what is the relation called " meaning." The word " Napoleon," we say, " means " a certain person. In saying this, we are asserting a relation between the word " Napoleon " and the person so designated. It is this relation that we must now investigate.

Let us first consider what sort of object a word is when considered simply as a physical thing, apart from its meaning. To begin with, there are many instances of a word, namely all the different occasions when it is employed. Thus a word is not something unique and particular, but a set of occurrences. If we confine ourselves to spoken words, a word has two aspects, according as we regard it from the point of view of the speaker or from that of the hearer. From the point of view of the speaker, a single instance of the use of a word consists of a certain set of movements in the throat and mouth, combined with breath. From the point of view of the hearer, a single instance of the use of a word consists of a certain series of sounds, each being approximately represented by a single letter in writing, though in practice a letter may represent several sounds, or several letters may represent one sound. The connection between the spoken word and the word as it reaches the hearer is causal. Let us confine ourselves to the spoken word, which is the more important for the analysis of what is called " thought." Then we may say that a single instance of the spoken word consists of a series of movements, and the word consists of a whole set of such series, each member of the set being very similar to each other member. That is to say, any two instances of the word " Napoleon " are very similar, and each instance consists of a series of movements in the mouth.

A single word, accordingly, is by no means simple : it is a class of similar series of movements (confining ourselves still to the spoken word). The degree of similarity required cannot be precisely defined : a man may pronounce the word " Napoleon " so badly that it can hardly be determined whether he has really pronounced it or not. The instances of a word shade off into other movements by imperceptible degrees. And exactly analogous observations apply to words heard or written or read. But in what has been said so far we have not even broached the question of the *definition* of a word, since " meaning " is clearly what distinguishes a word from other sets of similar movements, and " meaning " remains to be defined.

It is natural to think of the meaning of a word as something conventional. This, however, is only true with great limitations. A new word can be added to an existing language by a mere convention, as is done, for instance, with new scientific terms. But the basis of a language is not conventional, either from the point of view of the individual or from that of the community. A child learning to speak is learning habits and associations which are just as much determined by the environment as the habit of expecting dogs to bark and cocks to crow. The community that speaks a language has learnt it, and modified it by processes almost all of which are not deliberate, but the results of causes operating according to more or less ascertainable laws. If we trace any Indo-European language back far enough, we arrive hypothetically (at any rate according to some authorities) at the stage when language consisted only of the roots out of which subsequent words have grown. How these roots acquired their meanings is not known, but a conventional origin is clearly just as mythical as the social contract by which Hobbes and Rousseau supposed civil government to have been established. We can hardly suppose a parliament of hitherto speechless elders meeting together and agreeing to call a cow a cow and a wolf a wolf. The association of words with their meanings must have grown up by some natural process, though at present the nature of the process is unknown.

Spoken and written words are, of course, not the only way of conveying meaning. A large part of one of Wundt's two vast volumes on language in his *Völkerpsychologie* is concerned with gesture-language. Ants appear to be able to communicate a certain amount of information by means of their antennæ. Probably writing itself, which we now regard as merely a way of representing speech, was originally an independent language, as it has remained to this day in China. Writing seems to have consisted originally of pictures, which gradually became conventionalized, coming in time to represent syllables, and finally letters on the telephone principle of " T for Tommy." But it would seem that writing nowhere began as an attempt to represent speech :

it began as a direct pictorial representation of what was
to be expressed. The essence of language lies, not in
the use of this or that special means of communication,
but in the employment of fixed associations (however
these may have originated) in order that something now
sensible—a spoken word, a picture, a gesture, or what
not—may call up the " idea " of something else.   Whenever this is done, what is now sensible may be called
a " sign " or " symbol," and that of which it is intended
to call up the " idea " may be called its " meaning."
This is a rough outline of what constitutes " meaning."
But we must fill in the outline in various ways. And,
since we are concerned with what is called " thought,"
we must pay more attention than we otherwise should
do to the private as opposed to the social use of language.
Language profoundly affects our thoughts, and it is this
aspect of language that is of most importance to us in
our present inquiry. We are almost more concerned
with the internal speech that is never uttered than we are
with the things said out loud to other people.

When we ask what constitutes meaning, we are not
asking what is the meaning of this or that particular
word. The word " Napoleon " means a certain individual ; but we are asking, not who is the individual
meant, but what is the relation of the word to the individual which makes the one mean the other. But just
as it is useful to realize the nature of a word as part of
the physical world, so it is useful to realize the sort of
thing that a word may mean. When we are clear both
as to what a word is in its physical aspect, and as to what
sort of thing it can mean, we are in a better position to
discover the relation of the two which *is* meaning.

The things that words mean differ more than words

do. There are different sorts of words, distinguished by the grammarians ; and there are logical distinctions, which are connected to some extent, though not so closely as was formerly supposed, with the grammatical distinctions of parts of speech. It is easy, however, to be misled by grammar, particularly if all the languages we know belong to one family. In some languages, according to some authorities, the distinction of parts of speech does not exist ; in many languages it is widely different from that to which we are accustomed in the Indo-European languages. These facts have to be borne in mind if we are to avoid giving metaphysical importance to mere accidents of our own speech.

In considering what words mean, it is natural to start with proper names, and we will again take " Napoleon " as our instance. We commonly imagine, when we use a proper name, that we mean one definite entity, the particular individual who was called " Napoleon." But what we know as a person is not simple There *may* be a single simple ego which was Napoleon, and remained strictly identical from his birth to his death. There is no way of proving that this cannot be the case, but there is also not the slightest reason to suppose that it is the case. Napoleon as he was empirically known consisted of a series of gradually changing appearances : first a squalling baby, then a boy, then a slim and beautiful youth, then a fat and slothful person very magnificently dressed. This series of appearances, and various occurrences having certain kinds of causal connections with them, constitute Napoleon as empirically known, and therefore are Napoleon in so far as he forms part of the experienced world. Napoleon is a complicated series of occurrences, bound together by causal laws, not, like instances of a word, by similarities. For although a person changes gradually, and presents similar appearances on two nearly contemporaneous occasions, it is not these similarities that constitute the person, as appears from the *Comedy of Errors* for example.

Thus in the case of a proper name, while the word is a set of similar series of movements, what it means is a series of occurrences bound together by causal laws of that special kind that makes the occurrences taken together constitute what we call one person, or one animal or thing, in case the name applies to an animal or thing instead of to a person. Neither the word nor what it names is one of the ultimate indivisible constituents of the world. In language there is no direct way of designating one of the ultimate brief existents that go to make up the collections we call things or persons. If we want to speak of such existents—which hardly happens except in philosophy—we have to do it by means of some elaborate phrase, such as " the visual sensation which occupied the centre of my field of vision at noon on January 1, 1919." Such ultimate simples I call " particulars." Particulars *might* have proper names, and no doubt would have if language had been invented by scientifically trained observers for purposes of philosophy and logic. But as language was invented for practical ends, particulars have remained one and all without a name.

We are not, in practice, much concerned with the actual particulars that come into our experience in sensation ; we are concerned rather with whole systems to which the particulars belong and of which they are signs. What we see makes us say " Hullo, there's Jones," and the fact that what we see is a sign of Jones (which is the case because it is one of the particulars that make up Jones) is more interesting to us than the actual particular itself. Hence we give the name " Jones " to the whole set of particulars, but do not trouble to give separate names to the separate particulars that make up the set.

Passing on from proper names, we come next to general names, such as " man," " cat," " triangle." A word such as " man " means a whole class of such collections of particulars as have proper names. The several members of the class are assembled together in virtue of some similarity or common property. All men resemble each other in certain important respects ; hence we want a word which shall be equally applicable to all of them. We only give proper names to the individuals of a species when they differ *inter se* in practically important respects. In other cases we do not do this. A poker, for instance, is just a poker ; we do not call one " John " and another " Peter."

There is a large class of words, such as " eating," " walking," "speaking," which mean a set of similar occurrences. Two instances of walking have the same name because they resemble each other, whereas two instances of Jones have the same name because they are causally connected. In practice, however, it is difficult to make any precise distinction between a word such as " walking " and a general name such as " man." One instance of walking cannot be concentrated into an instant : it is a process in time, in which there is a causal connection between the earlier and later parts, as between the earlier and later parts of Jones. Thus an instance of walking differs from an instance of man solely by the fact that it has a shorter life. There is a notion that an instance of walking, as compared with Jones, is unsubstantial, but this seems to be a mistake. We think that Jones walks, and that there could not be any walking unless there were somebody like Jones to perform the walking. But it is equally true that there could be no Jones unless there were something like walking for him to do. The notion that actions are performed by an agent is liable to the same kind of criticism as the notion that thinking needs a subject or ego, which we rejected in Lecture I. To say that it is Jones who is walking is merely to say that the walking in question is part of the whole series of occurrences which is Jones. There is no *logical* impossibility in walking occurring as an isolated phenomenon, not forming part of any such series as we call a " person."

We may therefore class with " eating," " walking," " speaking " words such as " rain," " sunrise," " lightning," which do not denote what would commonly be called actions. These words illustrate, incidentally, how little we can trust to the grammatical distinction of parts of speech, since the substantive " rain " and the verb " to rain " denote precisely the same class of meteorological occurrences. The distinction between the class of objects denoted by such a word and the class of objects denoted by a general name such as " man," " vegetable," or " planet," is that the sort of object which is an instance of (say) " lightning " is much simpler than (say) an individual man. (I am speaking of lightning as a sensible phenomenon, not as it is described in physics.) The distinction is one of degree, not of kind. But there is, from the point of view of ordinary thought, a great difference between a process which, like a flash of lightning, can be wholly comprised within one specious present and a process which, like the life of a man, has to be pieced together by observation and memory and the apprehension of causal connections. We may say broadly, therefore, that a word of the kind we have been discussing denotes a set of similar occurrences, each (as a rule) much more brief and less complex than a perscn or thing. Words themselves, as we have seen, are sets of similar occurrences of this kind. Thus there is more logical affinity between a word and what it means in the case of words of our present sort than in any other case.

There is no very great difference between such words as we have just been considering and words denoting qualities, such as " white " or " round." The chief difference is that words of this latter sort do not denote processes, however brief, but static features of the world. Snow falls, and is white ; the falling is a process, the whiteness is not. Whether there is a universal, called " whiteness," or whether white things are to be defined as those having a certain kind of similarity to a standard thing, say freshly fallen snow, is a question which need not concern us, and which I believe to be strictly insoluble. For our purposes, we may take the word " white " as denoting a certain set of similar particulars or collections of particulars, the similarity being in respect of a static quality, not of a process.

From the logical point of view, a very important class of words are those that express relations, such as " in," " above," " before," " greater," and so on. The meaning of one of these words differs very fundamentally from the meaning of one of any of our previous classes, being more abstract and logically simpler than any of them. If our business were logic, we should have to spend much time on these words. But as it is psychology that concerns us, we will merely note their special character and pass on, since the logical classification of words is not our main business.

We will consider next the question what is implied by saying that a person " understands " a word, in the sense in which one understands a word in one's own language, but not in a language of which one is ignorant. We may say that a person understands a word when (a) suitable circumstances make him use it, (b) the hearing of it causes suitable behaviour in him. We may call these two active and passive understanding respectively. Dogs often have passive understanding of some words, but not active understanding, since they cannot use words.

It is not necessary, in order that a man should " understand " a word, that he should " know what it means," in the sense of being able to say " this word means so-and-so." Understanding words does not consist in knowing their dictionary definitions, or in being able to specify the objects to which they are appropriate. Such understanding as this may belong to lexicographers and students, but not to ordinary mortals in ordinary life. Understanding language is more like understanding cricket [1] : it is a matter of habits, acquired in oneself and rightly presumed in others. To say that a word has a meaning is not to say that those who use the word correctly have ever thought out what the meaning is : the use of the word comes first, and the meaning is to be distilled out of it by observation and analysis. Moreover, the meaning of a word is not absolutely definite : there is

---

[1] This point of view, extended to the analysis of " thought " is urged with great force by J. B. Watson, both in his *Behavior*, and in *Psychology from the Standpoint of a Behaviorist* (Lippincott, 1919), chap. ix.

always a greater or less degree of vagueness. The meaning is an area, like a target: it may have a bull's eye, but the outlying parts of the target are still more or less within the meaning, in a gradually diminishing degree as we travel further from the bull's eye. As language grows more precise, there is less and less of the target outside the bull's eye, and the bull's eye itself grows smaller and smaller; but the bull's eye never shrinks to a point, and there is always a doubtful region, however small, surrounding it.[1]

A word is used " correctly " when the average hearer will be affected by it in the way intended. This is a psychological, not a literary, definition of "correctness." The literary definition would substitute, for the average hearer, a person of high education living a long time ago; the purpose of this definition is to make it difficult to speak or write correctly.

The relation of a word to its meaning is of the nature of a causal law governing our use of the word and our actions when we hear it used. There is no more reason why a person who uses a word correctly should be able to tell what it means than there is why a planet which is moving correctly should know Kepler's laws.

To illustrate what is meant by " understanding " words and sentences, let us take instances of various situations.

[1] On the understanding of words, a very admirable little book is Ribot's *Evolution of General Ideas*, Open Court Co., 1899. Ribot says (p. 131): " We learn to understand a concept as we learn to walk, dance, fence or play a musical instrument: it is a habit, i.e. an organized memory. General terms cover an organized, latent knowledge which is the hidden capital without which we should be in a state of bankruptcy, manipulating false money or paper of no value. General ideas are habits in the intellectual order."

Suppose you are walking in London with an absent-minded friend, and while crossing a street you say, " Look out, there's a motor coming." He will glance round and jump aside without the need of any " mental " intermediary. There need be no " ideas," but only a stiffening of the muscles, followed quickly by action. He " understands " the words, because he does the right thing. Such " understanding " may be taken to belong to the nerves and brain, being habits which they have acquired while the language was being learnt. Thus understanding in this sense may be reduced to mere physiological causal laws.

If you say the same thing to a Frenchman with a slight knowledge of English he will go through some inner speech which may be represented by " Que dit-il ? Ah, oui, une automobile ! " After this, the rest follows as with the Englishman. Watson would contend that the inner speech must be incipiently pronounced ; we should argue that it *might* be merely imaged. But this point is not important in the present connection.

If you say the same thing to a child who does not yet know the word " motor," but does know the other words you are using, you produce a feeling of anxiety and doubt : you will have to point and say, " There, that's a motor." After that the child will roughly understand the word " motor," though he may include trains and steam-rollers If this is the first time the child has heard the word " motor," he may for a long time continue to recall this scene when he hears the word.

So far we have found four ways of understanding words :

(1) On suitable occasions you use the word properly.
(2) When you hear it you act appropriately

(3) You associate the word with another word (say in a different language) which has the appropriate effect on behaviour.

(4) When the word is being first learnt, you may associate it with an object, which is what it " means," or a representative of various objects that it " means."

In the fourth case, the word acquires, through association, some of the same causal efficacy as the object. The word " motor " can make you leap aside, just as the motor can, but it cannot break your bones. The effects which a word can share with its object are those which proceed according to laws other than the general laws of physics, i.e. those which, according to our terminology, involve vital movements as opposed to merely mechanical movements. The effects of a word that we understand are always mnemic phenomena in the sense explained in Lecture IV, in so far as they are identical with, or similar to, the effects which the object itself might have.

So far, all the uses of words that we have considered can be accounted for on the lines of behaviourism.

But so far we have only considered what may be called the " demonstrative " use of language, to point out some feature in the present environment. This is only one of the ways in which language may be used. There are also its narrative and imaginative uses, as in history and novels. Let us take as an instance the telling of some remembered event.

We spoke a moment ago of a child who hears the word " motor " for the first time when crossing a street along which a motor-car is approaching. On a later occasion, we will suppose, the child remembers the incident and

relates it to someone else.   In this case, both the active
and passive understanding of words is different from what
it is when words are used demonstratively.   The child is
not seeing a motor, but only remembering one ; the
hearer does not look round in expectation of seeing a
motor coming, but " understands " that a motor came at
some earlier time.   The whole of this occurrence is much
more difficult to account for on behaviourist lines.   It is
clear that, in so far as the child is genuinely remembering,
he has a picture of the past occurrence, and his words
are chosen so as to describe the picture ; and in so far
as the hearer is genuinely apprehending what is said, the
hearer is acquiring a picture more or less like that of the
child.   It is true that this process may be telescoped
through the operation of the word-habit.   The child may
not genuinely remember the incident, but only have the
habit of the appropriate words, as in the case of a poem
which we know by heart, though we cannot remember
learning it.   And the hearer also may only pay attention to
the words, and not call up any corresponding picture.
But it is, nevertheless, the possibility of a memory-image
in the child and an imagination-image in the hearer that
makes the essence of the narrative " meaning " of the
words.   In so far as this is absent, the words are mere
counters, capable of meaning, but not at the moment
possessing it.

Yet this might perhaps be regarded as something of
an over-statement. The words alone, without the use of
images, may cause appropriate emotions and appropriate
behaviour.   The words have been used in an environment
which produced certain emotions ; by a telescoped process, the words alone are now capable of producing
similar emotions.   On these lines it might be sought to

show that images are unnecessary. I do not believe, however, that we could account on these lines for the entirely different response produced by a narrative and by a description of present facts. Images, as contrasted with sensations, are the response expected during a narrative ; it is understood that present action is not called for. Thus it seems that we must maintain our distinction : words used demonstratively describe and are intended to lead to sensations, while the same words used in narrative describe and are only intended to lead to images.

We have thus, in addition to our four previous ways in which words can mean, two new ways, namely the way of memory and the way of imagination. That is to say :

(5) Words may be used to describe or recall a memory-image : to describe it when it already exists, or to recall it when the words exist as a habit and are known to be descriptive of some past experience.

(6) Words may be used to describe or create an imagination-image : to describe it, for example, in the case of a poet or novelist, or to create it in the ordinary case for giving information—though, in the latter case, it is intended that the imagination-image, when created, shall be accompanied by belief that something of the sort occurred.

These two ways of using words, including their occurrence in inner speech, may be spoken of together as the use of words in " thinking." If we are right, the use of words in thinking depends, at least in its origin, upon images, and cannot be fully dealt with on behaviourist lines. And this is really the most essential function of words, namely that, originally through their connection with images, they bring us into touch with what is remote in time or space. When they operate without the medium of images, this seems to be a telescoped process. Thus the problem of the meaning of words is brought into connection with the problem of the meaning of images.

To understand the function that words perform in what is called " thinking," we must understand both the causes and the effects of their occurrence. The causes of the occurrence of words require somewhat different treatment according as the object designated by the word is sensibly present or absent. When the object is present, it may itself be taken as the cause of the word, through association. But when it is absent there is more difficulty in obtaining a behaviourist theory of the occurrence of the word. The language-habit consists not merely in the use of words demonstratively, but also in their use to express narrative or desire. Professor Watson, in his account of the acquisition of the language-habit, pays very little attention to the use of words in narrative and desire. He says (*Behavior*, pp. 329–330) :

" The stimulus (object) to which the child often responds, a box, e.g. by movements such as opening and closing and putting objects into it, may serve to illustrate our argument. The nurse, observing that the child reacts with his hands, feet, etc., to the box, begins to say ' box ' when the child is handed the box, ' open box ' when the childs opens it, ' close box ' when he closes it, and ' put doll in box ' when that act is executed. This is repeated over and over again. In the process of time it comes about that without any other stimulus than that of the box which originally called out the bodily habits, he begins to say 'box' when he sees it, 'open box' when he opens it, etc. The visible box now becomes a stimulus capable of releasing either the bodily habits or the word-habit, i.e. development has brought about two things: (1) a series of functional connections among arcs which run from visual receptor to muscles of throat, and (2) a series of already earlier connected arcs which run from the same receptor to the bodily muscles. . . . The object meets the child's vision. He runs to it and tries to reach it and says 'box.' . . . Finally the word is uttered without the movement of going towards the box being executed. . . . Habits are formed of going to the box when the arms are full of toys. The child has been taught to deposit them there. When his arms are laden with toys and no box is there, the word-habit arises and he calls 'box'; it is handed to him, and he opens it and deposits the toys therein. This roughly marks what we would call the genesis of a true language-habit" (pp. 329–330).[1]

We need not linger over what is said in the above passage as to the use of the word "box" in the presence of the box. But as to its use in the absence of the box, there is only one brief sentence, namely: "When his arms are laden with toys and no box is there, the word-habit arises and he calls 'box.'" This is inadequate as it stands, since the habit has been to use the word when the box is present, and we have to explain its extension to cases in which the box is absent.

Having admitted images, we may say that the word "box," in the absence of the box, is caused by an image of the box. This may or may not be true—in fact, it is true in some cases but not in others. Even, however, if

---

[1] Just the same account of language is given in Professor Watson's more recent book (reference above).

it were true in all cases, it would only slightly shift our problem : we should now have to ask what causes an image of the box to arise. We might be inclined to say that desire for the box is the cause. But when this view is investigated, it is found that it compels us to suppose that the box can be desired without the child's having either an image of the box or the word " box." This will require a theory of desire which may be, and I think is, in the main true, but which removes desire from among things that actually occur, and makes it merely a convenient fiction, like force in mechanics.[1] With such a view, desire is no longer a true cause, but merely a short way of describing certain processes.

In order to explain the occurrence of either the word or the image in the absence of the box, we have to assume that there is something, either in the environment or in our own sensations, which has frequently occurred at about the same time as the word " box." One of the laws which distinguish psychology (or nerve-physiology ?) from physics is the law that, when two things have frequently existed in close temporal contiguity, either comes in time to cause the other.[2] This is the basis both of habit and of association. Thus, in our case, the arms full of toys have frequently been followed quickly by the box, and the box in turn by the word " box." The box itself is subject to physical laws, and does not tend to be caused by the arms full of toys, however often it may in the past have followed them—always provided that, in the case in question, its physical position is such that

[1] See Lecture III, above.

[2] For a more exact statement of this law, with the limitations suggested by experiment, see A. Wohlgemuth, " On Memory and the Direction of Associations," *British Journal of Psychology*, vol. v, part iv (March, 1913).

voluntary movements cannot lead to it. But the word " box " and the image of the box are subject to the law of habit ; hence it is possible for either to be caused by the arms full of toys. And we may lay it down generally that, whenever we use a word, either aloud or in inner speech, there is some sensation or image (either of which may be itself a word) which has frequently occurred at about the same time as the word, and now, through habit, causes the word. It follows that the law of habit is adequate to account for the use of words in the absence of their objects ; moreover, it would be adequate even without introducing images. Although, therefore, images seem undeniable, we cannot derive an additional argument in their favour from the use of words, which could, theoretically, be explained without introducing images.

When we understand a word, there is a reciprocal association between it and the images of what it " means." Images may cause us to use words which mean them, and these words, heard or read, may in turn cause the appropriate images. Thus speech is a means of producing in our hearers the images which are in us. Also, by a telescoped process, words come in time to produce directly the effects which would have been produced by the images with which they were associated. The general law of telescoped processes is that, if A causes B and B causes C, it will happen in time that A will cause C directly, without the intermediary of B. This is a characteristic of psychological and neural causation. In virtue of this law, the effects of images upon our actions come to be produced by words, even when the words do not call up appropriate images. The more familiar we are with words, the more our " thinking " goes on in words instead of images. We may, for example, be able to describe a person's appear-

ance correctly without having at any time had any image
of him, provided, when we saw him, we thought of words
which fitted him ; the words alone may remain with us
as a habit, and enable us to speak as if we could recall a
visual image of the man. In this and other ways the
understanding of a word often comes to be quite free
from imagery ; but in first learning the use of language
it would seem that imagery always plays a very important
part.

Images as well as words may be said to have " meaning " ; indeed, the meaning of images seems more primitive than the meaning of words. What we call (say) an
image of St. Paul's may be said to " mean " St. Paul's.
But it is not at all easy to say exactly what constitutes
the meaning of an image. A memory-image of a particular
occurrence, when accompanied by a memory-belief, may
be said to mean the occurrence of which it is an image.
But most actual images do not have this degree of definiteness. If we call up an image of a dog, we are very likely
to have a vague image, which is not representative of
some one special dog, but of dogs in general. When we
call up an image of a friend's face, we are not likely to
reproduce the expression he had on some one particular
occasion, but rather a compromise expression derived from
many occasions. And there is hardly any limit to the
vagueness of which images are capable. In such cases,
the meaning of the image, if defined by relation to the
prototype, is vague : there is not one definite prototype,
but a number, none of which is copied exactly.[1]

There is, however, another way of approaching the
meaning of images, namely through their causal efficacy.

[1] Cf. Semon, *Mnemische Empfindungen,* chap. xvi, especially
pp. 301–308.

What is called an image " of " some definite object, say
St. Paul's, has some of the effects which the object would
have. This applies especially to the effects that depend
upon association. The emotional effects, also, are often
similar : images may stimulate desire almost as strongly
as do the objects they represent. And conversely desire
may cause images [1] : a hungry man will have images of
food, and so on. In all these ways the causal laws concerning images are connected with the causal laws concerning the objects which the images " mean." An image
may thus come to fulfil the function of a general idea.
The vague image of a dog, which we spoke of a moment
ago, will have effects which are only connected with dogs
in general, not the more special effects which would be
produced by some dogs but not by others. Berkeley and
Hume, in their attack on general ideas, do not allow for
the vagueness of images : they assume that every image
has the definiteness that a physical object would have.
This is not the case, and a vague image may well have a
meaning which is general.

In order to define the " meaning " of an image, we have
to take account both of its resemblance to one or more
prototypes, and of its causal efficacy. If there were such
a thing as a pure imagination-image, without any prototype whatever, it would be destitute of meaning. But
according to Hume's principle, the simple elements in an
image, at least, are derived from prototypes—except
possibly in very rare exceptional cases. Often, in such
instances as our image of a friend's face or of a nondescript
dog, an image is not derived from one prototype, but from

---

[1] This phrase is in need of interpretation, as appears from the
analysis of desire. But the reader can easily supply the interpretation for himself.

many; when this happens, the image is vague, and blurs the features in which the various prototypes differ. To arrive at the meaning of the image in such a case, we observe that there are certain respects, notably associations, in which the effects of images resemble those of their prototypes. If we find, in a given case, that our vague image, say, of a nondescript dog, has those associative effects which all dogs would have, but not those belonging to any special dog or kind of dog, we may say that our image means " dog " in general. If it has all the associations appropriate to spaniels but no others, we shall say it means " spaniel " ; while if it has all the associations appropriate to one particular dog, it will mean that dog, however vague it may be as a picture. The meaning of an image, according to this analysis, is constituted by a combination of likeness and associations. It is not a sharp or definite conception, and in many cases it will be impossible to decide with any certainty what an image means. I think this lies in the nature of things, and not in defective analysis.

We may give somewhat more precision to the above account of the meaning of images, and extend it to meaning in general. We find sometimes that, *in mnemic causation*, an image or word, as stimulus, has the same effect (or very nearly the same effect) as would belong to some object, say, a certain dog. In that case we say that the image or word means that object. In other cases the mnemic effects are not all those of one object, but only those shared by objects of a certain kind, e.g. by all dogs. In this case the meaning of the image or word is general : it means the whole kind. Generality and particularity are a matter of degree. If two particulars differ sufficiently little, their mnemic effects will be the same ; therefore no image or word can mean the one as opposed to the other ; this sets a bound to the particularity of meaning. On the other hand, the mnemic effects of a number of sufficiently dissimilar objects will have nothing discoverable in common ; hence a word which aims at complete generality, such as " entity " for example, will have to be devoid of mnemic effects, and therefore of meaning. In practice, this is not the case : such words have *verbal* associations, the learning of which constitutes the study of metaphysics.

The meaning of a word, unlike that of an image, is wholly constituted by mnemic causal laws, and not in any degree by likeness (except in exceptional cases). The word " dog " bears no resemblance to a dog, but its effects, like those of an image of a dog, resemble the effects of an actual dog in certain respects. It is much easier to say definitely what a word means than what an image means, since words, however they originated, have been framed in later times for the purpose of having meaning, and men have been engaged for ages in giving increased precision to the meanings of words. But although it is easier to say what a word means than what an image means, the relation which constitutes meaning is much the same in both cases. A word, like an image, has the same associations as its meaning has. In addition to other associations, it is associated with images of its meaning, so that the word tends to call up the image and the image tends to call up the word. But this association is not essential to the intelligent use of words. If a word has the right associations with other objects, we shall be able to use it correctly, and understand its use by others, even if it evokes no image. The theoretical understanding of words involves only the power of associating them correctly with other words; the practical understanding involves associations with other bodily movements.

The use of words is, of course, primarily social, for the purpose of suggesting to others ideas which we entertain or at least wish them to entertain. But the aspect of words that specially concerns us is their power of promoting our own thought. Almost all higher intellectual activity is a matter of words, to the nearly total exclusion of everything else. The advantages of words for purposes of thought are so great that I should never end if I were to enumerate them. But a few of them deserve to be mentioned.

In the first place, there is no difficulty in producing a word, whereas an image cannot always be brought into existence at will, and when it comes it often contains much irrelevant detail. In the second place, much of our thinking is concerned with abstract matters which do not readily lend themselves to imagery, and are apt to be falsely conceived if we insist upon finding images that may be supposed to represent them. The word is always concrete and sensible, however abstract its meaning may be, and thus by the help of words we are able to dwell on abstractions in a way which would otherwise be impossible. In the third place, two instances of the same word are so similar that neither has associations not capable of being shared by the other. Two instances of the word " dog " are much more alike than (say) a pug and a great dane; hence the word " dog " makes it much easier to think about dogs in general. When a number of objects have a common property which is important but not obvious, the invention of a name for the common property helps us to remember it and to think of the whole set of objects that possess it.   But it is unnecessary to prolong the catalogue of the uses of language in thought.

At the same time, it is possible to conduct rudimentary thought by means of images, and it is important, sometimes, to check purely verbal thought by reference to what it means.   In philosophy especially the tyranny of traditional words is dangerous, and we have to be on our guard against assuming that grammar is the key to metaphysics, or that the structure of a sentence corresponds at all accurately with the structure of the fact that it asserts.   Sayce maintained that all European philosophy since Aristotle has been dominated by the fact that the philosophers spoke Indo-European languages, and therefore supposed the world, like the sentences they were used to, necessarily divisible into subjects and predicates. When we come to the consideration of truth and falsehood, we shall see how necessary it is to avoid assuming too close a parallelism between facts and the sentences which assert them.   Against such errors, the only safeguard is to be able, once in a way, to discard words for a moment and contemplate facts more directly through images. Most serious advances in philosophic thought result from some such comparatively direct contemplation of facts. But the outcome has to be expressed in words if it is to be communicable.   Those who have a relatively direct vision of facts are often incapable of translating their vision into words, while those who possess the words have usually lost the vision.   It is partly for this reason that the highest philosophical capacity is so rare : it requires a combination of vision with abstract words which is hard to achieve, and too quickly lost in the few who have for a moment achieved it.

LECTURE XI

GENERAL IDEAS AND THOUGHT

It is said to be one of the merits of the human mind that it is capable of framing abstract ideas, and of conducting non-sensational thought. In this it is supposed to differ from the mind of animals. From Plato onward the " idea " has played a great part in the systems of idealizing philosophers. The " idea " has been, in their hands, always something noble and abstract, the apprehension and use of which by man confers upon him a quite special dignity.

The thing we have to consider to-day is this : seeing that there certainly are words of which the meaning is abstract, and seeing that we can use these words intelligently, what must be assumed or inferred, or what can be discovered by observation, in the way of mental content to account for the intelligent use of abstract words ?

Taken as a problem in logic, the answer is, of course, that absolutely nothing in the way of abstract mental content is inferable from the mere fact that we can use intelligently words of which the meaning is abstract. It is clear that a sufficiently ingenious person could manufacture a machine moved by olfactory stimuli which, whenever a dog appeared in its neighbourhood, would say, " There is a dog," and when a cat appeared would throw stones at it. The act of saying " There is a dog," and the act of throwing stones, would in such a case be equally mechanical. Correct speech does not of itself afford any better evidence of mental content than the performance of any other set of biologically useful movements, such as those of flight or combat. All that is inferable from language is that two instances of a universal, even when they differ very greatly, may cause the utterance of two instances of the same word which only differ very slightly. As we saw in the preceding lecture, the word " dog " is useful, partly, because two instances of this word are much more similar than (say) a pug and a great dane. The use of words is thus a method of substituting for two particulars which differ widely, in spite of being instances of the same universal, two other particulars which differ very little, and which are also instances of a universal, namely the name of the previous universal. Thus, so far as logic is concerned, we are entirely free to adopt any theory as to general ideas which empirical observation may recommend.

Berkeley and Hume made a vigorous onslaught on " abstract ideas." They meant by an idea approximately what we should call an image. Locke having maintained that he could form an idea of triangle in general, without deciding what sort of triangle it was to be, Berkeley contended that this was impossible. He says :

" Whether others have this wonderful faculty of abstracting their ideas, they best can tell : for myself, I dare be confident I have it not. I find, indeed, I have indeed a faculty of imagining, or representing to myself, the ideas of those particular things I have perceived, and of variously compounding and dividing them. I can imagine a man with two heads, or the upper parts of a

man joined to the body of a horse. I can consider the
hand, the eye, the nose, each by itself abstracted or
separated from the rest of the body. But, then, whatever
hand or eye I imagine, it must have some particular
shape and colour. Likewise the idea of a man that I frame
to myself must be either of a white, or a black, or a tawny,
a straight, or a crooked, a tall, or a low, or a middle-sized
man. I cannot by any effort of thought conceive the
abstract idea above described. And it is equally impossible
for me to form the abstract idea of motion distinct from
the body moving, and which is neither swift nor slow,
curvilinear nor rectilinear ; and the like may be said of all
other abstract general ideas whatsoever. To be plain, I own
myself able to abstract in one sense, as when I consider
some particular parts of qualities separated from others,
with which, though they are united in some object, yet
it is possible they may really exist without them. But
I deny that I can abstract from one another, or conceive separately, those qualities which it is impossible
should exist so separated ; or that I can frame a general
notion, by abstracting from particulars in the manner
aforesaid—which last are the two proper acceptations of
abstraction. And there is ground to think most men will
acknowledge themselves to be in my case. The generality
of men which are simple and illiterate never pretend to
abstract notions. It is said they are difficult and not
to be attained without pains and study ; we may therefore reasonably conclude that, if such there be, they are
confined only to the learned.

" I proceed to examine what can be alleged in defence
of the doctrine of abstraction, and try if I can discover
what it is that inclines the men of speculation to embrace
an opinion so remote from common sense as that seems

to be. There has been a late excellent and deservedly esteemed philosopher who, no doubt, has given it very much countenance, by seeming to think the having abstract general ideas is what puts the widest difference in point of understanding betwixt man and beast. 'The having of general ideas,' saith he, 'is that which puts a perfect distinction betwixt man and brutes, and is an excellency which the faculties of brutes do by no means attain unto. For, it is evident we observe no footsteps in them of making use of general signs for universal ideas ; from which we have reason to imagine that they have not the faculty of abstracting, or making general ideas, since they have no use of words or any other general signs.' And a little after : ' Therefore, I think, we may suppose that it is in this that the species of brutes are discriminated from men, and it is that proper difference wherein they are wholly separated, and which at last widens to so wide a distance. For, if they have any ideas at all, and are not bare machines (as some would have them), we cannot deny them to have some reason. It seems as evident to me that they do, some of them, in certain instances reason as that they have sense ; but it is only in particular ideas, just as they receive them from their senses. They are the best of them tied up within those narrow bounds, and have not (as I think) the faculty to enlarge them by any kind of abstraction.' (*Essay on Human Understanding*, Bk. II, chap. xi, paragraphs 10 and 11.) I readily agree with this learned author, that the faculties of brutes can by no means attain to abstraction. But, then, if this be made the distinguishing property of that sort of animals, I fear a great many of those that pass for men must be reckoned into their number. The reason that is here assigned why we have no grounds to think brutes have abstract general ideas is, that we observe in them no use of words or any other general signs ; which is built on this supposition—that the making use of words implies the having general ideas. From which it follows that men who use language are able to abstract or generalize their ideas. That this is the sense and arguing of the author will further appear by his answering the question he in another place puts : ' Since all things that exist are only particulars, how come we by general terms ? ' His answer is : ' Words become general by being made the signs of general ideas.' (*Essay on Human Understanding*, Bk. III, chap. iii, paragraph 6.) But it seems that a word becomes general by being made the sign, not of an abstract general idea, but of several particular ideas, any one of which it indifferently suggests to the mind. For example, when it is said ' the change of motion is proportional to the impressed force,' or that ' whatever has extension is divisible,' these propositions are to be understood of motion and extension in general ; and nevertheless it will not follow that they suggest to my thoughts an idea of motion without a body moved, or any determinate direction and velocity, or that I must conceive an abstract general idea of extension, which is neither line, surface, nor solid, neither great nor small, black, white, nor red, nor of any other determinate colour. It is only implied that whatever particular motion I consider, whether it be swift or slow, perpendicular, horizontal, or oblique, or in whatever object, the axiom concerning it holds equally true. As does the other of every particular extension, it matters not whether line, surface, or solid, whether of this or that magnitude or figure.

" By observing how ideas become general, we may the better judge how words are made so. And here it is to be noted that I do not deny absolutely there are general ideas, but only that there are any *abstract* general ideas ; for, in the passages we have quoted wherein there is mention of general ideas, it is always supposed that they are formed by abstraction, after the manner set forth in sections 8 and 9. Now, if we will annex a meaning to our words, and speak only of what we can conceive, I believe we shall acknowledge that an idea which, considered in itself, is particular, becomes general by being made to represent or stand for all other particular ideas of the same sort. To make this plain by an example, suppose a geometrician is demonstrating the method of cutting a line in two equal parts. He draws, for instance, a black line of an inch in length : this, which in itself is a particular line, is nevertheless with regard to its signification general, since, as it is there used, it represents all particular lines whatsoever ; so that what is demonstrated of it is demonstrated of all lines, or, in other words, of a line in general. And, as *that particular line* becomes general by being made a sign, so the *name* ' line,' which taken absolutely is particular, by being a sign is made general. And as the former owes its generality not to its being the sign of an abstract or general line, but of all particular right lines that may possibly exist, so the latter must be thought to derive its generality from the same cause, namely, the various particular lines which it indifferently denotes." [1]

Berkeley's view in the above passage, which is essentially the same as Hume's, does not wholly agree with modern psychology, although it comes nearer to agreement than does the view of those who believe that there are in the mind single contents which can be called abstract

[1] Introduction to *A Treatise concerning the Principles of Human Knowledge*, paragraphs 10, 11, and 12.

ideas. The way in which Berkeley's view is inadequate is chiefly in the fact that images are as a rule not of one definite prototype, but of a number of related similar prototypes. On this subject Semon has written well. In *Die Mneme*, pp. 217 ff., discussing the effect of repeated similar stimuli in producing and modifying our images, he says : " We choose a case of mnemic excitement whose existence we can perceive for ourselves by introspection, and seek to ekphore the bodily picture of our nearest relation in his absence, and have thus a pure mnemic excitement before us. At first it may seem to us that a determinate quite concrete picture becomes manifest in us, but just when we are concerned with a person with whom we are in constant contact, we shall find that the ekphored picture has something so to speak generalized. It is something like those American photographs which seek to display what is general about a type by combining a great number of photographs of different heads over each other on one plate. In our opinion, the generalizations happen by the homophonic working of different pictures of the same face which we have come across in the most different conditions and situations, once pale, once reddened, once cheerful, once earnest, once in this light, and once in that. As soon as we do not let the whole series of repetitions resound in us uniformly, but give our attention to one particular moment out of the many . . . this particular mnemic stimulus at once overbalances its simultaneously roused predecessors and successors, and we perceive the face in question with concrete definiteness in that particular situation." A little later he says : " The result is—at least in man, but probably also in the higher animals—the development of a sort of *physiological* abstraction. Mnemic homophony gives us, without the addition of other processes of thought, a picture of our friend X which is in a certain sense abstract, not the concrete in any one situation, but X cut loose from any particular point of time. If the circle of ekphored engrams is drawn even more widely, abstract pictures of a higher order appear : for instance, a white man or a negro. In my opinion, the first form of abstract concepts in general is based upon such abstract pictures. The physiological abstraction which takes place in the above described manner is a predecessor of purely logical abstraction. It is by no means a monopoly of the human race, but shows itself in various ways also among the more highly organized animals." The same subject is treated in more detail in Chapter xvi of *Die mnemischen Empfindungen*, but what is said there adds nothing vital to what is contained in the above quotations.

It is necessary, however, to distinguish between the vague and the general. So long as we are content with Semon's composite image, we *may* get no farther than the vague. The question whether this image takes us to the general or not depends, I think, upon the question whether, in addition to the generalized image, we have also particular images of some of the instances out of which it is compounded. Suppose, for example, that on a number of occasions you had seen one negro, and that you did not know whether this one was the same or different on the different occasions. Suppose that in the end you had an abstract memory-image of the different appearances presented by the negro on different occasions, but no memory-image of any one of the single appearances. In that case your image would be vague. If, on the other hand, you have, in addition to the generalized image, particular images of the several appearances, sufficiently clear to be recognized as different, and as instances of the generalized picture, you will then not feel the generalized picture to be adequate to any one particular appearance, and you will be able to make it function as a general idea rather than a vague idea. If this view is correct, no new general content needs to be added to the generalized image. What needs to be added is particular images compared and contrasted with the generalized image. So far as I can judge by introspection, this does occur in practice. Take for example Semon's instance of a friend's face. Unless we make some special effort of recollection, the face is likely to come before us with an average expression, very blurred and vague, but we can at will recall how our friend looked on some special occasion when he was pleased or angry or unhappy, and this enables us to realize the generalized character of the vague image.

There is, however, another way of distinguishing between the vague, the particular and the general, and this is not by their content, but by the reaction which they produce. A word, for example, may be said to be vague when it is applicable to a number of different individuals, but to each as individuals ; the name Smith, for example, is vague : it is always meant to apply to one man, but there are many men to each of whom it applies.[1] The word " man," on the other hand, is general. We say, " This is Smith," but we do not say " This is man," but " This is a man." Thus we may say that a word embodies a vague idea when its effects are appropriate to an indi-

[1] " Smith " would only be a quite satisfactory representation of vague words if we failed to discriminate between different people called Smith.

vidual, but are the same for various similar individuals, while a word embodies a general idea when its effects are different from those appropriate to individuals. In what this difference consists it is, however, not easy to say. I am inclined to think that it consists merely in the knowledge that no one individual is represented, so that what distinguishes a general idea from a vague idea is merely the presence of a certain accompanying belief. If this view is correct, a general idea differs from a vague one in a way analogous to that in which a memory-image differs from an imagination-image. There also we found that the difference consists merely of the fact that a memory-image is accompanied by a belief, in this case as to the past.

It should also be said that our images even of quite particular occurrences have always a greater or a less degree of vagueness. That is to say, the occurrence might have varied within certain limits without causing our image to vary recognizably. To arrive at the general it is necessary that we should be able to contrast it with a number of relatively precise images or words for particular occurrences ; so long as all our images and words are vague, we cannot arrive at the contrast by which the general is defined. This is the justification for the view which I quoted on p. 184 from Ribot (*op. cit.*, p. 32), viz. that intelligence progresses from the indefinite to the definite, and that the vague appears earlier than either the particular or the general.

I think the view which I have been advocating, to the effect that a general idea is distinguished from a vague one by the presence of a judgment, is also that intended by Ribot when he says (*op. cit.*, p. 92) : " The generic image is never, the concept is always, a judgment. We know that for logicians (formerly at any rate) the concept is the simple and primitive element ; next comes the judgment, uniting two or several concepts ; then ratiocination, combining two or several judgments. For the psychologists, on the contrary, affirmation is the fundamental act ; the concept is the *result* of judgment (explicit or implicit), of similarities with exclusion of differences."

A great deal of work professing to be experimental has been done in recent years on the psychology of thought. A good summary of such work up to the year 1909 is contained in Titchener's *Lectures on the Experimental Psychology of the Thought Processes* (1909). Three articles in the *Archiv für die gesammte Psychologie* by Watt,[1] Messer [2] and Bühler [3] contain a great deal of the material amassed by the methods which Titchener calls experimental.

For my part I am unable to attach as much importance to this work as many psychologists do. The method employed appears to me hardly to fulfil the conditions of scientific experiment. Broadly speaking, what is done is, that a set of questions are asked of various people, their answers are recorded, and likewise their own accounts, based upon introspection, of the processes of thought which led them to give those answers. Much too much reliance seems to me to be placed upon the correctness of their introspection. On introspection as a method I have spoken earlier (Lecture VI). I am not prepared, like Professor Watson, to reject it wholly, but I do consider that it is exceedingly fallible and quite peculiarly

---

[1] Henry J. Watt, *Experimentelle Beiträge zu einer Theorie des Denkens*, vol. iv (1905), pp. 289–436.

[2] August Messer, *Experimentell-psychologische Untersuchungen über das Denken*, vol. iii (1906), pp. 1–224.

[3] Karl Bühler, *Über Gedanken*, vol. ix (1907), pp. 297–365.

liable to falsification in accordance with preconceived theory. It is like depending upon the report of a short-sighted person as to whom he sees coming along the road at a moment when he is firmly convinced that Jones is sure to come. If everybody were short-sighted and obsessed with beliefs as to what was going to be visible, we might have to make the best of such testimony, but we should need to correct its errors by taking care to collect the simultaneous evidence of people with the most divergent expectations. There is no evidence that this was done in the experiments in question, nor indeed that the influence of theory in falsifying the introspection was at all adequately recognized. I feel convinced that if Professor Watson had been one of the subjects of the *questionnaires*, he would have given answers totally different from those recorded in the articles in question. Titchener quotes an opinion of Wundt on these investigations, which appears to me thoroughly justified. " These experiments," he says, " are not experiments at all in the sense of a scientific methodology ; they are counterfeit experiments, that seem methodical simply because they are ordinarily performed in a psychological laboratory, and involve the co-operation of two persons, who purport to be experimenter and observer. In reality, they are as unmethodical as possible ; they possess none of the special features by which we distinguish the introspections of experimental psychology from the casual introspections of everyday life." [1] Titchener, of course, dissents from this opinion, but I cannot see that his reasons for dissent are adequate. My doubts are only increased by the fact that Bühler at any rate used trained psychologists as his subjects. A trained psychologist is,

[1] Titchener, *op. cit.*, p. 79.

of course, supposed to have acquired the habit of observation, but he is at least equally likely to have acquired
a habit of seeing what his theories require. We may
take Bühler's *Über Gedanken* to illustrate the kind of
results arrived at by such methods. Bühler says (p. 303) :
" We ask ourselves the general question : ' *What do
we experience when we think ?* ' Then we do not at all
attempt a preliminary determination of the concept
' thought,' but choose for analysis only such processes as
everyone would describe as processes of thought." The
most important thing in thinking, he says, is " awareness
that . . ." (*Bewusstheit dass*), which he calls a thought.
It is, he says, thoughts in this sense that are essential
to thinking. Thinking, he maintains, does not need
language or sensuous presentations. " I assert rather
that in principle every object can be thought (meant)
distinctly, without any help from sensuous presentation
(*Anschauungshilfen*). Every individual shade of blue
colour on the picture that hangs in my room I can think
with complete distinctness unsensuously (*unanschaulich*),
provided it is possible that the object should be given to
me in another manner than by the help of sensations.
How that is possible we shall see later." What he calls
a thought (*Gedanke*) cannot be reduced, according to
him, to other psychic occurrences. He maintains that
thoughts consist for the most part of known rules (p. 342).
It is clearly essential to the interest of this theory that
the thought or rule alluded to by Bühler should not need
to be expressed in words, for if it is expressed in words it
is immediately capable of being dealt with on the lines
with which the behaviourists have familiarized us. It is
clear also that the supposed absence of words rests solely
upon the introspective testimony of the persons experi-

mented upon. I cannot think that there is sufficient certainty of their reliability in this negative observation to make us accept a difficult and revolutionary view of thought, merely because they have failed to observe the presence of words or their equivalent in their thinking. I think it far more likely, especially in view of the fact that the persons concerned were highly educated, that we are concerned with telescoped processes, in which habit has caused a great many intermediate terms to be elided or to be passed over so quickly as to escape observation.

I am inclined to think that similar remarks apply to the general idea of "imageless thinking," concerning which there has been much controversy. The advocates of imageless thinking are not contending merely that there can be thinking which is purely verbal; they are contending that there can be thinking which proceeds neither in words nor in images. My own feeling is that they have rashly assumed the presence of thinking in cases where habit has rendered thinking unnecessary. When Thorndike experimented with animals in cages, he found that the associations established were between a sensory stimulus and a bodily movement (not the idea of it), without the need of supposing any non-physiological intermediary (*op. cit.*, p. 100 ff.). The same thing, it seems to me, applies to ourselves. A certain sensory situation produces in us a certain bodily movement. Sometimes this movement consists in uttering words. Prejudice leads us to suppose that between the sensory stimulus and the utterance of the words a process of thought must have intervened, but there seems no good reason for such a supposition. Any habitual action, such as eating or dressing, may be performed on the appropriate occasion, without any need of thought,

and the same seems to be true of a painfully large proportion of our talk. What applies to uttered speech
applies of course equally to the internal speech which is
not uttered. I remain, therefore, entirely unconvinced
that there is any such phenomenon as thinking which
consists neither of images nor of words, or that " ideas "
have to be added to sensations and images as part of the
material out of which mental phenomena are built.

The question of the nature of our consciousness of the
universal is much affected by our view as to the general
nature of the relation of consciousness to its object. If we
adopt the view of Brentano, according to which all mental
content has essential reference to an object, it is then
natural to suppose that there is some peculiar kind of
mental content of which the object is a universal, as
oppose to a particular. According to this view, a particular cat can be *per*ceived or imagined, while the universal
" cat " is *con*ceived. But this whole manner of viewing
our dealings with universals has to be abandoned when
the relation of a mental occurrence to its " object " is
regarded as merely indirect and causal, which is the view
that we have adopted. The mental content is, of course,
always particular, and the question as to what it " means "
(in case it means anything) is one which cannot be settled
by merely examining the intrinsic character of the mental
content, but only by knowing its causal connections in
the case of the person concerned. To say that a certain
thought " means " a universal as opposed to either a vague
or a particular, is to say something exceedingly complex.
A horse will behave in a certain manner whenever he smells
a bear, even if the smell is derived from a bearskin. That
is to say, any environment containing an instance of the
universal " smell of a bear " produces closely similar

behaviour in the horse, but we do not say that the horse is conscious of this universal. There is equally little reason to regard a man as conscious of the same universal, because under the same circumstances he can react by saying, " I smell a bear." This reaction, like that of the horse, is merely closely similar on different occasions where the environment affords instances of the same universal. Words of which the logical meaning is universal can therefore be employed correctly, without anything that could be called consciousness of universals. Such consciousness in the only sense in which it can be said to exist is a matter of reflective judgment consisting in the observation of similarities and differences. A universal never appears before the mind as a single object in the sort of way in which something perceived appears. I *think* a logical argument could be produced to show that universals are part of the structure of the world, but they are an inferred part, not a part of our data. What exists in us consists of various factors, some open to external observation, others only visible to introspection. The factors open to external observation are primarily habits, having the peculiarity that very similar reactions are produced by stimuli which are in many respects very different from each other. Of this the reaction of the horse to the smell of the bear is an instance, and so is the reaction of the man who says " bear " under the same circumstances. The verbal reaction is, of course, the most important from the point of view of what may be called knowledge of universals. A man who can always use the word " dog " when he sees a dog may be said, in a certain sense, to know the meaning of the word " dog," and *in that sense* to have knowledge of the universal " dog." But there is, of course, a further stage reached by the logician in which he not merely reacts with the word "dog," but sets to work to discover what it is in the environment that causes in him this almost identical reaction on different occasions. This further stage consists in knowledge of similarities and differences : similarities which are necessary to the applicability of the word "dog," and differences which are compatible with it. Our knowledge of these similarities and differences is never exhaustive, and therefore our knowledge of the meaning of a universal is never complete.

In addition to external observable habits (including the habit of words), there is also the generic image produced by the superposition, or, in Semon's phrase, homophony, of a number of similar perceptions. This image is vague so long as the multiplicity of its prototypes is not recognized, but becomes universal when it exists alongside of the more specific images of its instances, and is knowingly contrasted with them. In this case we find again, as we found when we were discussing words in general in the preceding lecture, that images are not logically necessary in order to account for observable behaviour, i.e. in this case intelligent speech. Intelligent speech could exist as a motor habit, without any accompaniment of images, and this conclusion applies to words of which the meaning is universal, just as much as to words of which the meaning is relatively particular. If this conclusion is valid, it follows that behaviourist psychology, which eschews introspective data, is capable of being an independent science, and of accounting for all that part of the behaviour of other people which is commonly regarded as evidence that they think. It must be admitted that this conclusion considerably weakens the reliance which can be placed upon introspective data. They must be accepted simply on account of the fact that we seem to perceive them, not on account of their supposed necessity for explaining the data of external observation.

This, at any rate, is the conclusion to which we are forced, so long as, with the behaviourists, we accept common-sense views of the physical world. But if, as I have urged, the physical world itself, as known, is infected through and through with subjectivity, if, as the theory of relativity suggests, the physical universe contains the diversity of points of view which we have been accustomed to regard as distinctively psychological, then we are brought back by this different road to the necessity for trusting observations which are in an important sense private. And it is the privacy of introspective data which causes much of the behaviourists' objection to them.

This is an example of the difficulty of constructing an adequate philosophy of any one science without taking account of other sciences. The behaviourist philosophy of psychology, though in many respects admirable from the point of view of method, appears to me to fail in the last analysis because it is based upon an inadequate philosophy of physics. In spite, therefore, of the fact that the evidence for images, whether generic or particular, is merely introspective, I cannot admit that images should be rejected, or that we should minimize their function in our knowledge of what is remote in time or space.

LECTURE XII

BELIEF

BELIEF, which is our subject to-day, is the central problem in the analysis of mind. Believing seems the most "mental" thing we do, the thing most remote from what is done by mere matter. The whole intellectual life consists of beliefs, and of the passage from one belief to another by what is called "reasoning." Beliefs give knowledge and error ; they are the vehicles of truth and falsehood. Psychology, theory of knowledge and metaphysics revolve about belief, and on the view we take of belief our philosophical outlook largely depends.

Before embarking upon the detailed analysis of belief, we shall do well to note certain requisites which any theory must fulfil.

(1) Just as words are characterized by meaning, so beliefs are characterized by truth or falsehood. And just as meaning consists in relation to the object meant, so truth and falsehood consist in relation to something that lies outside the belief. You may believe that such-and-such a horse will win the Derby. The time comes, and your horse wins or does not win ; according to the outcome, your belief was true or false. You may believe that six times nine is fifty-six ; in this case also there

is a fact which makes your belief false. You may believe that America was discovered in 1492, or that it was discovered in 1066. In the one case your belief is true, in the other false ; in either case its truth or falsehood depends upon the actions of Columbus, not upon anything present or under your control. What makes a belief true or false I call a " fact." The particular fact that makes a given belief true or false I call its " objective," [1] and the relation of the belief to its objective I call the " reference " or the " objective reference " of the belief. Thus, if I believe that Columbus crossed the Atlantic in 1492, the " objective " of my belief is Columbus's actual voyage, and the " reference " of my belief is the relation between my belief and the voyage—that relation, namely, in virtue of which the voyage makes my belief true (or, in another case, false). " Reference " of beliefs differs from " meaning " of words in various ways, but especially in the fact that it is of two kinds, " true " reference and " false " reference. The truth or falsehood of a belief does not depend upon anything intrinsic to the belief, but upon the nature of its relation to its objective. The intrinsic nature of belief can be treated without reference to what makes it true or false. In the remainder of the present lecture I shall ignore truth and falsehood, which will be the subject of Lecture XIII. It is the intrinsic nature of belief that will concern us to-day.

(2) We must distinguish between believing and what is believed. I may believe that Columbus crossed the Atlantic, that all Cretans are liars, that two and two are four, or that nine times six is fifty-six ; in all these

[1] This terminology is suggested by Meinong, but is not exactly the same as his.

cases the believing is just the same, and only the contents believed are different. I may remember my breakfast this morning, my lecture last week, or my first sight of New York. In all these cases the feeling of memory-belief is just the same, and only what is remembered differs. Exactly similar remarks apply to expectations. Bare assent, memory and expectation are forms of belief; all three are different from what is believed, and each has a constant character which is independent of what is believed.

In Lecture I we criticized the analysis of a presentation into act, content and object. But our analysis of belief contains three very similar elements, namely the believing, what is believed and the objective. The objections to the act (in the case of presentations) are not valid against the believing in the case of beliefs, because the believing is an actual experienced feeling, not something postulated, like the act. But it is necessary first to complete our preliminary requisites, and then to examine the content of a belief. After that, we shall be in a position to return to the question as to what constitutes believing.

(3) What is believed, and the believing, must both consist of present occurrences in the believer, no matter what may be the objective of the belief. Suppose I believe, for example, "that Cæsar crossed the Rubicon." The objective of my belief is an event which happened long ago, which I never saw and do not remember. This event itself is not in my mind when I believe that it happened. It is not correct to say that I am believing the actual event; what I am believing is something now in my mind, something related to the event (in a way which we shall investigate in Lecture XIII), but obviously not to be confounded with the event, since the event is not

occurring now but the believing is. What a man is believing at a given moment is wholly determinate if we know the contents of his mind at that moment ; but Cæsar's crossing of the Rubicon was an historical physical event, which is distinct from the present contents of every present mind. What is believed, however true it may be, is not the actual fact that makes the belief true, but a present event related to the fact. This present event, which is what is believed, I shall call the " content " of the belief. We have already had occasion to notice the distinction between content and objective in the case of memory-beliefs, where the content is " this occurred " and the objective is the past event.

(4) Between content and objective there is sometimes a very wide gulf, for example in the case of " Cæsar crossed the Rubicon." This gulf may, when it is first perceived, give us a feeling that we cannot really " know " anything about the outer world. All we can " know," it may be said, is what is now in our thoughts. If Cæsar and the Rubicon cannot be bodily in our thoughts, it might seem as though we must remain cut off from knowledge of them. I shall not now deal at length with this feeling, since it is necessary first to define " knowing," which cannot be done yet. But I will say, as a preliminary answer, that the feeling assumes an ideal of knowing which I believe to be quite mistaken : it assumes, if it is thought out, something like the mystic unity of knower and known. These two are often said to be combined into a unity by the fact of cognition ; hence when this unity is plainly absent, it may seem as if there were no genuine cognition. For my part, I think such theories and feelings wholly mistaken : I believe knowing to be a very external and complicated relation,

incapable of exact definition, dependent upon causal laws, and involving no more unity than there is between a signpost and the town to which it points. I shall return to this question on a later occasion ; for the moment these provisional remarks must suffice.

(5) The objective reference of a belief is connected with the fact that all or some of the constituents of its content have meaning. If I say " Cæsar conquered Gaul," a person who knows the meaning of the three words composing my statement knows as much as can be known about the nature of the objective which would make my statement true. It is clear that the objective reference of a belief is, in general, in some way derivative from the meanings of the words or images that occur in its content. There are, however, certain complications which must be borne in mind. In the first place, it might be contended that a memory-image acquires meaning only through the memory-belief, which would seem, at least in the case of memory, to make belief more primitive than the meaning of images. In the second place, it is a very singular thing that meaning, which is single, should generate objective reference, which is dual, namely true and false. This is one of the facts which any theory of belief must explain if it is to be satisfactory.

It is now time to leave these preliminary requisites, and attempt the analysis of the contents of beliefs.

The first thing to notice about what is believed, i.e. about the content of a belief, is that it is always complex. We believe that a certain thing has a certain property, or a certain relation to something else, or that it occurred or will occur (in the sense discussed at the end of Lecture IX) ; or we may believe that all the members of a certain class have a certain property, or that a certain property sometimes occurs among the members of a class ; or we may believe that if one thing happens, another will happen (for example, " if it rains I shall bring my umbrella "), or we may believe that something does not happen, or did not or will not happen (for example, " it won't rain ") ; or that one of two things must happen (for example, " either you withdraw your accusation, or I shall bring a libel action "). The catalogue of the sorts of things we may believe is infinite, but all of them are complex.

Language sometimes conceals the complexity of a belief. We say that a person believes in God, and it might seem as if God formed the whole content of the belief. But what is really believed is that God exists, which is very far from being simple. Similarly, when a person has a memory-image with a memory-belief, the belief is " this occurred," in the sense explained in Lecture IX; and " this occurred " is not simple. In like manner all cases where the content of a belief seems simple at first sight will be found, on examination, to confirm the view that the content is always complex.

The content of a belief involves not merely a plurality of constituents, but definite relations between them ; it is not determinate when its constituents alone are given. For example, " Plato preceded Aristotle " and " Aristotle preceded Plato " are both contents which may be believed, but, although they consist of exactly the same constituents, they are different, and even incompatible.

The content of a belief may consist of words only, or of images only, or of a mixture of the two, or of either or both together with one or more sensations. It must contain at least one constituent which is a word or an image, and it may or may not contain one or more sensations as constituents. Some examples will make these various possibilities clear.

We may take first recognition, in either of the forms " this is of such-and-such a kind " or " this has occurred before." In either case, present sensation is a constituent. For example, you hear a noise, and you say to yourself " tram." Here the noise and the word " tram " are both constituents of your belief; there is also a relation between them, expressed by " is " in the proposition " that is a tram." As soon as your act of recognition is completed by the occurrence of the word " tram," your actions are affected : you hurry if you want the tram, or cease to hurry if you want a bus. In this case the content of your belief is a sensation (the noise) and a word (" tram ") related in a way which may be called predication.

The same noise may bring into your mind the visual image of a tram, instead of the word " tram." In this case your belief consists of a sensation and an image suitable related. Beliefs of this class are what are called " judgments of perception." As we saw in Lecture VIII, the images associated with a sensation often come with such spontaneity and force that the unsophisticated do not distinguish them from the sensation ; it is only the psychologist or the skilled observer who is aware of the large mnemic element that is added to sensation to make perception. It may be objected that what is added consists merely of images without belief. This is no doubt sometimes the case, but is certainly sometimes not the case. That belief always occurs in perception as opposed to sensation it is not necessary for us to maintain ; it is enough for our purposes to note that it sometimes occurs, and that when it does, the content of our belief consists of a sensation and an image suitably related.

In a *pure* memory-belief only images occur. But a mixture of words and images is very common in memory. You have an image of the past occurrence, and you say to yourself: "Yes, that's how it was." Here the image and the words together make up the content of the belief. And when the remembering of an incident has become a habit, it may be purely verbal, and the memory-belief may consist of words alone.

The more complicated forms of belief tend to consist only of words. Often images of various kinds accompany them, but they are apt to be irrelevant, and to form no part of what is actually believed. For example, in thinking of the Solar System, you are likely to have vague images of pictures you have seen of the earth surrounded by clouds, Saturn and his rings, the sun during an eclipse, and so on ; but none of these form part of your belief that the planets revolve round the sun in elliptical orbits. The only images that form an actual part of such beliefs are, as a rule, images of words. And images of words, for the reasons considered in Lecture VIII, cannot be distinguished with any certainty from sensations, when, as is often, if not usually, the case, they are kinæsthetic images of pronouncing the words.

It is impossible for a belief to consist of sensations alone, except when, as in the case of words, the sensations have associations which make them signs possessed of meaning. The reason is that objective reference is of the essence of belief, and objective reference is derived from meaning. When I speak of a belief consisting partly of sensations and partly of words, I do not mean to deny that the words, when they are not mere images, are sensational, but that they occur as signs, not (so to speak) in their own right. To revert to the noise of the tram, when you hear it and say " tram," the noise and the word are both sensations (if you actually pronounce the word), but the noise is part of the fact which makes your belief true, whereas the word is not part of this fact. It is the *meaning* of the word " tram," not the actual word, that forms part of the fact which is the objective of your belief. Thus the word occurs in the belief as a symbol, in virtue of its meaning, whereas the noise enters into both the belief and its objective. It is this that distinguishes the occurrence of words as symbols from the occurrence of sensations in their own right : the objective contains the sensations that occur in their own right, but contains only the meanings of the words that occur as symbols.

For the sake of simplicity, we may ignore the cases in which sensations in their own right form part of the content of a belief, and confine ourselves to images and words. We may also omit the cases in which both images and words occur in the content of a belief. Thus we become confined to two cases : (a) when the content consists wholly of images, (b) when it consists wholly of words. The case of mixed images and words has no special importance, and its omission will do no harm.

Let us take in illustration a case of memory. Suppose you are thinking of some familiar room. You may call up an image of it, and in your image the window may be to the left of the door. Without any intrusion of words, you may believe in the correctness of your image. You then have a belief, consisting wholly of images, which becomes, when put into words, " the window is to the left of the door." You may yourself use these words and proceed to believe them. You thus pass from an image-content to the corresponding word-content. The content is different in the two cases, but its objective reference is the same. This shows the relation of image-beliefs to word-beliefs in a very simple case. In more elaborate cases the relation becomes much less simple.

It may be said that even in this very simple case the objective reference of the word-content is not quite the same as that of the image-content, that images have a wealth of concrete features which are lost when words are substituted, that the window in the image is not a mere window in the abstract, but a window of a certain shape and size, not merely to the left of the door, but a certain distance to the left, and so on. In reply, it may be admitted at once that there is, as a rule, a certain amount of truth in the objection. But two points may be urged to minimize its force. First, images do not, as a rule, have that wealth of concrete detail that would make it *impossible* to express them fully in words. They are vague and fragmentary : a finite number of words, though perhaps a large number, would exhaust at least their *significant* features. For—and this is our second point—images enter into the content of a belief through the fact that they are capable of meaning, and their meaning does not, as a rule, have as much complexity as they have : some of their characteristics are usually devoid of meaning. Thus it may well be possible to extract in words all that has meaning in an image-content ; in that case the word-content and the image-content will have exactly the same objective reference.

The content of a belief, when expressed in words, is the same thing (or very nearly the same thing) as what in

logic is called a " proposition." A proposition is a series
of words (or sometimes a single word) expressing the
kind of thing that can be asserted or denied. " That all
men are mortal," " that Columbus discovered America,"
" that Charles I died in his bed," " that all philosophers
are wise," are propositions. Not any series of words is
a proposition, but only such series of words as have
" meaning," or, in our phraseology, " objective reference."
Given the meanings of separate words, and the rules of
syntax, the meaning of a proposition is determinate.
This is the reason why we can understand a sentence
we never heard before. You probably never heard
before the proposition " that the inhabitants of the
Andaman Islands habitually eat stewed hippopotamus
for dinner," but there is no difficulty in understanding
the proposition. The question of the relation between
the meaning of a sentence and the meanings of the
separate words is difficult, and I shall not pursue it now;
I brought it up solely as being illustrative of the nature
of propositions.

We may extend the term " proposition " so as to cover
the image-contents of beliefs consisting of images. Thus,
in the case of remembering a room in which the window
is to the left of the door, when we believe the image-
content the proposition will consist of the image of the
window on the left together with the image of the door
on the right. We will distinguish propositions of this
kind as " image-propositions " and propositions in words
as " word-propositions." We may identify propositions in
general with the contents of actual and possible beliefs,
and we may say that it is propositions that are true or
false. In logic we are concerned with propositions rather
than beliefs, since logic is not interested in what people

do in fact believe, but only in the conditions which determine the truth or falsehood of possible beliefs. Whenever possible, except when actual beliefs are in question, it is generally a simplification to deal with propositions.

It would seem that image-propositions are more primitive than word-propositions, and may well ante-date language. There is no reason why memory-images, accompanied by that very simple belief-feeling which we decided to be the essence of memory, should not have occurred before language arose ; indeed, it would be rash to assert positively that memory of this sort does not occur among the higher animals. Our more elementary beliefs, notably those that are added to sensation to make perception, often remain at the level of images. For example, most of the visual objects in our neighbourhood rouse tactile images : we have a different feeling in looking at a sofa from what we have in looking at a block of marble, and the difference consists chiefly in different stimulation of our tactile imagination. It may be said that the tactile images are merely present, without any accompanying belief ; but I think this view, though sometimes correct, derives its plausibility as a general proposition from our thinking of explicit conscious belief only. Most of our beliefs, like most of our wishes, are " unconscious," in the sense that we have never told ourselves that we have them. Such beliefs display themselves when the expectations that they arouse fail in any way. For example, if someone puts tea (without milk) into a glass, and you drink it under the impression that it is going to be beer ; or if you walk on what appears to be a tiled floor, and it turns out to be a soft carpet made to look like tiles. The shock of surprise on an occasion of this kind makes us aware of the expectations that habitually enter into our perceptions; and such expectations must be classed as beliefs, in spite of the fact that we do not normally take note of them or put them into words. I remember once watching a cock pigeon running over and over again to the edge of a looking-glass to try to wreak vengeance on the particularly obnoxious bird whom he expected to find there, judging by what he saw in the glass. He must have experienced each time the sort of surprise on finding nothing, which is calculated to lead in time to the adoption of Berkeley's theory that objects of sense are only in the mind. His expectation, though not expressed in words, deserved, I think, to be called a belief.

I come now to the question what constitutes believing, as opposed to the content believed.

To begin with, there are various different attitudes that may be taken towards the same content. Let us suppose, for the sake of argument, that you have a visual image of your breakfast-table. You may expect it while you are dressing in the morning; remember it as you go to your work; feel doubt as to its correctness when questioned as to your powers of visualizing; merely entertain the image, without connecting it with anything external, when you are going to sleep; desire it if you are hungry, or feel aversion for it if you are ill. Suppose, for the sake of definiteness, that the content is " an egg for breakfast." Then you have the following attitudes: " I expect there will be an egg for breakfast "; " I remember there was an egg for breakfast"; "Was there an egg for breakfast ? " " An egg for breakfast: well, what of it ? " " I hope there will be an egg for breakfast "; " I am afraid there will be an egg for breakfast and it is sure to be bad." I do not suggest that this is a list of all possible attitudes on the subject; I say only that they are different attitudes, all concerned with the one content "an egg for breakfast."

These attitudes are not all equally ultimate. Those that involve desire and aversion have occupied us in Lecture III. For the present, we are only concerned with such as are cognitive. In speaking of memory, we distinguished three kinds of belief directed towards the same content, namely memory, expectation and bare assent without any time-determination in the belief-feeling. But before developing this view, we must examine two other theories which might be held concerning belief, and which, in some ways, would be more in harmony with a behaviourist outlook than the theory I wish to advocate.

(1) The first theory to be examined is the view that the differentia of belief consists in its causal efficacy I do not wish to make any author responsible for this theory: I wish merely to develop it hypothetically so that we may judge of its tenability.

We defined the meaning of an image or word by causal efficacy, namely by associations: an image or word acquires meaning, we said, through having the same associations as what it means.

We propose hypothetically to define "belief" by a different kind of causal efficacy, namely efficacy in causing voluntary movements. (Voluntary movements are defined as those vital movements which are distinguished from reflex movements as involving the higher nervous centres. I do not like to distinguish them by means of such notions as "consciousness" or "will," because I do not think these notions, in any definable sense, are always applicable. Moreover, the purpose of the theory we are examining is to be, as far as possible, physiological and behaviourist, and this purpose is not achieved if we introduce such a conception as " consciousness " or " will." Nevertheless, it is necessary for our purpose to find some way of distinguishing between voluntary and reflex movements, since the results would be too paradoxical, if we were to say that reflex movements also involve beliefs.) According to this definition, a content is said to be " believed " when it causes us to move. The images aroused are the same if you say to me, " Suppose there were an escaped tiger coming along the street," and if you say to me, " There is an escaped tiger coming along the street." But my actions will be very different in the two cases : in the first, I shall remain calm ; in the second, it is possible that I may not. It is suggested, by the theory we are considering, that this difference of effects constitutes what is meant by saying that in the second case I believe the proposition suggested, while in the first case I do not. According to this view, images or words are " believed " when they cause bodily movements.

I do not think this theory is adequate, but I think it is suggestive of truth, and not so easily refutable as it might appear to be at first sight.

It might be objected to the theory that many things which we certainly believe do not call for any bodily movements. I believe that Great Britain is an island, that whales are mammals, that Charles I was executed, and so on ; and at first sight it seems obvious that such beliefs, as a rule, do not call for any action on my part. But when we investigate the matter more closely, it becomes more doubtful. To begin with, we must distinguish belief as a mere *disposition* from actual active belief. We speak as if we always believed that Charles I was executed, but that only means that we are always ready to believe it when the subject comes up. The phenomenon we are concerned to analyse is the active belief, not the permanent disposition. Now, what are the occasions when we actively believe that Charles I was executed ? Primarily : examinations, when we perform the bodily movement of writing it down ; conversation, when we assert it to display our historical erudition ; and political discourses, when we are engaged in showing what Soviet government leads to. In all these cases bodily movements (writing or speaking) result from our belief.

But there remains the belief which merely occurs in " thinking." One may set to work to recall some piece of history one has been reading, and what one recalls is believed, although it probably does not cause any bodily movement whatever. It is true that what we believe always *may* influence action. Suppose I am invited to become King of Georgia : I find the prospect attractive, and go to Cook's to buy a third-class ticket to my new realm. At the last moment I remember Charles I and all the other monarchs who have come to a bad end ; I change my mind, and walk out without completing the transaction. But such incidents are rare, and cannot constitute the whole of my belief that Charles I was executed. The conclusion seems to be that, although a belief always *may* influence action if it becomes relevant to a practical issue, it often exists actively (not as a mere disposition) without producing any voluntary movement whatever. If this is true, we cannot define belief by the effect on voluntary movements.

There is another, more theoretical, ground for rejecting the view we are examining. It is clear that a proposition can be either believed or merely considered, and that the content is the same in both cases. We can expect an egg for breakfast, or merely entertain the supposition that there may be an egg for breakfast. A moment ago I considered the possibility of being invited to become King of Georgia, but I do not believe that this will happen. Now, it seems clear that, since believing and considering have different effects if one produces bodily movements while the other does not, there must be some intrinsic difference between believing and considering [1]; for if they were precisely similar, their effects also would be precisely similar. We have seen that the difference between believing a given proposition and merely considering it does not lie in the content; therefore there must be, in one case or in both, something additional to the content which distinguishes the occurrence of a belief from the occurrence of a mere consideration of the same content. So far as the theoretical argument goes, this additional element may exist only in belief, or only in consideration, or there may be one sort of additional element in the case of belief, and another in the case of consideration. This brings us to the second view which we have to examine.

(2) The theory which we have now to consider regards belief as belonging to every idea which is entertained, except in so far as some positive counteracting force interferes. In this view belief is not a positive phenomenon, though doubt and disbelief are so. What we call belief, according to this hypothesis, involves only

[1] Cf. Brentano, *Psychologie vom empirischen Standpunkte*, p. 268 (criticizing Bain, *The Emotions and the Will*).

the appropriate content, which will have the effects characteristic of belief unless something else operating simultaneously inhibits them. James (*Psychology*, vol. ii, p. 288) quotes with approval, though inaccurately, a passage from Spinoza embodying this view :

" Let us conceive a boy imagining to himself a horse, and taking note of nothing else. As this imagination involves the existence of the horse, *and the boy has no perception which annuls its existence* [James's italics], he will necessarily contemplate the horse as present, nor will he be able to doubt of its existence, however little certain of it he may be. I deny that a man in so far as he imagines [percipit] affirms nothing. For what is it to imagine a winged horse but to affirm that the horse [that horse, namely] has wings ? For if the mind had nothing before it but the winged horse, it would contemplate the same as present, would have no cause to doubt of its existence, nor any power of dissenting from its existence, unless the imagination of the winged horse were joined to an idea which contradicted [tollit] its existence " (*Ethics*, vol. ii, p. 49, Scholium).

To this doctrine James entirely assents, adding in italics :

" *Any object which remains uncontradicted is ipso facto believed and posited as absolute reality.*"

If this view is correct, it follows (though James does not draw the inference) that there is no need of any specific feeling called " belief," and that the mere existence of images yields all that is required. The state of mind in which we merely consider a proposition, without believing or disbelieving it, will then appear as a sophisticated product, the result of some rival force adding to the image-proposition a positive feeling which may be called suspense or non-belief—a feeling which may be compared to that of a man about to run a race waiting for the signal. Such a man, though not moving, is in a very different condition from that of a man quietly at rest. And so the man who is considering a proposition without believing it will be in a state of tension, restraining the natural tendency to act upon the proposition which he would display if nothing interfered. In this view belief primarily consists merely in the existence of the appropriate images without any counteracting forces.

There is a great deal to be said in favour of this view, and I have some hesitation in regarding it as inadequate. It fits admirably with the phenomena of dreams and hallucinatory images, and it is recommended by the way in which it accords with mental development. Doubt, suspense of judgment and disbelief all seem later and more complex than a wholly unreflecting assent. Belief as a positive phenomenon, if it exists, may be regarded, in this view, as a product of doubt, a decision after debate, an acceptance, not merely of *this*, but of *this-rather-than-that*. It is not difficult to suppose that a dog has images (possible olfactory) of his absent master, or of the rabbit that he dreams of hunting. But it is very difficult to suppose that he can entertain mere imagination-images to which no assent is given.

I think it must be conceded that a mere image, without the addition of any positive feeling that could be called "belief," is apt to have a certain dynamic power, and in this sense an uncombated image has the force of a belief. But although this may be true, it accounts only for some of the simplest phenomena in the region of belief. It will not, for example, explain memory. Nor can it explain beliefs which do not issue in any proximate action, such as those of mathematics. I conclude, therefore, that there must be belief-feelings of the same order as those of doubt or disbelief, although phenomena closely analogous to those of belief can be produced by mere uncontradicted images.

(3) I come now to the view of belief which I wish to advocate. It seems to me that there are at least three kinds of belief, namely memory, expectation and bare assent. Each of these I regard as constituted by a certain feeling or complex of sensations, attached to the content believed. We may illustrate by an example. Suppose I am believing, by means of images, not words, that it will rain. We have here two interrelated elements, namely the content and the expectation. The content consists of images of (say) the visual appearance of rain, the feeling of wetness, the patter of drops, interrelated, roughly, as the sensations would be if it were raining. Thus the content is a complex fact composed of images. Exactly the same content may enter into the memory " it was raining " or the assent " rain occurs." The difference of these cases from each other and from expectation does not lie in the content. The difference lies in the nature of the belief-feeling. I, personally, do not profess to be able to analyse the sensations constituting respectively memory, expectation and assent ; but I am not prepared to say that they cannot be analysed. There may be other belief-feelings, for example in disjunction and implication ; also a disbelief-feeling.

It is not enough that the content and the belief-feeling should co-exist : it is necessary that there should be a specific relation between them, of the sort expressed by saying that the content is what is believed. If this were not obvious, it could be made plain by an argument. If the mere co-existence of the content and the belief-feeling sufficed, whenever we were having (say) a memory-feeling we should be remembering any proposition which came into our minds at the same time. But this is not the case, since we may simultaneously remember one proposition and merely consider another.

We may sum up our analysis, in the case of bare assent to a proposition not expressed in words, as follows : (a) We have a proposition, consisting of interrelated images, and possibly partly of sensations ; (b) we have the feeling of assent, which is presumably a complex sensation demanding analysis ; (c) we have a relation, actually subsisting, between the assent and the proposition, such as is expressed by saying that the proposition in question is what is assented to. For other forms of belief-feeling or of content, we have only to make the necessary substitutions in this analysis.

If we are right in our analysis of belief, the use of words in expressing beliefs is apt to be misleading. There is no way of distinguishing, in words, between a memory and an assent to a proposition about the past : " I ate my breakfast " and " Cæsar conquered Gaul " have the same verbal form, though (assuming that I remember my breakfast) they express occurrences which are psychologically very different. In the one case, what happens is that I remember the content " eating my breakfast " ; in the other case, I assent to the content " Cæsar's conquest of Gaul occurred." In the latter case, but not in the former, the pastness is part of the content believed. Exactly similar remarks apply to the difference between expectation, such as we have when waiting for the thunder after a flash of lightning, and assent to a proposition about the future, such as we have in all the usual cases of inferential knowledge as to what will occur. I think this difficulty in the verbal expression of the temporal aspects of beliefs is one among the causes which have hampered philosophy in the consideration of time.

The view of belief which I have been advocating contains little that is novel except the distinction of kinds of belief-feeling such as memory and expectation. Thus James says : " Everyone knows the difference between imagining a thing and believing in its existence, between supposing a proposition and acquiescing in its truth. . . . *In its inner nature, belief, or the sense of reality, is a sort of feeling more allied to the emotions than to anything else* " (*Psychology*, vol. ii, p. 283. James's italics). He proceeds to point out that drunkenness, and, still more, nitrous-oxide intoxication, will heighten the sense of belief : in the latter case, he says, a man's very soul may sweat with conviction, and he be all the time utterly unable to say what he is convinced of. It would seem that, in such cases, the feeling of belief exists unattached, without its usual relation to a content believed, just as the feeling of familiarity may sometimes occur without being related to any definite familiar object. The feeling of belief, when it occurs in this separated heightened form, generally leads us to look for a content to which to attach it. Much of what passes for revelation or mystic insight probably comes in this way : the belief-feeling, in abnormal strength, attaches itself, more or less accidentally, to some content which we happen to think of at the appropriate moment. But this is only a speculation, upon which I do not wish to lay too much stress.

LECTURE XIII

TRUTH AND FALSEHOOD

THE definition of truth and falsehood, which is our topic to-day, lies strictly outside our general subject, namely the analysis of mind. From the psychological standpoint, there may be different kinds of belief, and different degrees of certainty, but there cannot be any purely psychological means of distinguishing between true and false beliefs. A belief is rendered true or false by relation to a fact, which may lie outside the experience of the person entertaining the belief. Truth and falsehood, except in the case of beliefs about our own minds, depend upon the relations of mental occurrences to outside things, and thus take us beyond the analysis of mental occurrences as they are in themselves. Nevertheless, we can hardly avoid the consideration of truth and falsehood. We wish to believe that our beliefs, sometimes at least, yield *knowledge*, and a belief does not yield knowledge unless it is true. The question whether our minds are instruments of knowledge, and, if so, in what sense, is so vital that any suggested analysis of mind must be examined in relation to this question. To ignore this question would be like describing a chronometer without regard to its accuracy as a time-keeper, or a thermometer without mentioning the fact that it measures temperature.

Many difficult questions arise in connection with knowledge. It is difficult to define knowledge, difficult to decide whether we have any knowledge, and difficult, even if it is conceded that we sometimes have knowledge, to discover whether we can ever know that we have knowledge in this or that particular case. I shall divide the discussion into four parts :

I. We may regard knowledge, from a behaviourist standpoint, as exhibited in a certain kind of response to the environment. This response must have some characteristics which it shares with those of scientific instruments, but must also have others that are peculiar to knowledge. We shall find that this point of view is important, but not exhaustive of the nature of knowledge.

II. We may hold that the beliefs that constitute knowledge are distinguished from such as are erroneous or uncertain by properties which are intrinsic either to single beliefs or to systems of beliefs, being in either case discoverable without reference to outside fact. Views of this kind have been widely held among philosophers, but we shall find no reason to accept them.

III. We believe that some beliefs are true, and some false. This raises the problem of *verifiability* : are there any circumstances which can justifiably give us an unusual degree of certainty that such and such a belief is true ? It is obvious that there are circumstances which in fact cause a certainty of this sort, and we wish to learn what we can from examining these circumstances.

IV. Finally, there is the formal problem of defining truth and falsehood, and deriving the objective reference of a proposition from the meanings of its component words.

We will consider these four problems in succession.

I. We may regard a human being as an instrument, which makes various responses to various stimuli. If we observe these responses from outside, we shall regard them as showing knowledge when they display two characteristics, *accuracy* and *appropriateness*. These two are quite distinct, and even sometimes incompatible. If I am being pursued by a tiger, accuracy is furthered by turning round to look at him, but appropriateness by running away without making any search for further knowledge of the beast. I shall return to the question of appropriateness later; for the present it is accuracy that I wish to consider.

When we are viewing a man from the outside, it is not his beliefs, but his bodily movements, that we can observe. His knowledge must be inferred from his bodily movements, and especially from what he says and writes. For the present we may ignore beliefs, and regard a man's knowledge as actually consisting in what he says and does. That is to say, we will construct, as far as possible, a purely behaviouristic account of truth and falsehood.

If you ask a boy " What is twice two ? " and the boy says " four," you take that as *prima facie* evidence that the boy knows what twice two is. But if you go on to ask what is twice three, twice four, twice five, and so on, and the boy always answers " four," you come to the conclusion that he knows nothing about it. Exactly similar remarks apply to scientific instruments. I know a certain weather-cock which has the pessimistic habit of always pointing to the north-east. If you were to see it first on a cold March day, you would think it an excellent weather-cock ; but with the first warm day of spring your confidence would be shaken. The boy and the weather-cock have the same defect : they do not vary their response when the stimulus is varied. A good instrument, or a person with much knowledge, will give different responses to stimuli which differ in relevant ways. This is the first point in defining accuracy of response.

We will now assume another boy, who also, when you first question him, asserts that twice two is four. But with this boy, instead of asking him different questions, you make a practice of asking him the same question every day at breakfast. You find that he says five, or six, or seven, or any other number at random, and you conclude that he also does not know what twice two is, though by good luck he answered right the first time. This boy is like a weather-cock which, instead of being stuck fast, is always going round and round, changing without any change of wind. This boy and weather-cock have the opposite defect to that of the previous pair : they give different responses to stimuli which do not differ in any relevant way.

In connection with vagueness in memory, we already had occasion to consider the definition of accuracy. Omitting some of the niceties of our previous discussion, we may say that an instrument is *accurate* when it avoids the defects of the two boys and weather-cocks, that is to say, when—

(*a*) It gives different responses to stimuli which differ in relevant ways ;

(*b*) It gives the same response to stimuli which do not differ in relevant ways.

What are relevant ways depends upon the nature and purpose of the instrument. In the case of a weather-cock, the direction of the wind is relevant, but not its strength ; in the case of the boy, the meaning of the words of your question is relevant, but not the loudness of your voice, or whether you are his father or his school-master. If, however, you were a boy of his own age, that would be relevant, and the appropriate response would be different.

It is clear that knowledge is displayed by accuracy of response to certain kinds of stimuli, e.g. examinations. Can we say, conversely, that it consists wholly of such accuracy of response ? I do not think we can ; but we can go a certain distance in this direction. For this purpose we must define more carefully the kind of accuracy and the kind of response that may be expected where there is knowledge.

From our present point of view, it is difficult to exclude perception from knowledge ; at any rate, knowledge is displayed by actions based upon perception. A bird flying among trees avoids bumping into their branches ; its avoidance is a response to visual sensations. This response has the characteristic of accuracy, in the main, and leads us to say that the bird " knows," by sight, what objects are in its neighbourhood. For a behaviourist, this must certainly count as knowledge, however it may be viewed by analytic psychology. In this case, what is known, roughly, is the stimulus ; but in more advanced knowledge the stimulus and what is known become different. For example, you look in your calendar and find that Easter will be early next year. Here the stimulus is the calendar, whereas the response concerns the future. Even this can be paralleled among instru-ments : the behaviour of the barometer has a present stimulus, but foretells the future, so that the barometer might be said, in a sense, to know the future. However that may be, the point I am emphasizing as regards knowledge is that what is known may be quite different from the stimulus, and no part of the cause of the knowledge-response. It is only in sense-knowledge that the stimulus and what is known are, with qualifications, identifiable. In knowledge of the future, it is obvious that they are totally distinct, since otherwise the response would precede the stimulus. In abstract knowledge also they are distinct, since abstract facts have no date. In knowledge of the past there are complications, which we must briefly examine.

Every form of memory will be, from our present point of view, in one sense a delayed response. But this phrase does not quite clearly express what is meant. If you light a fuse and connect it with a heap of dynamite, the explosion of the dynamite may be spoken of, in a sense, as a delayed response to your lighting of the fuse. But that only means that it is a somewhat late portion of a continuous process of which the earlier parts have less emotional interest. This is not the case with habit. A display of habit has two sorts of causes : (*a*) the past occurrences which generated the habit, (*b*) the present occurrence which brings it into play. When you drop a weight on your toe, and say what you do say, the habit has been caused by imitation of your undesirable associates, whereas it is brought into play by the dropping of the weight. The great bulk of our knowledge is a habit in this sense : whenever I am asked when I was born, I reply correctly by mere habit. It would hardly be correct to say that getting born was the stimulus, and that my reply is a delayed response But in cases of memory this way of speaking would have an element of truth. In an habitual memory, the event remembered was clearly an essential part of the stimulus to the formation of the habit. The present stimulus which brings the habit into play produces a different response from that which it would produce if the habit did not exist. Therefore the habit enters into the causation of the response, and so do, at one remove, the causes of the habit. It follows that an event remembered is an essential part of the causes of our remembering.

In spite, however, of the fact that what is known is *sometimes* an indispensable part of the cause of the knowledge, this circumstance is, I think, irrelevant to the general question with which we are concerned, namely: What sort of response to what sort of stimulus can be regarded as displaying knowledge? There is one characteristic which the response must have, namely, it must consist of voluntary movements. The need of this characteristic is connected with the characteristic of *appropriateness*, which I do not wish to consider as yet. For the present I wish only to obtain a clearer idea of the sort of *accuracy* that a knowledge-response must have. It is clear from many instances that accuracy, in other cases, may be purely mechanical. The most complete form of accuracy consists in giving correct answers to questions, an achievement in which calculating machines far surpass human beings. In asking a question of a calculating machine, you must use its language: you must not address it in English, any more than you would address an Englishman in Chinese. But if you address it in the language it understands, it will tell you what is 34521 times 19987, without a moment's hesitation or a hint of inaccuracy. We do not say the machine *knows* the answer, because it has no purpose of its own in giving the answer: it does not wish to impress you with its cleverness, or feel proud of being such a good machine. But as far as mere accuracy goes, the machine leaves nothing to be desired.

Accuracy of response is a perfectly clear notion in the case of answers to questions, but in other cases it is much more obscure. We may say generally that an object whether animate or inanimate, is " sensitive " to a certain feature of the environment if it behaves differently according to the presence or absence of that feature. Thus iron is sensitive to anything magnetic. But sensitiveness does not constitute knowledge, and knowledge of a fact which is not sensible is not sensitiveness to *that* fact, as we have seen in distinguishing the fact known from the stimulus. As soon as we pass beyond the simple case of question and answer, the definition of knowledge by means of behaviour demands the consideration of purpose. A carrier pigeon flies home, and so we say it " knows " the way. But if it merely flew to some place at random, we should not say that it " knew " the way to that place, any more than a stone rolling down hill knows the way to the valley.

On the features which distinguish knowledge from accuracy of response in general, not much can be said from a behaviourist point of view without referring to purpose. But the necessity of *something* besides accuracy of response may be brought out by the following consideration : Suppose two persons, of whom one believed whatever the other disbelieved, and disbelieved whatever the other believed. So far as accuracy and sensitiveness of response alone are concerned, there would be nothing to choose between these two persons. A thermometer which went down for warm weather and up for cold might be just as accurate as the usual kind ; and a person who always believes falsely is just as sensitive an instrument as a person who always believes truly. The observable and practical difference between them would be that the one who always believed falsely would quickly come to a bad end. This illustrates once more that accuracy of response to stimulus does not alone show knowledge, but must be reinforced by appropriateness, i.e. suitability for realizing one's purpose. This applies even in the apparently simple case of answering questions : if the purpose of the answers is to deceive, their falsehood, not their truth, will be evidence of knowledge. The proportion of the combination of appropriateness with accuracy in the definition of knowledge is difficult ; it seems that both enter in, but that appropriateness is only required as regards the general type of response, not as regards each individual instance.

II. I have so far assumed as unquestionable the view that the truth or falsehood of a belief consists in a relation to a certain fact, namely the objective of the belief. This view has, however, been often questioned. Philosophers have sought some intrinsic criterion by which true and false beliefs could be distinguished.[1] I am

---

[1] The view that such a criterion exists is generally held by those whose views are in any degree derived from Hegel. It may be illustrated by the following passage from Lossky, *The Intuitive Basis of Knowledge* (Macmillan, 1919), p. 268 : " Strictly speaking, a false judgment is not a judgment at all. The predicate does not follow from the subject S alone, but from the subject plus a certain addition C, *which in no sense belongs to the content of the judgment.* What takes place may be a process of association of ideas, of imagining, or the like, but is not a process of judging. An experienced psychologist will be able by careful observation to detect that in this process there is wanting just the specific element of the objective dependence of the predicate upon the subject which is characteristic of a judgment. It must be admitted,

afraid their chief reason for this search has been the wish to feel more certainty than seems otherwise possible as to what is true and what is false. If we could discover the truth of a belief by examining its intrinsic characteristics, or those of some collection of beliefs of which it forms part, the pursuit of truth, it is thought, would be a less arduous business than it otherwise appears to be. But the attempts which have been made in this direction are not encouraging. I will take two criteria which have been suggested, namely, (1) self-evidence, (2) mutual coherence. If we can show that these are inadequate, we may feel fairly certain that no intrinsic criterion hitherto suggested will suffice to distinguish true from false beliefs.

(1) *Self-evidence.*—Some of our beliefs seem to be peculiarly indubitable. One might instance the belief that two and two are four, that two things cannot be in the same place at the same time, nor one thing in two places, or that a particular buttercup that we are seeing is yellow. The suggestion we are to examine is that such beliefs have some recognizable quality which secures their truth, and the truth of whatever is deduced from them according to self-evident principles of inference. This theory is set forth, for example, by Meinong in his book, *Ueber die Erfahrungsgrundlagen unseres Wissens.*

If this theory is to be logically tenable, self-evidence must not consist merely in the fact that we believe a proposition. We believe that our beliefs are sometimes erroneous, and we wish to be able to select a certain class of beliefs which are never erroneous. If we are

however, that an exceptional power of observation is needed in order to distinguish, by means of introspection, mere combinations of ideas from judgments."

to do this, it must be by some mark which belongs only
to certain beliefs, not to all ; and among those to which
it belongs there must be none that are mutually inconsistent.   If, for example, two propositions p and q were
self-evident, and it were also self-evident that p and q
could not both be true, that would condemn self-evidence
as a guarantee of truth.   Again, self-evidence must not
be the same thing as the absence of doubt or the presence
of complete certainty.   If we are completely certain of
a proposition, we do not seek a ground to support our
belief.   If self-evidence is alleged as a ground of belief,
that implies that doubt has crept in, and that our self-
evident proposition has not wholly resisted the assaults
of scepticism.   To say that any given person believes
some things so firmly that he cannot be made to doubt
them is no doubt true.   Such beliefs he will be willing
to use as premisses in reasoning, and to him personally
they will seem to have as much evidence as any belief
can need.   But among the propositions which one man
finds indubitable there will be some that another man
finds it quite possible to doubt.   It used to seem self-
evident that there could not be men at the Antipodes,
because they would fall off, or at best grow giddy from
standing on their heads.   But New Zealanders find the
falsehood of this proposition self-evident.   Therefore, if
self-evidence is a guarantee of truth, our ancestors must
have been mistaken in thinking their beliefs about the
Antipodes self-evident.   Meinong meets this difficulty
by saying that some beliefs are falsely thought to be
self-evident, but in the case of others it is self-evident
that they are self-evident, and these are wholly reliable.
Even this, however, does not remove the practical risk
of error, since we may mistakenly believe it self-evident

that a certain belief is self-evident. To remove all risk of error, we shall need an endless series of more and more complicated self-evident beliefs, which cannot possibly be realized in practice. It would seem, therefore, that self-evidence is useless as a practical criterion for insuring truth.

The same result follows from examining instances. If we take the four instances mentioned at the beginning of this discussion, we shall find that three of them are logical, while the fourth is a judgment of perception. The proposition that two and two are four follows by purely logical deduction from definitions : that means that its truth results, not from the properties of objects, but from the meanings of symbols. Now symbols, in mathematics, mean what we choose ; thus the feeling of self-evidence, in this case, seems explicable by the fact that the whole matter is within our control. I do not wish to assert that this is the whole truth about mathematical propositions, for the question is complicated, and I do not know what the whole truth is. But I do wish to suggest that the feeling of self-evidence in mathematical propositions has to do with the fact that they are concerned with the meanings of symbols, not with properties of the world such as external observation might reveal.

Similar considerations apply to the impossibility of a thing being in two places at once, or of two things being in one place at the same time. These impossibilities result logically, if I am not mistaken, from the definitions of one thing and one place. That is to say, they are not laws of physics, but only part of the intellectual apparatus which we have manufactured for manipulating physics. Their self-evidence, if this is so, lies merely in the fact that they represent our decision as to the use of words, not a property of physical objects.

Judgments of perception, such as "this buttercup is yellow," are in a quite different position from judgments of logic, and their self-evidence must have a different explanation. In order to arrive at the nucleus of such a judgment, we will eliminate, as far as possible, the use of words which take us beyond the present fact, such as "buttercup" and "yellow." The simplest kind of judgment underlying the perception that a buttercup is yellow would seem to be the perception of similarity in two colours seen simultaneously. Suppose we are seeing two buttercups, and we perceive that their colours are similar. This similarity is a physical fact, not a matter of symbols or words; and it certainly seems to be indubitable in a way that many judgments are not.

The first thing to observe, in regard to such judgments, is that as they stand they are vague. The word "similar" is a vague word, since there are degrees of similarity, and no one can say where similarity ends and dissimilarity begins. It is unlikely that our two buttercups have *exactly* the same colour, and if we judged that they had we should have passed altogether outside the region of self-evidence. To make our proposition more precise, let us suppose that we are also seeing a red rose at the same time. Then we may judge that the colours of the buttercups are more similar to each other than to the colour of the rose. This judgment seems more complicated, but has certainly gained in precision. Even now, however, it falls short of complete precision, since similarity is not *prima facie* measurable, and it would require much discussion to decide what we mean by greater or less similarity. To this process of the pursuit of precision there is strictly no limit.

The next thing to observe (although I do not personally doubt that most of our judgments of perception are true) is that it is very difficult to define any class of such judgments which can be known, by its intrinsic quality, to be always exempt from error. Most of our judgments of perception involve correlations, as when we judge that a certain noise is that of a passing cart. Such judgments are all obviously liable to error, since there is no correlation of which we have a right to be certain that it is invariable. Other judgments of perception are derived from recognition, as when we say " this is a buttercup," or even merely " this is yellow." All such judgments entail some risk of error, though sometimes perhaps a very small one ; some flowers that look like buttercups are marigolds, and colours that some would call yellow others might call orange. Our subjective certainty is usually a result of habit, and may lead us astray in circumstances which are unusual in ways of which we are unaware.

For such reasons, no form of self-evidence seems to afford an absolute criterion of truth. Nevertheless, it is perhaps true that judgments having a high degree of subjective certainty are more apt to be true than other judgments. But if this be the case, it is a result to be demonstrated, not a premiss from which to start in defining truth and falsehood. As an initial guarantee, therefore, neither self-evidence nor subjective certainty can be accepted as adequate.

(2) *Coherence.*—Coherence as the definition of truth is advocated by idealists, particularly by those who in the main follow Hegel. It is set forth ably in Mr. Joachim's

book, *The Nature of Truth* (Oxford, 1906). According to this view, any set of propositions other than the whole of truth can be condemned on purely logical grounds, as internally inconsistent ; a single proposition, if it is what we should ordinarily call false, contradicts itself irremediably, while if it is what we should ordinarily call true, it has implications which compel us to admit other propositions, which in turn lead to others, and so on, until we find ourselves committed to the whole of truth. One might illustrate by a very simple example : if I say " so-and-so is a married man," that is not a self-subsistent proposition. We cannot logically conceive of a universe in which this proposition constituted the whole of truth. There must be also someone who is a married woman, and who is married to the particular man in question. The view we are considering regards everything that can be said about any one object as relative in the same sort of way as " so-and-so is a married man." But everything, according to this view, is relative, not to one or two other things, but to all other things, so that from one bit of truth the whole can be inferred.

The fundamental objection to this view is logical, and consists in a criticism of its doctrine as to relations. I shall omit this line of argument, which I have developed elsewhere.[1] For the moment I will content myself with saying that the powers of logic seem to me very much less than this theory supposes. If it were taken seriously, its advocates ought to profess that any one truth is logically inferable from any other, and that, for example, the fact that Cæsar conquered Gaul, if

---

[1] In the article on " The Monistic Theory of Truth " in *Philosophical Essays* (Longmans, 1910), reprinted from the Proceedings of the Aristotelian Society, 1906–7.

adequately considered, would enable us to discover what the weather will be to-morrow. No such claim is put forward in practice, and the necessity of empirical observation is not denied; but according to the theory it ought to be.

Another objection is that no endeavour is made to show that we cannot form a consistent whole composed partly or wholly of false propositions, as in a novel. Leibniz's conception of many possible worlds seems to accord much better with modern logic and with the practical empiricism which is now universal. The attempt to deduce the world by pure thought is attractive, and in former times was largely supposed capable of success. But nowadays most men admit that beliefs must be tested by observation, and not merely by the fact that they harmonize with other beliefs. A consistent fairy-tale is a different thing from truth, however elaborate it may be. But to pursue this topic would lead us into difficult technicalities; I shall therefore assume, without further argument, that coherence is not sufficient as a definition of truth.

III. Many difficult problems arise as regards the verifiability of beliefs. We believe various things, and while we believe them we think we know them. But it sometimes turns out that we were mistaken, or at any rate we come to think we were. We must be mistaken either in our previous opinion or in our subsequent re-cantation; therefore our beliefs are not all correct, and there are cases of belief which are not cases of knowledge. The question of verifiability is in essence this: can we discover any set of beliefs which are never mistaken or any test which, when applicable, will always enable us to discriminate between true and false beliefs? Put thus broadly and abstractly, the answer must be negative. There is no way hitherto discovered of wholly eliminating the risk of error, and no infallible criterion. If we believe we have found a criterion, this belief itself may be mistaken ; we should be begging the question if we tried to test the criterion by applying the criterion to itself.

But although the notion of an absolute criterion is chimerical, there may be relative criteria, which increase the probability of truth. Common sense and science hold that there are. Let us see what they have to say.

One of the plainest cases of verification, perhaps ultimately the only case, consists in the happening of something expected. You go to the station believing that there will be a train at a certain time ; you find the train, you get into it, and it starts at the expected time This constitutes verification, and is a perfectly definite experience. It is, in a sense, the converse of memory : instead of having first sensations and then images accompanied by belief, we have first images accompanied by belief and then sensations. Apart from differences as to the time-order and the accompanying feelings, the relation between image and sensation is closely similar in the two cases of memory and expectation ; it is a relation of similarity, with difference as to causal efficacy— broadly, the image has the psychological but not the physical effects that the sensation would have. When an image accompanied by an expectation-belief is thus succeeded by a sensation which is the " meaning " of the image, we say that the expectation-belief has been verified. The experience of verification in this sense is exceedingly familiar ; it happens every time that accustomed activities have results that are not surprising, in eating and walking and talking and all our daily pursuits.

But although the experience in question is common, it is not wholly easy to give a theoretical account of it. How do we know that the sensation resembles the previous image ? Does the image persist in presence of the sensation, so that we can compare the two ? And even if *some* image does persist, how do we know that it is the previous image unchanged ? It does not seem as if this line of inquiry offered much hope of a successful issue. It is better, I think, to take a more external and causal view of the relation of expectation to expected occurrence. If the occurrence, when it comes, gives us the feeling of expectedness, and if the expectation, beforehand, enabled us to act in a way which proves appropriate to the occurrence, that must be held to constitute the maximum of verification. We have first an expectation, then a sensation with the feeling of expectedness related to memory of the expectation. This whole experience, when it occurs, may be defined as verification, and as constituting the truth of the expectation. Appropriate action, during the period of expectation, may be regarded as additional verification, but is not essential. The whole process may be illustrated by looking up a familiar quotation, finding it in the expected words, and in the expected part of the book. In this case we can strengthen the verification by writing down beforehand the words which we expect to find.

I think all verification is ultimately of the above sort. We verify a scientific hypothesis indirectly, by deducing consequences as to the future, which subsequent experience confirms. If somebody were to doubt whether Cæsar had crossed the Rubicon, verification could only be obtained from the future. We could proceed to display manuscripts to our historical sceptic, in which it was said that Cæsar had behaved in this way. We could advance arguments, verifiable by future experience, to prove the antiquity of the manuscript from its texture, colour, etc. We could find inscriptions agreeing with the historian on other points, and tending to show his general accuracy. The causal laws which our arguments would assume could be verified by the future occurrence of events inferred by means of them. The existence and persistence of causal laws, it is true, must be regarded as a fortunate accident, and how long it will continue we cannot tell. Meanwhile verification remains often practically possible. And since it is sometimes possible, we can gradually discover what kinds of beliefs tend to be verified by experience, and what kinds tend to be falsified; to the former kinds we give an increased degree of assent, to the latter kinds a diminished degree. The process is not absolute or infallible, but it has been found capable of sifting beliefs and building up science. It affords no theoretical refutation of the sceptic, whose position must remain logically unassailable; but if complete scepticism is rejected, it gives the practical method by which the system of our beliefs grows gradually towards the unattainable ideal of impeccable knowledge.

IV. I come now to the purely formal definition of the truth or falsehood of a belief. For this definition it is necessary first of all to consider the derivation of the objective reference of a proposition from the meanings of its component words or images.

Just as a word has meaning, so a proposition has an objective reference. The objective reference of a proposition is a function (in the mathematical sense) of the meanings of its component words. But the objective reference differs from the meaning of a word through the duality of truth and falsehood. You may believe the proposition " to-day is Tuesday " both when, in fact, to-day is Tuesday, and when to-day is not Tuesday. If to-day is not Tuesday, this fact is the objective of your belief that to-day is Tuesday. But obviously the relation of your belief to the fact is different in this case from what it is in the case when to-day is Tuesday. We may say, metaphorically, that when to-day is Tuesday, your belief that it is Tuesday points *towards* the fact, whereas when to-day is not Tuesday your belief points *away from* the fact. Thus the objective reference of a belief is not determined by the fact alone, but by the direction of the belief towards or away from the fact.[1] If, on a Tuesday, one man believes that it is Tuesday while another believes that it is not Tuesday, their beliefs have the same objective, namely the fact that it is Tuesday, but the true belief points towards the fact while the false one points away from it. Thus, in order to define the reference of a proposition we have to take account not only of the objective, but also of the direction of pointing, towards the objective in the case of a true proposition and away from it in the case of a false one.

This mode of stating the nature of the objective reference of a proposition is necessitated by the circumstance that there are true and false propositions, but not true and false facts. If to-day is Tuesday, there is not a false objective " to-day is not Tuesday," which could be the objective of the false belief " to-day is not Tuesday." This is the reason why two beliefs which are each other's contradictories have the same objective. There is, however, a practical inconvenience, namely that we cannot

[1] I owe this way of looking at the matter to my friend Ludwig Wittgenstein.

determine the objective reference of a proposition, according to this definition, unless we know whether the proposition is true or false. To avoid this inconvenience, it is better to adopt a slightly different phraseology, and say: The " meaning " of the proposition " to-day is Tuesday " consists in pointing to the fact " to-day is Tuesday " if that is a fact, or away from the fact " to-day is not Tuesday " if that is a fact. The " meaning " of the proposition " to-day is not Tuesday " will be exactly the opposite. By this hypothetical form we are able to speak of the meaning of a proposition without knowing whether it is true or false. According to this definition, we know the meaning of a proposition when we know what would make it true and what would make it false, even if we do not know whether it is in fact true or false.

The meaning of a proposition is derivative from the meanings of its constituent words. Propositions occur in pairs, distinguished (in simple cases) by the absence or presence of the word " not." Two such propositions have the same objective, but opposite meanings : when one is true, the other is false, and when one is false, the other is true.

The purely formal definition of truth and falsehood offers little difficulty. What is required is a formal expression of the fact that a proposition is true when it points towards its objective, and false when it points away from it. In very simple cases we can give a very simple account of this : we can say that true propositions actually resemble their objectives in a way in which false propositions do not. But for this purpose it is necessary to revert to image-propositions instead of word-propositions. Let us take again the illustration of a memory-image of a familiar room, and let us suppose

that in the image the window is to the left of the door.
If in fact the window is to the left of the door, there is
a correspondence between the image and the objective;
there is the same relation between the window and the
door as between the images of them. The image-memory
consists of the image of the window to the left of the
image of the door. When this is true, the very same
relation relates the terms of the objective (namely the
window and the door) as relates the images which mean
them. In this case the correspondence which constitutes
truth is very simple.

In the case we have just been considering the objective consists of two parts with a certain relation (that
of left-to-right), and the proposition consists of images
of these parts with the very same relation. The same
proposition, if it were false, would have a less simple
formal relation to its objective. If the image-proposition
consists of an image of the window to the left of an image
of the door, while in fact the window is not to the left
of the door, the proposition does not result from the
objective by the mere substitution of images for their
prototypes. Thus in this unusually simple case we can
say that a true proposition " corresponds " to its objective
in a formal sense in which a false proposition does not.
Perhaps it may be possible to modify this notion of formal
correspondence in such a way as to be more widely applicable, but if so, the modifications required will be
by no means slight. The reasons for this must now be
considered.

To begin with, the simple type of correspondence we
have been exhibiting can hardly occur when words are
substituted for images, because, in word-propositions,
relations are usually expressed by words, which are

not themselves relations. Take such a proposition as " Socrates precedes Plato." Here the word " precedes " is just as solid as the words " Socrates " and " Plato " ; it *means* a relation, but is not a relation. Thus the objective which makes our proposition true consists of *two* terms with a relation between them, whereas our proposition consists of *three* terms with a relation of order between them. Of course, it would be perfectly possible, theoretically, to indicate a few chosen relations, not by words, but by relations between the other words. " Socrates–Plato " might be used to mean " Socrates precedes Plato " ; " Pla-Socrates-to " might be used to mean " Plato was born before Socrates and died after him " ; and so on. But the possibilities of such a method would be very limited. For aught I know, there may be languages that use it, but they are not among the languages with which I am acquainted. And in any case, in view of the multiplicity of relations that we wish to express, no language could advance far without words for relations. But as soon as we have words for relations, word-propositions have necessarily more terms than the facts to which they refer, and cannot therefore correspond so simply with their objectives as some image-propositions can.

The consideration of negative propositions and negative facts introduces further complications. An image-proposition is necessarily positive : we can image the window to the left of the door, or to the right of the door, but we can form no image of the bare negative " the window not to the left of the door." We can *disbelieve* the image-proposition expressed by " the window to the left of the door," and our disbelief will be true if the window is not to the left of the door. But we can form no image of the fact that the window is not to the left of the door. Attempts have often been made to deny such negative facts, but, for reasons which I have given elsewhere,[1] I believe these attempts to be mistaken, and I shall assume that there are negative facts.

Word-propositions, like image-propositions, are always positive facts. The fact that Socrates precedes Plato is symbolized in English by the fact that the word " precedes " occurs between the words "Socrates" and "Plato." But we cannot symbolize the fact that Plato does not precede Socrates by not putting the word "precedes" between "Plato" and "Socrates." A negative fact is not sensible, and language, being intended for communication, has to be sensible. Therefore we symbolize the fact that Plato does not precede Socrates by putting the words "does not precede" between "Plato" and "Socrates." We thus obtain a series of words which is just as positive a fact as the series "Socrates precedes Plato." The propositions asserting negative facts are themselves positive facts; they are merely different positive facts from those asserting positive facts.

We have thus, as regards the opposition of positive and negative, three different sorts of duality, according as we are dealing with facts, image-propositions, or word-propositions. We have, namely :

(1) Positive and negative facts ;
(2) Image-propositions, which may be believed or disbelieved, but do not allow any duality of content corresponding to positive and negative facts ;

[1] *Monist*, January, 1919, p. 42 ff.

(3) Word-propositions, which are always positive facts, but are of two kinds: one verified by a positive objective, the other by a negative objective.

Owing to these complications, the simplest type of correspondence is impossible when either negative facts or negative propositions are involved.

Even when we confine ourselves to relations between two terms which are both imaged, it may be impossible to form an image-proposition in which the relation of the terms is represented by the same relation of the images. Suppose we say " Cæsar was 2,000 years before Foch," we express a certain temporal relation between Cæsar and Foch ; but we cannot allow 2,000 years to elapse between our image of Cæsar and our image of Foch. This is perhaps not a fair example, since " 2,000 years before " is not a direct relation. But take a case where the relation is direct, say, " the sun is brighter than the moon." We can form visual images of sunshine and moonshine, and it may happen that our image of the sunshine is the brighter of the two, but this is by no means either necessary or sufficient. The act of comparison, implied in our judgment, is something more than the mere co-existence of two images, one of which is in fact brighter than the other. It would take us too far from our main topic if we were to go into the question what actually occurs when we make this judgment. Enough has been said to show that the correspondence between the belief and its objective is more complicated in this case than in that of the window to the left of the door, and this was all that had to be proved.

In spite of these complications, the general nature of

the formal correspondence which makes truth is clear from our instances. In the case of the simpler kind of propositions, namely those that I call "atomic" propositions, where there is only one word expressing a relation, the objective which would verify our proposition, assuming that the word "not" is absent, is obtained by replacing each word by what it means, the word meaning a relation being replaced by this relation among the meanings of the other words. For example, if the proposition is "Socrates precedes Plato," the objective which verifies it results from replacing the word "Socrates" by Socrates, the word "Plato" by Plato, and the word "precedes" by the relation of preceding between Socrates and Plato. If the result of this process is a fact, the proposition is true; if not, it is false. When our proposition is "Socrates does not precede Plato," the conditions of truth and falsehood are exactly reversed. More complicated propositions can be dealt with on the same lines. In fact, the purely formal question, which has occupied us in this last section, offers no very formidable difficulties.

I do not believe that the above formal theory is untrue, but I do believe that it is inadequate. It does not, for example, throw any light upon our preference for true beliefs rather than false ones. This preference is only explicable by taking account of the causal efficacy of beliefs, and of the greater appropriateness of the responses resulting from true beliefs. But appropriateness depends upon purpose, and purpose thus becomes a vital part of theory of knowledge.

LECTURE XIV

EMOTIONS AND WILL

On the two subjects of the present lecture I have nothing original to say, and I am treating them only in order to complete the discussion of my main thesis, namely that all psychic phenomena are built up out of sensations and images alone.

Emotions are traditionally regarded by psychologists as a separate class of mental occurrences : I am, of course, not concerned to deny the obvious fact that they have characteristics which make a special investigation of them necessary. What I am concerned with is the analysis of emotions. It is clear that an emotion is essentially complex, and we have to inquire whether it ever contains any non-physiological material not reducible to sensations and images and their relations.

Although what specially concerns us is the analysis of emotions, we shall find that the more important topic is the physiological causation of emotions. This is a subject upon which much valuable and exceedingly interesting work has been done, whereas the bare analysis of emotions has proved somewhat barren. In view of the fact that we have defined perceptions, sensations, and images by their physiological causation, it is evident that our problem of the analysis of the emotions is bound up with the problem of their physiological causation.

Modern views on the causation of emotions begin with what is called the James-Lange theory. James states this view in the following terms (*Psychology*, vol. ii, p. 449) :

" Our natural way of thinking about these coarser emotions, grief, fear, rage, love, is that the mental perception of some fact excites the mental affection called the emotion, and that this latter state of mind gives rise to the bodily expression.   My theory, on the contrary, is that *the bodily changes follow directly the perception of the exciting fact, and that our feeling of the same changes as they occur IS the emotion* (James's italics).   Common sense says : we lose our fortune, are sorry and weep ; we meet a bear, are frightened and run ; we are insulted by a rival, are angry and strike.   The hypothesis here to be defended says that this order of sequence is incorrect, that the one mental state is not immediately induced by the other, that the bodily manifestations must first be interposed between, and that the more rational statement is that we feel sorry because we cry, angry because we strike, afraid because we tremble, and not that we cry, strike, or tremble, because we are sorry, angry, or fearful, as the case may be.   Without the bodily states following on the perception, the latter would be purely cognitive in form, pale, colourless, destitute of emotional warmth."

Round this hypothesis a very voluminous literature has grown up.   The history of its victory over earlier criticism, and its difficulties with the modern experimental work of Sherrington and Cannon, is well told by James R. Angell in an article called " A Reconsideration of

James's Theory of Emotion in the Light of Recent Criticisms."[1] In this article Angell defends James's theory and to me—though I speak with diffidence on a question as to which I have little competence—it appears that his defence is on the whole successful.

Sherrington, by experiments on dogs, showed that many of the usual marks of emotion were present in their behaviour even when, by severing the spinal cord in the lower cervical region, the viscera were cut off from all communication with the brain except that existing through certain cranial nerves. He mentions the various signs which "contributed to indicate the existence of an emotion as lively as the animal had ever shown us before the spinal operation had been made."[2] He infers that the physiological condition of the viscera cannot be the cause of the emotion displayed under such circumstances, and concludes : " We are forced back toward the likelihood that the visceral expression of emotion is *secondary* to the cerebral action occurring with the psychical state. . . . We may with James accept visceral and organic sensations and the memories and associations of them as contributory to primitive emotion, but we must regard them as re-enforcing rather than as initiating the psychosis."[2]

Angell suggests that the display of emotion in such cases may be due to past experience, generating habits which would require only the stimulation of cerebral reflex arcs. Rage and some forms of fear, however, may, he thinks, gain expression without the brain. Rage and fear have been especially studied by Cannon, whose work is of the greatest importance. His results are given in

[1] *Psychological Review*, 1916.
[2] Quoted by Angell, *loc. cit.*

his book, *Bodily Changes in Pain, Hunger, Fear and Rage*
(D. Appleton and Co., 1916).

The most interesting part of Cannon's book consists
in the investigation of the effects produced by secretion
of adrenin. Adrenin is a substance secreted into the
blood by the adrenal glands. These are among the
ductless glands, the functions of which, both in physiology
and in connection with the emotions, have only come to
be known during recent years. Cannon found that pain,
fear and rage occurred in circumstances which affected
the supply of adrenin, and that an artificial injection
of adrenin could, for example, produce all the symptoms
of fear. He studied the effects of adrenin on various
parts of the body ; he found that it causes the pupils to
dilate, hairs to stand erect, bloodvessels to be constricted,
and so on. These effects were still produced if the parts
in question were removed from the body and kept alive
artificially.[1]

Cannon's chief argument against James is, if I understand him rightly, that similar affections of the viscera
may accompany dissimilar emotions, especially fear and
rage. Various different emotions make us cry, and
therefore it cannot be true to say, as James does, that
we " feel sorry because we cry," since sometimes we cry
when we feel glad. This argument, however, is by no
means conclusive against James, because it cannot be
shown that there are *no* visceral differences for different
emotions, and indeed it is unlikely that this is the case.

[1] Cannon's work is not unconnected with that of Mosso, who
maintains, as the result of much experimental work, that " the
seat of the emotions lies in the sympathetic nervous system."
An account of the work of both these men will be found in God-
dard's *Psychology of the Normal and Sub-normal* (Kegan Paul,
1919), chap. vii and Appendix.

As Angell says (*loc. cit.*) : " Fear and joy may both cause cardiac palpitation, but in one case we find high tonus of the skeletal muscles, in the other case relaxation and the general sense of weakness."

Angell's conclusion, after discussing the experiments of Sherrington and Cannon, is : " I would therefore submit that, so far as concerns the critical suggestions by these two psychologists, James's essential contentions are not materially affected." If it were necessary for me to take sides on this question, I should agree with this conclusion ; but I think my thesis as to the analysis of emotion can be maintained without coming to a probably premature conclusion upon the doubtful parts of the physiological problem.

According to our definitions, if James is right, an emotion may be regarded as involving a confused perception of the viscera concerned in its causation, while if Cannon and Sherrington are right, an emotion involves a confused perception of its external stimulus. This follows from what was said in Lecture VII. We there defined a perception as an appearance, however irregular, of one or more objects external to the brain. And in order to be an appearance of one or more objects, it is only necessary that the occurrence in question should be connected with them by a continuous chain, and should vary when they are varied sufficiently. Thus the question whether a mental occurrence can be called a perception turns upon the question whether anything can be inferred from it as to its causes outside the brain : if such inference is possible, the occurrence in question will come within our definition of a perception. And in that case, according to the definition in Lecture VIII, its non-mnemic elements will be sensations. Accordingly, whether emotions are caused by changes in the viscera or by sensible objects, they contain elements which are sensations according to our definition.

An emotion in its entirety is, of course, something much more complex than a perception. An emotion is essentially a process, and it will be only what one may call a cross-section of the emotion that will be a perception, of a bodily condition according to James, or (in certain cases) of an external object according to his opponents. An emotion in its entirety contains dynamic elements, such as motor impulses, desires, pleasures and pains. Desires and pleasures and pains, according to the theory adopted in Lecture III, are characteristics of processes, not separate ingredients. An emotion—rage, for example—will be a certain kind of process, consisting of perceptions and (in general) bodily movements. The desires and pleasures and pains involved are properties of this process, not separate items in the stuff of which the emotion is composed. The dynamic elements in an emotion, if we are right in our analysis, contain, from our point of view, no ingredients beyond those contained in the processes considered in Lecture III. The ingredients of an emotion are only sensations and images and bodily movements succeeding each other according to a certain pattern. With this conclusion we may leave the emotions and pass to the consideration of the will.

The first thing to be defined when we are dealing with Will is a *voluntary movement*. We have already defined vital movements, and we have maintained that, from a behaviourist standpoint, it is impossible to distinguish which among such movements are reflex and which voluntary. Nevertheless, there certainly is a distinction. When we decide in the morning that it is time to get up, our consequent movement is voluntary. The beating of the heart, on the other hand, is involuntary : we can neither cause it nor prevent it by any decision of our own, except indirectly, as e.g. by drugs. Breathing is intermediate between the two : we normally breathe without the help of the will, but we can alter or stop our breathing if we choose.

James (*Psychology*, chap. xxvi) maintains that the only distinctive characteristic of a voluntary act is that it involves an idea of the movement to be performed, made up of memory-images of the kinæsthetic sensations which we had when the same movement occurred on some former occasion. He points out that, on this view, no movement can be made voluntarily unless it has previously occurred involuntarily.[1]

I see no reason to doubt the correctness of this view. We shall say, then, that movements which are accompanied by kinæsthetic sensations tend to be caused by the images of those sensations, and when so caused are called *voluntary*.

Volition, in the emphatic sense, involves something more than voluntary movement. The sort of case I am thinking of is decision after deliberation. Voluntary movements are a part of this, but not the whole. There is, in addition to them, a judgment : " This is what I shall do " ; there is also a sensation of tension during doubt, followed by a different sensation at the moment of deciding. I see no reason whatever to suppose that there is any specifically new ingredient ; sensations and images, with their relations and causal laws, yield all that seems to be wanted for the analysis of the will, together with the fact that kinæsthetic images tend to cause

[1] *Psychology*, vol. ii, pp. 492-3.

the movements with which they are connected. Conflict of desires is of course essential in the causation of the emphatic kind of will : there will be for a time kinæsthetic images of incompatible movements, followed by the exclusive image of the movement which is said to be willed. Thus will seems to add no new irreducible ingredient to the analysis of the mind.

LECTURE XV

CHARACTERISTICS OF MENTAL PHENOMENA

AT the end of our journey it is time to return to the
question from which we set out, namely: What is it
that characterizes mind as opposed to matter? Or,
to state the same question in other terms: How is
psychology to be distinguished from physics? The
answer provisionally suggested at the outset of our inquiry was that psychology and physics are distinguished
by the nature of their causal laws, not by their subject
matter. At the same time we held that there is a certain
subject matter, namely images, to which only psychological causal laws are applicable; this subject matter,
therefore, we assigned exclusively to psychology. But we
found no way of defining images except through their
causation; in their intrinsic character they appeared
to have no universal mark by which they could be
distinguished from sensations.

In this last lecture I propose to pass in review various
suggested methods of distinguishing mind from matter.
I shall then briefly sketch the nature of that fundamental
science which I believe to be the true metaphysic, in
which mind and matter alike are seen to be constructed
out of a neutral stuff, whose causal laws have no such
duality as that of psychology, but form the basis upon
which both physics and psychology are built.

In search for the definition of "mental phenomena," let us begin with "consciousness," which is often thought to be the essence of mind.   In the first lecture I gave various arguments against the view that consciousness is fundamental, but I did not attempt to say what consciousness is. We must find a definition of it, if we are to feel secure in deciding that it is not fundamental. It is for the sake of the proof that it is not fundamental that we must now endeavour to decide what it is.

"Consciousness," by those who regard it as fundamental, is taken to be a character diffused throughout our mental life, distinct from sensations and images, memories, beliefs and desires, but present in all of them.[1] Dr. Henry Head, in an article which I quoted in Lecture III, distinguishing sensations from purely physiological occurrences, says : "Sensation, in the strict sense of the term, demands the existence of consciousness" (p. 184). This statement, at first sight, is one to which we feel inclined to assent, but I believe we are mistaken if we do so. Sensation is the sort of thing of which we *may* be conscious, but not a thing of which we *must* be conscious. We have been led, in the course of our inquiry, to admit unconscious beliefs and unconscious desires. There is, so far as I can see, no class of mental or other occurrences of which we are always conscious whenever they happen.

The first thing to notice is that consciousness must be *of* something.   In view of this, I should define "consciousness" in terms of that relation of an image or a word to an object which we defined, in Lecture XI, as "meaning."   When a sensation is followed by an

[1] Cf. Lecture VI.

image which is a " copy " of it, I think it may be said that the existence of the image constitutes consciousness of the sensation, provided it is accompanied by that sort of belief which, when we reflect upon it, makes us feel that the image is a " sign " of something other than itself. This is the sort of belief which, in the case of memory, we expressed in the words " this occurred " ; or which, in the case of a judgment of perception, makes us believe in qualities correlated with present sensations, as e.g., tactile and visual qualities are correlated. The addition of some element of belief seems required, since mere imagination does not involve consciousness of anything, and there can be no consciousness which is not of something. If images alone constituted consciousness of their prototypes, such imagination-images as in fact have prototypes would involve con-sciousness of them ; since this is not the case, an element of belief must be added to the images in defining consciousness. The belief must be of that sort that constitutes objective reference, past or present. An image, together with a belief of this sort concerning it, constitutes, according to our definition, consciousness of the prototype of the image.

But when we pass from consciousness of sensations to consciousness of objects of perception, certain further points arise which demand an addition to our definition. A judgment of perception, we may say, consists of a core of sensation, together with associated images, with belief in the present existence of an object to which sensation and images are referred in a way which is difficult to analyse. Perhaps we might say that the belief is not fundamentally in any *present* existence, but is of the nature of an expectation : for example, when we see an object, we expect certain sensations to result if we proceed to touch it. Perception, then, will consist of a present sensation together with expectations of future sensations. (This, of course, is a reflective analysis, not an account of the way perception appears to unchecked introspection.) But all such expectations are liable to be erroneous, since they are based upon correlations which are usual but not invariable. Any such correlation may mislead us in a particular case, for example, if we try to touch a reflection in a looking-glass under the impression that it is " real." Since memory is fallible, a similar difficulty arises as regards consciousness of past objects. It would seem odd to say that we can be " conscious " of a thing which does not or did not exist. The only way to avoid this awkward-ness is to add to our definition the proviso that the beliefs involved in consciousness must be *true*.

In the second place, the question arises as to whether we can be conscious of images. If we apply our definition to this case, it seems to demand images of images. In order, for example, to be conscious of an image of a cat, we shall require, according to the letter of the defini-tion, an image which is a copy of our image of the cat, and has this image for its prototype. Now, it hardly seems probable, as a matter of observation, that there are images of images, as opposed to images of sensations. We may meet this difficulty in two ways, either by boldly denying consciousness of images, or by finding a sense in which, by means of a different accompanying belief, an image, instead of meaning its prototype, can mean another image of the same prototype.

The first alternative, which denies consciousness of images, has already been discussed when we were dealing with Introspection in Lecture VI. We then decided that there must be, in some sense, consciousness of images. We are therefore left with the second suggested way of dealing with knowledge of images. According to this second hypothesis, there may be two images of the same prototype, such that one of them means the other, instead of meaning the prototype. It will be remembered that we defined meaning by association: a word or image means an object, we said, when it has the same associations as the object. But this definition must not be interpreted too absolutely: a word or image will not have *all* the same associations as the object which it means. The word "cat" may be associated with the word "mat," but it would not happen except by accident that a cat would be associated with a mat. And in like manner an image may have certain associations which its prototype will not have, e.g. an association with the word "image." When these associations are active, an image means an image, instead of meaning its prototype. If I have had images of a given prototype many times, I can mean one of these, as opposed to the rest, by recollecting the time and place or any other distinctive association of that one occasion. This happens, for example, when a place recalls to us some thought we previously had in that place, so that we remember a thought as opposed to the occurrence to which it referred. Thus we may say that we think of an image A when we have a similar image B associated with recollections of circumstances connected with A, but not with its prototype or with other images of the same prototype. In this way we become aware of images without the need of any new store of mental contents, merely by the help of new associations. This theory, so far as I can see, solves the problems of introspective knowledge, without requiring heroic measures such as those proposed by Knight Dunlap, whose views we discussed in Lecture VI.

According to what we have been saying, sensation itself is not an instance of consciousness, though the immediate memory by which it is apt to be succeeded is so. A sensation which is remembered becomes an object of consciousness as soon as it begins to be remembered, which will normally be almost immediately after its occurrence (if at all) ; but while it exists it is not an object of consciousness. If, however, it is part of a perception, say of some familiar person, we may say that the person perceived is an object of consciousness. For in this case the sensation is a *sign* of the perceived object in much the same way in which a memory-image is a sign of a remembered object. The essential practical function of " consciousness " and " thought " is that they enable us to act with reference to what is distant in time or space, even though it is not at present stimulating our senses. This reference to absent objects is possible through association and habit. Actual sensations, in themselves, are not cases of consciousness, because they do not bring in this reference to what is absent. But their connection with consciousness is very close, both through immediate memory, and through the correlations which turn sensations into perceptions.

Enough has, I hope, been said to show that consciousness is far too complex and accidental to be taken as the fundamental characteristic of mind. We have seen that belief and images both enter into it. Belief itself, as we saw in an earlier lecture, is complex. Therefore, if any definition of mind is suggested by our analysis of consciousness, images are what would naturally suggest themselves. But since we found that images can only be defined causally, we cannot deal with this suggestion, except in connection with the difference between physical and psychological causal laws.

I come next to those characteristics of mental phenomena which arise out of mnemic causation. The possibility of action with reference to what is not sensibly present is one of the things that might be held to characterize mind. Let us take first a very elementary example. Suppose you are in a familiar room at night, and suddenly the light goes out. You will be able to find your way to the door without much difficulty by means of the picture of the room which you have in your mind. In this case visual images serve, somewhat imperfectly it is true, the purpose which visual sensations would otherwise serve. The stimulus to the production of visual images is the desire to get out of the room, which, according to what we found in Lecture III, consists essentially of present sensations and motor impulses caused by them. Again, words heard or read enable you to act with reference to the matters about which they give information ; here, again, a present sensible stimulus, in virtue of habits formed in the past, enables you to act in a manner appropriate to an object which is not sensibly present. The whole essence of the practical efficiency of " thought " consists in sensitiveness to *signs*: the sensible presence of A, which is a sign of the present or future existence of B, enables us to act in a manner appropriate to B. Of this, words are the supreme example, since their effects as signs are prodigious, while their intrinsic interest as sensible occurrences on their own account is usually very slight.

The operation of signs may or may not be accompanied by consciousness. If a sensible stimulus A calls up an image of B, and we then act with reference to B, we have what may be called consciousness of B. But habit may enable us to act in a manner appropriate to B as soon as A appears, without ever having an image of B. In that case, although A operates as a sign, it operates without the help of consciousness. Broadly speaking, a very familiar sign tends to operate directly in this manner, and the intervention of consciousness marks an imperfectly established habit.

The power of acquiring experience, which characterizes men and animals, is an example of the general law that, in mnemic causation, the causal unit is not one event at one time, but two or more events at two or more times.[1] A burnt child fears the fire, that is to say, the neighbourhood of fire has a different effect upon a child which has had the sensations of burning than upon one which has not. More correctly, the observed effect, when a child which has been burnt is put near a fire, has for its cause, not merely the neighbourhood of the fire, but this together with the previous burning. The general formula, when an animal has acquired experience through some event A, is that, when B occurs at some future time, the animal to which A has happened acts differently from an animal which A has not happened. Thus A and B together, not either separately, must be regarded as the cause of the animal's behaviour, unless we take account of the effect which A has had in altering the animal's nervous tissue, which is a matter not patent to external observation except under very special circumstances. With this possibility, we are brought back to causal laws,

[1] Cf. Lecture IV.

and to the suggestion that many things which seem essentially mental are really neural. Perhaps it is the nerves that acquire experience rather than the mind. If so, the possibility of acquiring experience cannot be used to define mind.[1]

Very similar considerations apply to memory, if taken as the essence of mind. A recollection is aroused by something which is happening now, but is different from the effect which the present occurrence would have produced if the recollected event had not occurred. This may be accounted for by the physical effect of the past event on the brain, making it a different instrument from that which would have resulted from a different experience. The causal peculiarities of memory *may*, therefore, have a physiological explanation. With every special class of mental phenomena this possibility meets us afresh. If psychology is to be a separate science at all, we must seek a wider ground for its separateness than any that we have been considering hitherto.

We have found that "consciousness" is too narrow to characterize mental phenomena, and that mnemic causation is too wide. I come now to a characteristic which, though difficult to define, comes much nearer to what we require, namely subjectivity.

Subjectivity, as a characteristic of mental phenomena, was considered in Lecture VII, in connection with the definition of perception. We there decided that those particulars which constitute the physical world can be collected into sets in two ways, one of which makes a bundle of all those particulars that are appearances of a given thing from different places, while the other makes a bundle of all those particulars which are appear-

[1] Cf. Lecture IV.

ances of different things from a given place. A bundle of this latter sort, at a given time, is called a " perspective"; taken throughout a period of time, it is called a " biography." Subjectivity is the characteristic of perspectives and biographies, the characteristic of giving the view of the world from a certain place. We saw in Lecture VII that this characteristic involves none of the other characteristics that are commonly associated with mental phenomena, such as consciousness, experience and memory. We found in fact that it is exhibited by a photographic plate, and, strictly speaking, by any particular taken in conjunction with those which have the same " passive " place in the sense defined in Lecture VII. The particulars forming one perspective are connected together primarily by simultaneity ; those forming one biography, primarily by the existence of direct time-relations between them. To these are to be added relations derivable from the laws of perspective. In all this we are clearly not in the region of psychology, as commonly understood ; yet we are also hardly in the region of physics. And the definition of perspectives and biographies, though it does not yet yield anything that would be commonly called " mental," is presupposed in mental phenomena, for example in mnemic causation : the causal unit in mnemic causation, which gives rise to Semon's engram, is the whole of one perspective—not of *any* perspective, but of a perspective in a place where there is nervous tissue, or at any rate living tissue of some sort. Perception also, as we saw, can only be defined in terms of perspectives. Thus the conception of subjectivity, i.e. of the " passive " place of a particular, though not alone sufficient to define mind, is clearly an essential element in the definition.

I have maintained throughout these lectures that the data of psychology do not differ in their intrinsic character from the data of physics. I have maintained that sensations are data for psychology and physics equally, while images, which may be in some sense exclusively psychological data, can only be distinguished from sensations by their correlations, not by what they are in themselves. It is now necessary, however, to examine the notion of a " datum," and to obtain, if possible, a definition of this notion.

The notion of " data " is familiar throughout science, and is usually treated by men of science as though it were perfectly clear. Psychologists, on the other hand, find great difficulty in the conception. " Data " are naturally defined in terms of theory of knowledge : they are those propositions of which the truth is known without demonstration, so that they may be used as premisses in proving other propositions. Further, when a proposition which is a datum asserts the existence of something, we say that the something is a datum, as well as the proposition asserting its existence. Thus those objects of whose existence we become certain through perception are said to be data.

There is some difficulty in connecting this epistemological definition of " data " with our psychological analysis of knowledge ; but until such a connection has been effected, we have no right to use the conception " data."

It is clear, in the first place, that there can be no datum apart from a belief. A sensation which merely comes and goes is not a datum ; it only becomes a datum when it is remembered. Similarly, in perception, we do not have a datum unless we have a *judgment* of perception. In the sense in which objects (as opposed to propositions) are data, it would seem natural to say that those objects of which we are conscious are data. But consciousness, as we have seen, is a complex notion, involving beliefs, as well as mnemic phenomena such as are required for perception and memory. It follows that no datum is theoretically indubitable, since no belief is infallible; it follows also that every datum has a greater or less degree of vagueness, since there is always some vagueness in memory and the meaning of images.

Data are not those things of which our consciousness is earliest in time. At every period of life, after we have become capable of thought, some of our beliefs are obtained by inference, while others are not. A belief may pass from either of these classes into the other, and may therefore become, or cease to be, a belief giving a datum. When, in what follows, I speak of data, I do not mean the things of which we feel sure before scientific study begins, but the things which, when a science is well advanced, appear as affording grounds for other parts of the science, without themselves being believed on any ground except observation. I assume, that is to say, a trained observer, with an analytic attention, knowing the sort of thing to look for, and the sort of thing that will be important. What he observes is, at the stage of science which he has reached, a datum for his science. It is just as sophisticated and elaborate as the theories which he bases upon it, since only trained habits and much practice enable a man to make the kind of observation that will be scientifically illuminating. Nevertheless, when once it has been observed, belief in it is not based on inference and reasoning, but merely upon its having been seen. In this way its logical status differs from that of the theories which are proved by its means.

In any science other than psychology the datum is primarily a perception, in which only the sensational core is ultimately and theoretically a datum, though some such accretions as turn the sensation into a perception are practically unavoidable. But if we postulate an ideal observer, he will be able to isolate the sensation, and treat this alone as datum. There is, therefore, an important sense in which we may say that, if we analyse as much as we ought, our data, outside psychology, consist of sensations, which include within themselves certain spatial and temporal relations.

Applying this remark to physiology, we see that the nerves and brain as physical objects are not truly data ; they are to be replaced, in the ideal structure of science, by the sensations through which the physiologist is said to perceive them. The passage from these sensations to nerves and brain as physical objects belongs really to the initial stage in the theory of physics, and ought to be placed in the reasoned part, not in the part supposed to be observed. To say we see the nerves is like saying we hear the nightingale ; both are convenient but inaccurate expressions. We hear a sound which we believe to be causally connected with the nightingale, and we see a sight which we believe to be causally connected with a nerve. But in each case it is only the sensation that ought, in strictness, to be called a datum. Now, sensations are certainly among the data of psychology. Therefore all the data of the physical sciences are also psychological data. It remains to inquire whether all the data of psychology are also data of physical science, and especially of physiology.

If we have been right in our analysis of mind, the ultimate data of psychology are only sensations and images and their relations. Beliefs, desires, volitions, and so on, appeared to us to be complex phenomena consisting of sensations and images variously interrelated. Thus (apart from certain relations) the occurrences which seem most distinctively mental, and furthest removed from physics, are, like physical objects, constructed or inferred, not part of the original stock of data in the perfected science. From both ends, therefore, the difference between physical and psychological data is diminished. Is there ultimately no difference, or do images remain as irreducibly and exclusively psychological? In view of the causal definition of the difference between images and sensations, this brings us to a new question, namely: Are the causal laws of psychology different from those of any other science, or are they really physiological?

Certain ambiguities must be removed before this question can be adequately discussed.

First, there is the distinction between rough approximate laws and such as appear to be precise and general. I shall return to the former presently; it is the latter that I wish to discuss now.

Matter, as defined at the end of Lecture V, is a logical fiction, invented because it gives a convenient way of stating causal laws. Except in cases of perfect regularity in appearances (of which we can have no experience), the actual appearances of a piece of matter are not members of that ideal system of regular appearances which is defined as being the matter in question. But the matter is, after all, inferred from its appearances, which are used to *verify* physical laws. Thus, in so far as physics is an empirical and verifiable science, it must assume or prove that the inference from appearances to matter is, in general, legitimate, and it must be able to tell us, more or less, what appearances to expect. It is through this question of verifiability and empirical applicability to experience that we are led to a theory of matter such as I advocate. From the consideration of this question it results that physics, in so far as it is an empirical science, not a logical phantasy, is concerned with particulars of just the same sort as those which psychology considers under the name of sensations. The causal laws of physics, so interpreted, differ from those of psychology only by the fact that they connect a particular with other appearances in the same piece of matter, rather than with other appearances in the same perspective. That is to say, they group together particulars having the same " active " place, while psychology groups together those having the same " passive " place. Some particulars, such as images, have no " active " place, and therefore belong exclusively to psychology.

We can now understand the distinction between physics and psychology. The nerves and brain are matter : our visual sensations when we look at them may be, and I think are, members of the system constituting irregular appearances of this matter, but are not the whole of the system. Psychology is concerned, *inter alia*, with our sensations when we see a piece of matter, as opposed to the matter which we see. Assuming, as we must, that our sensations have physical causes, their causal laws are nevertheless radically different from the laws of physics, since the consideration of a single sensation requires the breaking up of the group of which it is a member. When a sensation is used to verify physics, it is used merely as a sign of a certain material phenomenon, i.e. of a group of particulars of which it is a member. But when it is studied by psychology, it is taken away from that group and put into quite a different context, where it causes images or voluntary movements. It is primarily this different grouping that is characteristic of psychology as opposed to all the physical sciences, including physiology ; a secondary difference is that images, which belong to psychology, are not easily to be included among the aspects which constitute a physical thing or piece of matter.

There remains, however, an important question, namely: Are mental events causally dependent upon physical events in a sense in which the converse dependence does not hold ? Before we can discuss the answer to this question, we must first be clear as to what our question means.

When, given A, it is possible to infer B, but given B, it is not possible to infer A, we say that B is dependent upon A in a sense in which A is not dependent upon B. Stated in logical terms, this amounts to saying that, when we know a many-one relation of A to B, B is dependent upon A in respect of this relation. If the relation is a causal law, we say that B is causally dependent upon A. The illustration that chiefly concerns us is the system of appearances of a physical object. We can, broadly speaking, infer distant appearances from near ones, but not vice versa. All men look alike when they are a mile away, hence when we see a man a mile off we cannot tell what he will look like when he is only a yard away. But when we see him a yard away, we can tell what he will look like a mile away. Thus the nearer view gives us more valuable information, and the distant view is causally dependent upon it in a sense in which it is not causally dependent upon the distant view.

It is this greater causal potency of the near appearance that leads physics to state its causal laws in terms of that system of regular appearances to which the nearest appearances increasingly approximate, and that makes it value information derived from the microscope or telescope. It is clear that our sensations, considered as irregular appearances of physical objects, share the causal dependence belonging to comparatively distant appearances; therefore in our sensational life we are in causal dependence upon physical laws.

This, however, is not the most important or interesting part of our question. It is the causation of images that is the vital problem. We have seen that they are subject to mnenic causation, and that mnenic causation may be reducible to ordinary physical causation in nervous tissue. This is the question upon which our attitude must turn towards what may be called materialism. One sense of materialism is the view that all mental phenomena are causally dependent upon physical phenomena in the above-defined sense of causal dependence. Whether this is the case or not, I do not profess to know. The question seems to me the same as the question whether mnemic causation is ultimate, which we considered without deciding in Lecture IV. But I think the bulk of the evidence points to the materialistic answer as the more probable.

In considering the causal laws of psychology, the distinction between rough generalizations and exact laws is important. There are many rough generalizations in psychology, not only of the sort by which we govern our ordinary behaviour to each other, but also of a more nearly scientific kind. Habit and association belong among such laws. I will give an illustration of the kind of law that can be obtained. Suppose a person has frequently experienced A and B in close temporal contiguity, an association will be established, so that A, or an image of A, tends to cause an image of B. The question arises : will the association work in either direction, or only from the one which has occurred earlier to the one which has occurred later ? In an article by Mr. Wohlgemuth, called "The Direction of Associations" (*British Journal of Psychology*, vol. v, part iv, March, 1913), it is claimed to be proved by experiment that, in so far as motor memory (i.e. memory of movements) is concerned, association works only from earlier to later, while in visual and auditory memory this is not the case, but the later of two neighbouring experiences may recall the earlier as well as the earlier the later. It is suggested that motor memory is physiological, while visual and auditory memory are more truly psychological. But that is not the point which concerns us in the illustration. The point which concerns us is that a law of association, established by purely psychological observation, is a purely psychological law, and may serve as a sample of what is possible in the way of discovering such laws. It is, however, still no more than a rough generalization, a statistical average. It cannot tell us what will result from a given cause on a given occasion. It is a law of tendency, not a precise and invariable law such as those of physics aim at being.

If we wish to pass from the law of habit, stated as a tendency or average, to something more precise and invariable, we seem driven to the nervous system. We can more or less guess how an occurrence produces a change in the brain, and how its repetition gradually produces something analogous to the channel of a river, along which currents flow more easily than in neighbouring paths. We can perceive that in this way, if we had more knowledge, the tendency to habit through repetition might be replaced by a precise account of the effect of each occurrence in bringing about a modification of the sort from which habit would ultimately result. It is such considerations that make students of psychophysiology materialistic in their methods, whatever they may be in their metaphysics. There are, of course, exceptions, such as Professor J. S. Haldane,[1] who maintains that it is theoretically impossible to obtain physiological explanations of psychical phenomena, or physical explanations of physiological phenomena. But I think the bulk of expert opinion, in practice, is on the other side.

The question whether it is possible to obtain precise causal laws in which the causes are psychological, not material, is one of detailed investigation. I have done what I could to make clear the nature of the question, but I do not believe that it is possible as yet to answer it with any confidence. It seems to be by no means an insoluble question, and we may hope that science will be able to produce sufficient grounds for regarding one answer as much more probable than the other. But for the moment I do not see how we can come to a decision.

I think, however, on grounds of the theory of matter explained in Lectures V and VII, that an ultimate scientific account of what goes on in the world, if it were ascertainable, would resemble psychology rather than physics in what we found to be the decisive difference between them. I think, that is to say, that such an account would not be content to speak, even formally, as though

[1] See his book, *The New Physiology and Other Addresses* (Charles Griffin & Co., 1919).

matter, which is a logical fiction, were the ultimate reality. I think that, if our scientific knowledge were adequate to the task, which it neither is nor is likely to become, it would exhibit the laws of correlation of the particulars constituting a momentary condition of a material unit, and would state the causal laws [1] of the world in terms of these particulars, not in terms of matter. Causal laws so stated would, I believe, be applicable to psychology and physics equally; the science in which they were stated would succeed in achieving what metaphysics has vainly attempted, namely a unified account of what really happens, wholly true even if not the whole of truth, and free from all convenient fictions or unwarrantable assumptions of metaphysical entities. A causal law applicable to particulars would count as a law of physics if it could be stated in terms of those fictitious systems of regular appearances which are matter; if this were not the case, it would count as a law of psychology if one of the particulars were a sensation or an image, i.e. were subject to mnemic causation. I believe that the realization of the complexity of a material unit, and its analysis into constituents analogous to sensations, is of the utmost importance to philosophy, and vital for any understanding of the relations between mind and matter, between our perceptions and the world which they perceive. It is in this direction, I am convinced, that we must look for the solution of many ancient perplexities.

It is probable that the whole science of mental occurrences, especially where its initial definitions are

---

[1] In a perfected science, causal laws will take the form of differential equations—or of finite-difference equations, if the theory of quanta should prove correct.

concerned, could be simplified by the development of the fundamental unifying science in which the causal laws of particulars are sought, rather than the causal laws of those systems of particulars that constitute the material units of physics. This fundamental science would cause physics to become derivative, in the sort of way in which theories of the constitution of the atom make chemistry derivative from physics; it would also cause psychology to appear less singular and isolated among sciences. If we are right in this, it is a wrong philosophy of matter which has caused many of the difficulties in the philosophy of mind—difficulties which a right philosophy of matter would cause to disappear.

The conclusions at which we have arrived may be summed up as follows:

I. Physics and psychology are not distinguished by their material. Mind and matter alike are logical constructions; the particulars out of which they are constructed, or from which they are inferred, have various relations, some of which are studied by physics, others by psychology. Broadly speaking, physics group particulars by their active places, psychology by their passive places.

II. The two most essential characteristics of the causal laws which would naturally be called psychological are *subjectivity* and *mnemic causation*; these are not unconnected, since the causal unit in mnemic causation is the group of particulars having a given passive place at a given time, and it is by this manner of grouping that subjectivity is defined.

III. Habit, memory and thought are all developments of mnemic causation. It is probable, though not certain, that mnemic causation is derivative from ordinary physical causation in nervous (and other) tissue.

IV. Consciousness is a complex and far from universal characteristic of mental phenomena.

V. Mind is a matter of degree, chiefly exemplified in number and complexity of habits.

VI. All our data, both in physics and psychology, are subject to psychological causal laws; but physical causal laws, at least in traditional physics, can only be stated in terms of matter, which is both inferred and constructed, never a datum. In this respect psychology is nearer to what actually exists.

INDEX